RETRIEVING FUNDAMENTAL THEOLOGY

The Three Styles of Contemporary Theology

Gerald O'Collins, S.J.

PAULIST PRESS
New York/Mahwah

Library of Congress Cataloging-in-Publication Data

O'Collins, Gerald.
    Retrieving fundamental theology : the three styles of contemporary theology / Gerald O'Collins.
      p. cm.
    Includes bibliographical references and index.
    ISBN 0-8091-3418-7 (pbk.)
    1. Theology, Doctrinal. 2. Theology, Doctrinal—History—20th century. 3. Apologetics—20th century. 4. Vatican Council (2nd : 1962–1965). Constitutio dogmatica de divina revelatione.
5. Revelation. 6. Catholic Church—Doctrines. 7. Catholic Church—Doctrines—History—20th century. 8. Catholic Church—Apologetic works. I. Title. II. Title: Fundamental theology.
BX1751.202937 1993
230′.2′01—dc20   93-28251
                                                CIP

Published by Paulist Press
997 Macarthur Boulevard
Mahwah, N.J. 07430

Printed and bound in the United States of America

CONTENTS

DE LICENTIA SUPERIORUM ORDINIS

INTRODUCTION

"I suffer, therefore I may be."

Samuel Beckett

"Only where there are tombs are there resurrections."
Friedrich Wilhelm Nietzsche

"If you don't believe, you don't see anything."
*Retired farmworker in
the East Anglian fens*

The Second Vatican Council (1962–65) has been seen as the most significant event in the history of the Catholic Church since the Protestant reformation. The four sessions of the council, its sixteen documents and the practical results it brought about have also enjoyed an important impact on the Anglican, Orthodox and Protestant Churches, as well as on the followers of non-Christian religions.

But has the teaching of the council been adequately heard and received from the point of view of fundamental theology (hereafter FT)? Only those who ignore or defy the evidence would answer in the affirmative. The situation is different in the case of other such areas as the liturgy, the church, and ecumenism. There one could argue that the council's liturgical, ecclesial and ecumenical teaching has been substantially heard and given serious attention—not only by Roman Catholics but also by many other Christians. In those areas there is already a solid history of the interpretation and application of the council's documents. The reception of the conciliar documents in their significance for FT is, however, quite another question.

For years we have lacked an adequate bibliography for the Dogmatic Constitution on Divine Revelation (*Dei Verbum*), on any showing the central document for FT. No one has really examined what the other fifteen conciliar documents might have to say about such key themes for FT as revelation, faith and tradition. Even *Dei Verbum* has not been properly received and, in many quarters, now tends to be half-forgotten.

1

Profound dissatisfaction at this failure has prompted my attempt to retrieve, interpret and develop the council's teaching that is significant for FT. I have undertaken this book conscious of two lessons from the history of Christianity. Not much theology survives the age in which it was written. But the best official church teaching happily survives the erosion of time. Taken together, the sixteen documents of the Second Vatican Council constitute a doctrinal masterpiece of the twentieth century. Their full reception from the point of view of FT has been long in coming. In this book I aim at trying to remedy at least in part that situation, convinced that those texts should "increase," while mine must inevitably "decrease."[1]

Nearly three decades have elapsed since the end of the council in 1965. The closing years of the twentieth century have been rich in church teaching and theological reflection. The election in 1978 of the first non-Italian pope for over 450 years, the demolition of the Berlin wall in 1989, the end of the cold war, the August coup of 1991, the break-up of the Soviet Union and many other events have radically changed the course of church and world history. From the vantage point of the 1990s we look back through those events and texts to the council's documents, reading and retrieving the conciliar teaching in the light of our questions and context. Our temporal distance from 1965 offers productive possibilities for understanding and interpretation. Our new experiences and a changed climate of opinion in the church and the world have brought fresh questions which help to unfold further the meaning of the conciliar texts. Every major event since 1965 has inevitably affected the meaning we find in the council's documents, requiring us to see them at least partly in a new light.

To set the stage for the central core of this book, I first scan the shifts in Catholic (and Christian) theology since 1965. Then two chapters are dedicated, respectively, to the nature of theology in general and to FT in particular. The great theme for FT is the divine self-revelation in Christ. Hence I examine *Dei Verbum* (Chapter 4), the other conciliar documents' teaching on revelation (Chapter 5), and the council's teaching on saving revelation for all peoples (Chapter 6). The core chapters of this work will be completed by more systematic approaches to revelation as past and present (Chapter 7), the nature of revelation as God's symbolic self-communication (Chapter 8), the human experience of this symbolic self-communication (Chapter 9), and love as the key content of the divine revelation (Chapter 10).

My hope is that this book's retrieval and development of the full conciliar contribution to the theme of theology and revelation will stir others into attempting the same for such further key themes of FT as faith, tradition and the credibility of the Christian message. (The council's full teaching on tradition, for example, is in no way limited just to *Dei Verbum*.[2]) One further area of FT beyond theology and revelation could not, however, be left out: the link between revelation and the inspired scriptures. The last part of this work explores the relationship between the Bible and revelation (Chapter 11) and some lessons to be drawn for contemporary exegesis from *Dei Verbum* (Chapter 12).

An appendix offers an English translation of an important conciliar speech that might have enjoyed a fuller impact on the text of *Dei Verbum*.

My special thanks go to Hilva Martorana and Catherine Pattenden for typing drafts of this book, and to Frank Sullivan, S.J. and Jared Wicks, S.J., whose criticism and suggestions have once again improved what I have written. I express my deep thanks also to the administrators of the McCarthy Family Foundation for their support toward the writing of this book. Their generosity enabled me to finish the work during a sabbatical semester back at Pembroke College, Cambridge University. Finally, I wish to register my gratitude to the Master and Fellows of the College for the chance of enjoying once again the joy and privilege of their company.

Right from the outset I realize (a) that its concentration on the creative reception of the conciliar documents will give this book a strongly Roman Catholic look, and (b) that for years Christians of other denominations have made up part of my readership. To them I say: Yes, the form (and title) of this book are Roman Catholic. But the questions I face about such matters as revelation, the role of theologians and the interpretation of the Bible are common to us all, and, in fact, common to members of other world religions. If you want a salutary warning about the need to explore these questions in depth, you could read J.S. Spong, *Rescuing the Bible from Fundamentalism* (San Francisco, 1991). That book suffers greatly from the author's lack of clarity about basic themes of FT like inspiration, meaning, truth and the integral interpretation of biblical texts. My non-Catholic audience might care to begin at Chapter 8. What they read there and in subsequent chapters could send them back later to Chapter 1.

With much affection this book is dedicated to Nola, Sue, Jill, Rick, Bob and Andy, who have entered my life and greatly enriched it by becoming the wives and husbands of my nephews and nieces.

Gerald O'Collins, S.J.
Rome, February 3, 1992

ABBREVIATIONS

ABBREVIATIONS FOR DOCUMENTS OF THE
SECOND VATICAN COUNCIL

AA   *Apostolicam Actuositatem* (Decree on the Apostolate of Lay People)

AG   *Ad Gentes Divinitus* (Decree on the Church's Missionary Activity)

CD   *Christus Dominus* (Decree on the Pastoral Office of Bishops in the Church)

DH   *Dignitatis Humanae* (Declaration on Religious Liberty)

DV   *Dei Verbum* (Dogmatic Constitution on Divine Revelation)

GE   *Gravissimum Educationis* (Declaration on Christian Education)

GS   *Gaudium et Spes* (Pastoral Constitution on the Church in the Modern World)

IM   *Inter Mirifica* (Decree on the Means of Social Communication)

LG   *Lumen Gentium* (Dogmatic Constitution on the Church)

NA   *Nostra Aetate* (Declaration on the Relation of the Church to Non-Christian Religions)

OE   *Orientalium Ecclesiarum* (Decree on the Catholic Eastern Churches)

OT   *Optatam Totius* (Decree on the Training of Priests)

PC   *Perfectae Caritatis* (Decree on the Up-to-Date Renewal of Religious Life)

PO   *Presbyterorum Ordinis* (Decree on the Ministry and Life of Priests)

SC   *Sacrosanctum Concilium* (The Constitution on the Sacred Liturgy)

UR   *Unitatis Redintegratio* (Decree on Ecumenism)

OTHER ABBREVIATIONS

AAS   *Acta Apostolicae Sedis*

CIC   1983 Code of Canon Law

DS   H. Denzinger and A. Schönmetzer, *Enchiridion Symbolorum, Definitionum et Declarationum de Rebus Fidei et Morum* (Freiburg, 1976)

FT   Fundamental Theology

NCE   *New Catholic Encyclopedia,* 18 vols. (1967–89)

NJBC   *The New Jerome Biblical Commentary,* ed. R.E. Brown et al. (Englewood Cliffs, 1990)

NT   New Testament

OT   Old Testament

PG   *Patrologia Graeca,* ed. J.P. Migne

RH   John Paul II, *Redemptor Hominis* (1979)

ThInv K. Rahner, *Theological Investigations,* 22 vols. (1961–92)

TRE   *Theologische Realenzyklopädie* (1977–   )

TS   *Theological Studies*

1. CATHOLIC THEOLOGY SINCE 1965

Those who wish to record the major changes in Catholic theology since the Second Vatican Council (1962–65) will certainly not lack material for their project.[1] A few questions point at once to important shifts and areas of growth. Who is doing theology today? How are they doing it nearly three decades after the council? What progress has been made? What theological issues engage our attention in the 1990s?

In the aftermath of the council, Catholic theology has, to a greater or lesser extent, ceased to be a clerical monopoly. In many countries, prior to the council, theological colleges and seminaries trained only male students for the ordained ministry and were often situated in the countryside. Now they have opened their doors to others and often enough shifted from the isolated countryside to city settings. In Brazil, Canada, England, Italy, the United States and many other countries religious women, laymen and laywomen are much more involved as students and teachers of theology.[2]

In the preconciliar days philosophy, and in particular some form of Thomism, played its traditional role as the handmaid of theology. Since 1965 Catholic theologians have more and more drawn on a broader range of philosophies: for example, various forms of existentialism, common language philosophy and process thought. Thomism, along with the Platonic and Aristotelian traditions, is still influential in Catholic theology, but these streams of philosophy hardly enjoy a monopoly anywhere nowadays. In an interdisciplinary way theologians have engaged in serious dialogue with cultural anthropologists, biologists, physicists, psychologists, sociologists and colleagues in other fields. The steady progress made in biblical studies has had an obvious impact on how theology is done.

Concern for the spiritual life and pastoral activity has everywhere influenced the way Catholic theologians go about their work. Like the council's Pastoral Constitution on the Church in the Modern World,

Gaudium et Spes, theology has also come to operate somewhat more inductively[3] and experientially. (To an extent, this has been true of some major documents of the church's magisterium such as John Paul II's *Sollicitudo Rei Socialis* [1987].) Commitment to the ecumenical movement has widely affected the way Catholics teach, study and think their theology. Often they are studying and teaching theology alongside colleagues of other Christian communities. Depending on their geographical context, Catholic theologians (and church leaders) have entered into much more serious dialogue with Judaism, Buddhism, Hinduism, Islam and other major religions, as well as with modern secularism. This is not a dialogue with religious groups who live thousands of miles away. In the western world contact with Jews and Jewish thought has deeply affected much teaching and writing of theology. The presence of millions of Moslems in France symbolizes the new presence and challenge of Islam to serious Christian reflection. To have a living encounter with other great world religions it is no longer necessary to go to Asia (or Africa). Ecumenism, in the broader or narrower sense, has refashioned the way many Catholics do their theology.

Without attempting to draw up a complete list, one can readily note areas in which progress occurred over the last twenty-five years. Many Catholic theologians have become aware of the challenges involved in selecting and interpreting texts, whether biblical or otherwise. Hermeneutical issues dominate some theologies. Second, by and large, theology is more christological and anthropological—a development encouraged by Pope John Paul II's first encyclical, *Redemptor Hominis* (1979). Third, along with such other forces as increased contacts with Orthodox Christians, the charismatic renewal has stimulated Catholic theologians to reflect much more about the Holy Spirit's work in the church and the world. Fourth, the interconfessional dialogues have helped to clarify Catholic beliefs in the area of sacraments (baptism, eucharist and the ordained ministry) and in other such areas as justification and church authority.

At the beginning of the 1990s theological attention is focused on a variety of issues. Inculturation has become a concern for many theologians. How can we express the message of Catholic Christianity through symbols, traditions, languages and value systems that shape particular cultures? What should one say about Christ's presence in the history and cultures of the world? Along with other influences, the huge growth of the Catholic Church in Africa, Korea and elsewhere has encouraged serious attention to the issues of inculturation. More and more theologians, instead of seeing the chuch as centered in the west and represented elsewhere by satellite communities, have shifted to a vision of local churches spread around the world. That ecclesial vision brings with it the need to contextualize and indigenize the Christian message and way of life for all cultures and peoples.

Second, various kinds of moral issues have emerged with great urgency. I am thinking here of issues of bioethics, ecology, social and economic justice, human rights and international peace. Third, questions about ministry within the church (like the ministry of women and the teaching role of episcopal conferences) clearly figure large on the current theological agenda.

Up to this point I have offered preliminary answers to my four opening questions. However, instead of pressing ahead with detailed responses to those opening questions, I believe reflection on an underlying diversity of method may in fact prove more illuminating about the nature and directions of postconciliar Catholic theology. Any classification will play down significant variations and exceptions. Nevertheless, a scheme of three types or styles cover much of what is currently happening in post-Vatican II Catholic (and indeed Christian) theology.

First Style. The cultivated use of reason bulks large in the first style of theology which predominates in the universities, colleges, and faculties of Europe and North America. The heirs of a tradition which stretches back through the enlightenment, the renaissance and the medieval universities to the intellectual glories of Greece, the exponents of this style pursue the meaning and truth of Christian revelation. Through research, hard thinking and serious dialogue with academic colleagues in other disciplines, they pursue fresh knowledge and new insights.

This North Atlantic style of theology is carried on among well educated persons or at least by those who aspire to be well educated. To change John Henry Newman's classic title, it is a style that would encourage us to consult the experts in matters of theology. Learned experts, including not only believers but also non-believers, are the desirable dialogue-partners.

This first way of doing theology characteristically finds its sources in writings from the past: in the Bible; in the works of Greek, Latin and Syrian fathers; in church documents; in the books of medieval or reformation theologians; and in other traditional texts that indicate how Christians, with varying degrees of authority, have understood and interpreted the content of revelation. In their passion for truth, the protagonists of this style of theology take up dialogue and debate with their intellectual contemporaries. Yet the normative voices and texts generally remain those of the past.

Second Style. The desire to promote justice and the common good shapes
the second style, best exemplified by liberation theology. It is a practical
way of doing theology, concerned to struggle against the massive injustice
found in our world. It characteristically questions itself: What does our
theology lead us to do or leave undone in the world? Although it aims to
stimulate, interpret and critique action in the present, this style of theology also bears witness to a Jewish-Christian tradition that reaches back to
the Old Testament and the prophetic denunciation of social evil and
oppression. It draws inspiration from Jesus' solidarity with the oppressed
and marginalized of his society.

This kind of theology thrives on contact with the poor: the Christian
poor in Latin America, the non-Christian poor in India and the disinte-
grating victims of western consumer societies. The second style of theology encourages us to consult the poor and suffering in matters of faith,
doctrine and morality.

A glance at any of the better works from liberation theologians
indicates their respect for the normative voices from the past: above all,
the scriptures and official church teaching. Nevertheless, this style of
theology typically looks to the contemporary situation: in particular, to
the millions of victimized non-persons of our world. Its primary *locus
theologicus* is found in the suffering people of today.

Third Style. Prayer and worship[4] form the context for the third style of
theology which finds its classic home in eastern Christianity. Instead of
being naturally located in a university (the first style) or in a poor *barrio*
(the second style), this third style works out of the setting of the church
at public prayer. It bears witness to the triune God, revealed and reflected in liturgical celebration.

Where the first style of theology focuses characteristically on truth
(understood more "theoretically") and the second on justice and the
common good, the third style centers on the divine beauty.

This third style of theology prods theologians into consulting worshipers in matters of faith and doctrine. According to the geographical
situation, these worshipers will be Christians (for example, in eastern
Europe) or non-Christians (for example, Jews, Hindus, Buddhists and
Moslems). Rather than looking to learned experts (the first style) or
suffering victims (the second style), the third style of theology aligns
itself with persons at prayer. It looks not only at solemn, official worship
but also at expressions of popular religiosity in feasts, pilgrimages, devotions, images and other things that mirror underlying beliefs, attitudes
and experiences of God.

Finally, the third style obviously does not ignore the present and the past. Traditions, inherited from the past, bulk large for eastern Christians who, like the rest of us, must worship now or not at all. All the same the future plays a special role for their prayer and theology.[5] With the exalted and heavenly Christ presiding, worship anticipates the final glory of heaven. Through prayer, icons and architecture, our eschatological future with God shines through.

The Three Styles. Thus far I have identified and sketched academic, practical and contemplative styles of theology.[6] The classic language about the faith involved in theology can be adapted to illustrate the different emphases in these three styles. Faith expresses itself as knowledge, action and worship. Hence we might contrast faith seeking scientific knowledge or understanding (*fides quaerens intellectum scientificum,* the first style) with faith seeking social justice (*fides quaerens iustitiam socialem,* the second style) and with faith seeking adoration (*fides quaerens adorationem,* the third style). In all three descriptions, the word "seeking" (*quaerens*) has a significant function. Faith seeks a knowledge and understanding that in this life will never be conclusive and exhaustive. It seeks a just society that can never completely come in this world. It seeks an adoration of God that will be fully realized only in the final kingdom.

Faith, love and hope offer an alternate version of what has just been suggested. Faith seeking understanding characterizes the first style of theology; love seeking a more just society expresses the second; and hope seeking to anticipate liturgically the final vision of God suggests the third.

Pontius Pilate asked "*What* is truth?" (Jn 18:38) but did not wait for an answer. In the context of this chapter it might be better to ask: *Where* is (theological) truth? The Socratic method, exemplified classically in Plato's dialogues, would encourage us to deploy all the resources of our human reason illuminated by faith and look for truth *within* ourselves—through the working of our understanding and judgment. As distinguishable from this first style of theology, the second style hopes to find and live human and Christian truth working with and for *other* men and women. The place of truth for the third style is above all *in God,* the Father, Son and Holy Spirit. Thus the characteristic place of truth for the three styles of theology is, respectively, in our reasoned judgment, in our practice and in our praise of God.[7]

Here one could enlarge a patristic adage and speak of theological truth emerging through the laws of believing, living and praying (the *lex credendi* for knowledge, the *lex vivendi* of Christian morality and the *lex orandi* of worship). The *lex credendi,* which looks back to and draws on normative texts of faith, guides and illuminates the study and knowledge involved in our first style of theology. The *lex vivendi* gives us the truth through the practice of a Christian life in the service of suffering people. The *lex orandi* lets us grow in the divine life communicated through baptism, fostered in Christian worship and to be consummated at the end. It is the difference between the academic, practical and contemplative approaches to truth—as primarily something, respectively, to be known or believed (*lex credendi*), done (*lex vivendi*) or worshiped (*lex orandi*).[8]

In its 1964 Dogmatic Constitution on the Church (*Lumen Gentium*), the Second Vatican Council listed "the preaching of the gospel," pastoral government and the sacramental ministry as the three great duties of bishops (LG, 25–27). One can apply this scheme *analogically* to theologians as yet another way of elucidating the three styles of theologizing open to them. They can speak out as prophetic interpreters of the gospel's truth (first style). They can work pastorally for the good of those who suffer (second style). They can put their share in Christ's priestly ministry at the service of prayer and worship (third style). To use the classic terminology, a theologian can come forward primarily as prophet, king/queen or priest.

Far from being free-lance operators, theologians are called to be prophets, kings or priests at the service of the church. One might describe in ecclesial terms the threefold role open to them. They can represent and personify the church at study (*ecclesia ratiocinans,* first style), the church at work for those who suffer (*ecclesia laborans,* second style), or the church at prayer and adoration (*ecclesia orans et adorans,* third style). The varying character of their ecclesial engagement gives their respective theologies its different quality.

The Second Vatican Council's 1965 Dogmatic Constitution on Divine Revelation (*Dei Verbum*) called the study of scripture "the soul of sacred theology" (DV, 24). Any theology can be understood and assessed by the characteristic way it highlights certain texts and goes on to interpret and use them. For our three styles of theology, the Bible is a book, respectively, for study, practice and prayer. The first style studies the biblical text and asks: What did it mean? What does it mean? The second style finds in the Bible a practical and local program for life, and asks: How do the scriptures challenge us? What should they lead us to do in our local situation? The third style takes up the Bible as *the* guide to worship and asks: How does it turn into prayer and liturgy? Biblical hermeneutics offers a major way of recognizing and assessing styles of theology, whether the exponents themselves explicitly clarify their hermeneutics (as is often now the case with those who develop the first and second styles) or do not do so.

This sketch of the three styles of theology can find in two official Catholic documents supportive hints and suggestions. In *Redemptor Hominis* John Paul II comments on St Augustine's classic phrase about the restlessness of the human heart: "In this creative restlessness beats and pulsates what is most deeply human—the search for truth, the insatiable need for the good, hunger for freedom, nostalgia for the beautiful and the voice of conscience" (18; see 14). To the traditional schema of the search for the true, the good and the beautiful, the pope has added our hunger for freedom and the voice of conscience. His reflection on the human condition bears application to the styles of theologizing: the search for truth (style one), the need for the good and hunger for freedom (style two) and the divine beauty and voice of conscience, to be encountered in common worship and personal prayer (style three).

The Constitution on Divine Revelation from the Second Vatican Council is the other document I have in mind. Apropos of tradition, *Dei Verbum* speaks of the church "in her teaching, life and worship" handing on to "all generations all that she herself is, all that she believes" (8). Undoubtedly there is a danger of discovering support for one's thesis everywhere. Nevertheless, this triple scheme of "teaching, life and worship" enjoys some analogy to my three types of theology. The intellectual type expounds and hands on true teaching. The practical type concerns itself particularly with the church's life and struggles on behalf of the suffering. The contemplative type of theology finds its inspiration in the church's worship.

Dangers and Possibilities. Thus far this chapter has highlighted the positive aspects of each style of theology. Experience suggests a word of warning. Developed one-sidedly by itself, each style can fail to be fully faithful and Christian.

The cultivated use of reason that is a feature of the first style may produce an erudition that simply resists and avoids any form of change. Its academic exponents can fail to be outward-looking and remain blind to issues that cry out for remedy in the church and the world. Endorsing a "neutral" theological standpoint, they may be tempted to remain socially, politically and ecclesiastically somewhat "apart." Since the holocaust there is a new awareness that such *"praxisferne Theologie"* (theology distanced from praxis) is unacceptable. In general, the first style's concern for scientific precision may cause it to lose contact with life and worship. Those who do not know God in prayer and do not know human beings through a loving compassion which searches for justice can hardly hope to be scientifically precise in theology.

The second style can fail to test its conclusions stringently in the light of the normative voices of scripture and tradition. Some kinds of commitment to suffering people can end up in an activism, violent or otherwise, that has forgotten its roots in Christian faith and worship.

When taken to extremes the third style may neglect sound scholarship (style one) and social commitment (style two). It can turn into a flight toward timeless worship, cut off from life and study. This would be to ignore, for example, how sharing in the eucharistic body of Christ carries a radical commitment to the suffering body of Christ in the world (see 1 Cor 11:17–34). These are "dangers," if one wants to think that way.

Positively speaking, Catholic theology—and indeed, Christian theology in general—will happily survive and serve the people of God to the extent that it can combine the three styles. We need David Tracy (style one), Jon Sobrino (style two) and Hans Urs von Balthasar (style three). Of course, classifying these and further theologians in this way risks ignoring the variety of ways their work has been developed. At the same time, however, characteristic elements allow us to categorize them as somewhat more oriented toward the true (style one), the good (style two) or the beautiful (style three).

Christianity needs an inclusive approach that allows these three styles to complement and mutually enrich each other. At the heart of all Christian theology is its doctrine of Jesus Christ.[9] He is not confined to past, present or future. As the one who is, who was and who is to come, he is Christ yesterday, today and the same forever (Heb 13:8): the Christ of the scriptures and the Christian tradition, the Christ whose passion continues today, and the Christ of coming glory. In christology and other branches of theology we need an openness to three styles of approach that take up, respectively, "what is past, or passing, or to come" (W.B. Yeats, "On Sailing to Byzantium").

A theologian from Manila once expressed for me in Filipino his hopes for a theology that "knows how to walk (*na marunong lumakad*), knows how to sit (*na marunong umupo*), and knows how to kneel (*na marunong lumukod*)." His three requirements can be aligned with my three styles of theology. We need and have theologies that know how to sit studying the past, that know how to walk the streets with the poor, and that know how to kneel in adoration of our Savior who is to come.

A Coda. Whether in clothes or theological productions, style can be a subtle and elusive thing. One might enlist further questions to clarify more successfully the three styles I have identified. At the beginning of this chapter I wrote of theology in general becoming more experiential and ecumenical. What counts then as *the* privileged experiences for the practitioners of the three theological styles? Second, how does the ecumenical movement, understood more strictly or more broadly, affect the theology of the three styles? In particular, what role does the Jewish/Christian dialogue play for each style? Third, what impact do the personal faith and moral practice (including their political stance) of theologians have on their work? How, for instance, does their courage manifest itself (or fail to manifest itself) in their theology, whether it belongs to the first, second or third style?

To conclude. In an address to the members of an international symposium on Jesus' resurrection (April 1–5, 1970), Pope Paul VI exhorted those present to look for "solutions by joining study and prayer." He went on to cite St Augustine's advice to biblical scholars that "they should pray in order to understand."[10] Augustine's advice, which points us toward the third style of theology, could be adjusted to express the other two styles. "They should study, think and dialogue in order to understand" (first style). "They should act and transform society in order to understand" (second style).

2. THEOLOGY, ITS NATURE AND METHODS

To clarify further theology, its nature and methods, this chapter will concentrate, albeit not exclusively, on the Second Vatican Council's teaching on theology and on some postconciliar documents of the Catholic Church. I shall conclude with some observations about theology in the 1990s. To begin the chapter, however, I would like to turn back to the First Vatican Council (1869-70) and some enduringly valuable guidelines it proposed for theology.

First Vatican Council. The fourth chapter of the council's Dogmatic Constitution on Catholic Faith (*Dei Filius*), in dealing with the interaction between faith and reason (DS 3015–43), presupposed the earlier teaching of that document about a) God's free revelation of divine mysteries and b) the faith by which we believe in the truth of the things revealed by God (DS 3004–05, 3008). The Second Vatican Council preferred to speak of God's personal self-revelation and our encounter with the divine "mystery" (in the singular). Nevertheless, in and through its language about the "mysteries" hidden in God but now revealed in Christ (DS 3015–17, 3041) the First Vatican Council set out some important principles that bear on the work of theologians. Let me highlight four of these principles, all found together in one paragraph of the chapter on faith and reason (DS 3016).[1]

The first principle concerns a "most fruitful" understanding of the divine mysteries which can come by examining their "analogy" with "the objects" of our "natural knowledge." Here the council is not addressing so much the constant appeal to analogies or similarities in our *language,* nor even the way analogical imagining and thinking helps to shape human knowledge and understanding. Rather than having in mind such linguistic and epistemological considerations, the council is appealing to the analogical structures of reality, those inbuilt similarities between God the creator and the created objects which all human beings can know. Such similarities can fruitfully illuminate what through revelation we know of God and the divine plan for human salvation.

One example can serve to illustrate how this principle of analogy with "the objects" of our "natural knowledge" could actually work. Chapter One of the Second Vatican Council's Dogmatic Constitution on the Church (*Lumen Gentium*), in reflecting on the mystery of the church, notes how her "inner nature" is "now made known to us in various images," which are "taken either from the life of the shepherd or from cultivation of the land, from the art of building or from family life and marriage." *Lumen Gentium* goes on to list such biblical images of the church as a sheepfold, a cultivated field, the house or holy temple of God, our mother and the spouse of Christ (LG 6). In the language of the First Vatican Council sheepfolds, cultivated fields, houses, temples, mothers and spouses are all "objects" of our "natural knowledge." Such "objects," taken up into biblical imagery, "fruitfully" illuminate what we know through revelation about Christ's body which is the church.

As two further guidelines for theological understanding *Dei Filius* invites us to link the revealed "mysteries with one another" and with our "ultimate end." The first of these procedures amounts to systematically looking for *coherence*. What coherent patterns of meaning show up when we examine the connection between various truths of revelation? By bringing into relationship with each other the revealed mysteries about the Trinity, Christ, the church and the human condition, we can organize into some kind of coherent whole the "content" of revelation. This is to ask how particular revealed "mysteries" fit in with other "mysteries" in a pattern that is satisfying, attractive and even beautiful. We are helped to understand and accept these divine "mysteries" when we find them relating beautifully in a whole pattern of meaning. Beyond doubt, views differ on whether and to what extent something which is "shapely" and beautiful points to what is true (and good). But Keats, Shakespeare and other classic poets, not to mention St. Augustine, Hans Urs von Balthasar and many theologians of eastern Christianity, have little difficulty in recognizing how we grasp truth, including divine truth, in and through beauty. By calling on us to relate the revealed "mysteries with one another," *Dei Filius* is encouraging us to detect coherent patterns of meaning. By so doing we will be led to contemplate and marvel at the shape and beauty manifested in the whole of revelation.

The third guideline encourages us to reflect on the revealed "mysteries" by linking them to our "ultimate end." In twentieth century terms, this is to respect and struggle with the essentially eschatological force of God's revelation (and redemption).[2] What has been communicated to us

through the history of Israel, Christ's incarnation, life, death and resurrection, and the outpouring of the Holy Spirit has inaugurated the end of
time. But the full, future revelation and salvation is not yet here (Rom
8:18–23; 1 Cor 15:20–28; 1 Jn 3:2). An eschatological outlook, which
recognizes the partial and provisional nature of God's proleptic self-
revelation in Christ, should characterize all theological thinking (first
style), acting (second style) and praying (third style). The attitude of
waiting in hope is at the heart of all authentic theology. Where the
council's first guideline (analogy with the objects of our "natural knowledge") draws help from the order of creation, this third guideline points
to the order of redemption and its final consummation.

To exemplify such an eschatological outlook we can go back to a
case mentioned above, the teaching of *Lumen Gentium* on "the mystery
of the holy church" (LG 5). Before completing this document, the Second Vatican Council included a whole chapter on "the pilgrim church"
(LG 48–51), a clear reminder that in grappling with the revealed mystery of the church, we should not ignore her eschatological nature or
that "ultimate end" which essentially characterizes her nature and function. Analogies taken from the created order must be qualified by our
hope for the church's final goal, when God will complete the work of
redemption and make all things new (Rev 21:1–22:5).

The fourth and last principle that I wish to note is taken from the
same paragraph we are examining in the fourth chapter of *Dei Filius*.
After recalling three positive guidelines for theology, the First Vatican
Council ends the paragraph by noting the radical inadequacy in our
present knowledge of the revealed mysteries of God.

> Divine mysteries by their very nature so transcend the created
> intellect, that, even when they have been communicated in
> revelation and received by faith, they remain covered by the
> veil of faith itself and shrouded as it were in darkness as long as
> in this mortal life "we are away from the Lord; for we walk by
> faith, not by sight" (2 Cor 5:6–7) (DS 3016).

Without using the term, the council is here endorsing apophatic or negative theology. Any statements about God have to be qualified by a
corresponding negation and the recognition that the divine mysteries
transcend in an infinite way our knowledge and understanding.[3]

Such then are four major guidelines that one can glean from the
First Vatican Council's teaching on the interaction of faith and reason.
In dealing with the "mysteries" of revelation, theology needs to be
analogical, coherent, eschatological and apophatic. Having taken read-

ers back to *Dei Filius,* let me now take them forward to the Second Vatican Council.

Second Vatican Council. In one way or another all sixteen documents of the Second Vatican Council have something to say about theology, its sources, methods, audiences and function in the life of the church. We still lack an accurate, full-scale study about the council's teaching on theology. For the purposes of this chapter I will attend, albeit not exclusively, to explicit statements about theology and theologians found in the conciliar documents. That explicit teaching is, by and large, summarized by one document, the Decree on the Training of Priests (*Optatam Totius*). Let me use that document to organize matters, while recognizing how *Optatam Totius* goes beyond "merely" theological and academic training to attend also to the spiritual and pastoral preparation of future priests.[4]

1) A "sacred science" (PO 19; see GS 62), theology reflects on divine revelation (OT 16; GE 11), or—to put things in equivalent terms—does its work "in the light of faith" (OT 15,16). From the standpoint of belief, it draws on the divine revelation which was specifically communicated through the history of Israel and reached its absolute climax with Christ's death, resurrection and the coming of the Holy Spirit. The "deposit of faith" (DV 10) is the classical term for this definitive revelation of God which has been entrusted to the church to be proclaimed and preserved with fidelity.

2) Since God's self-disclosure aims to redeem us from evil and communicate life, it follows that revelation and salvation through Christ are practically synonymous. In *Dei Verbum* the Second Vatican Council uses the terms almost interchangeably (DV 2,3,4). Hence it is no surprise that the council sees theology as studying not only "revealed truths" but also "the mysteries of salvation" (OT 15,16). As "faith (in divine revelation) seeking understanding," theology considers "the history of salvation" which centers on "the mystery of Christ" (OT 16; see DV 2–4). All theological disciplines are to "expound the mystery of Christ and the history of salvation" (SC 16; see AG 16). "They search out, under the light of faith, every truth stored up in the mystery of Christ" (DV 24). Thus the council moves back and forth between the divine self-revelation (or the deposit of faith) and the history of salvation (or the mystery of Christ) as the essential "given" for theological teaching and study.

3) Under the special inspiration of the Holy Spirit the story of God's revealing and saving activity has been recorded and interpreted in

the Bible. No other theological sources, not even infallibly true statements of the magisterium, can claim to be written under that special
guidance of the Spirit which gives the scriptures their specifically normative character as "the word of God" (DV 9,21), books that not only have
human authors but also "God as their author" (DV 11). Hence the Bible
"should be the soul, as it were, of all theology" (OT 16; see DV 24).[5] In
three ways *Dei Verbum* witnesses to the impact of the scriptures. They
provide "a permanent foundation," which "most firmly strengthens"
and "constantly rejuvenates" theology (DV 24).[6]

Not only the "exegetes" but also "other students of sacred theology" are to "zealously combine their efforts" in "examining and explaining" the Bible (DV 23). *Optatam Totius* singles out two branches of
theology which should be strengthened and rejuvenated by the scriptures. In "the treatment of dogmatic theology biblical themes should
have first place." In its "scientific presentation" moral theology "should
draw more nourishment from the teaching of sacred scripture" (OT 16).
Nevertheless, it is clear that the council expects that not only dogmatic
and moral theologians but also all workers in the field of theology should
look constantly to the scriptures for strength and rejuvenation. After all,
as we have just seen, the council calls the Bible "the soul of all theology." The scriptures should be not only *the* norm but also the primary
inspiration of all theology.

4) After the primary study of biblical themes, *Optatam Totius* proposes that

> students should be shown what the fathers of the eastern and
> western church contributed to the fruitful *transmission* and illu-
> mination of the individual truths of revelation, and also [what
> was] the later history of dogma and its relationship to the gen-
> eral history of the Church (OT 16; italics mine).[7]

This study of the church's living tradition, along with the scriptures,
plays a foundational role in the study of theology: "Sacred theology
relies on the written word of God, taken together with sacred tradition,
as on a permanent foundation" (DV 24).

This lapidary statement echoes what *Dei Verbum* has already said
about the scriptures together with "sacred tradition" constituting "the
supreme rule of faith" (DV 21) and applies to theology the teaching
about the "close connection and communication between sacred tradition and sacred scripture. For both of them, flowing from the same
divine wellspring, in a certain way merge into a unity and tend toward
the same end" (DV 9). Given that tradition and scripture are so inti-

mately connected in their past origin, present function and future goal, it is obvious that in relying on scripture, theologians must also take into account tradition.

Dei Verbum draws attention to a reciprocal relationship between theology and tradition. On the one hand, theology relies and draws on tradition (DV 24). On the other hand, theological "study" is named as one of the factors effecting, under the Holy Spirit, development in tradition—in the sense of a "growth in understanding" and progress "toward the fullness of divine truth" (DV 8).

5) As well as maintaining that "sacred tradition and sacred scripture form one sacred deposit of the word of God," *Dei Verbum* recognizes that "the task of authentically interpreting the word of God" has been "entrusted only to the living magisterium of the church." This magisterium

> is not above the word of God, but serves it, teaching only what has been handed on, listening to it devoutly, guarding it scrupulously, and explaining it faithfully by divine commission and with the help of the Holy Spirit.

This is a beautiful vision of the teaching office of the church as a living ministry. But the council does not intend thereby to weaken the links with tradition and scripture.

> Sacred tradition, sacred scripture and the magisterium of the church, in accord with God's most wise design, are so linked and joined together that one cannot stand without the others, and that all together and each in its own way, under the action of the one Holy Spirit, contribute effectively to the salvation of souls (DV 10).

We might add: "and also contribute effectively to the fruitful practice of theology."

Applying to theology what has been said in Chapter Two, the final chapter of *Dei Verbum* speaks of "Catholic exegetes" and "other students of sacred theology" devoting their energies to exploring and expounding the scriptures "under the watchful care of the sacred magisterium" (DV 23). In similarly general terms *Optatam Totius* recalls the function of the magisterium under whose "guidance" theology should be taught (OT 16).[8]

6) However, the ecclesial quality of theology is not limited to its being cared for and guided by the official teaching office. Six times the

key article of *Optatam Totius* speaks of the "church" (and once of "churches"), and does so in a variety of ways which indicate how the ecclesial context of theology includes, but is not restricted to, the guidance of the magisterium (OT 16). It is in the living community of the whole church that Christian theology really exists.

The Constitution on the Church in the Modern World (*Gaudium et Spes*) outlines some broader roles theologians can play for the church in the world. They should engage in "new investigations" demanded by fresh questions coming from "science, history and philosophy." They "are invited to seek for more suitable ways of communicating doctrine" to the people of our time. *Gaudium et Spes* obviously includes theologians among "all the faithful" who "possess a lawful freedom of inquiry and of thought, and the freedom to express their minds humbly and courageously about those matters in which they enjoy competence" (GS 62).

7) *Optatam Totius* faithfully gathers together further characteristics of theological teaching and learning encouraged by other documents of the council—first of all, the liturgical "style" of theology.

Students of dogmatic theology should be taught to recognize how "the mysteries of salvation" are "always present and operative" in "the liturgical actions" (OT 16; see 19). To put matters in equivalent terms, theologians should never forget how God's salvific self-revelation in Christ is now expressed and effective all through the liturgy. By reflecting on the history of salvation, theologians will think in a more liturgical way. As the Constitution on the Sacred Liturgy (*Sacrosanctum Concilium*) indicates, the encouragement of such a liturgical outlook should come not only from the professors of liturgy (SC 15) but also from other faculty members.

> The teachers of other disciplines, especially of dogmatic theology, sacred scripture, and spiritual and pastoral theology, should take care . . . to expound the mystery of Christ and the history of salvation in a way that will already bring out the connection between their subjects and the liturgy (SC 16).

8) Furthermore, theological teaching and training is to be ecumenical in the stricter and (as we shall see) in a broader sense.

Optatam Totius asks for students of theology to "be led to a more adequate understanding of the churches and ecclesial communities separated from the Roman apostolic see" (OT 16). Here this document applies to theology what the Decree on Ecumenism (*Unitatis Redintegratio*) says about the common responsibility for Christian unity:

Concern for restoring Christian unity pertains to the whole church, faithful and clergy alike. It extends to everyone, according to the potential of each, whether it be exercised in daily Christian living or in *theological* and historical studies (UR 5; italics mine).

Theology and history are linked together in a later article which stresses the ecumenical point of view in teaching and learning:

Instruction in sacred theology and other branches of knowledge, especially those of a historical nature, must also be presented from an ecumenical point of view . . . it is highly important that future bishops and priests should have mastered a theology carefully worked out in this way and not polemically, especially in what concerns the relations of separated brethren with the Catholic Church (UR 10).

Such an ecumenical approach, which should pervade all theological studies, entails, among other things, four guidelines. It calls for profound and precise scholarship that "at every point" aims to "correspond more accurately with the facts of the case." Second, Catholic doctrine should be "clearly presented in its entirety," and without "a false irenicism which harms the purity of Catholic doctrine and obscures its assured genuine meaning." Third, in their ecumenical dialogue Catholic theologians do well to remember the "order or 'hierarchy' of truths" (UR 11), in which the "basic dogmas" of the Trinity and the incarnation (UR 14; see 12) form the foundation of Christian faith. Fourth, "a proper freedom" and "variety" in "the theological elaboration of revealed truth" can give "richer expression to the authentic catholicity of the church" (UR 4). Later on the same document applies to eastern and western Christianity the principle of acceptable diversity in unity or of legitimate "differences in theological expression of doctrine": their "various theological formulations are often to be considered complementary rather than conflicting" (UR 17).

9) In a wider sense of ecumenism *Optatam Totius* recommends also the study of non-Christian religions for the syllabus of Catholic theological students.

They should also be introduced to a knowledge of the other religions which are more widely spread through individual areas. In this way, they can better understand the elements of goodness and truth which such religions possess by God's provi-

dence, and will learn how to disprove the errors in them and to
share the full light of truth with those who lack it (OT 16).

The language about "elements of goodness and truth" matches that of
another conciliar document promulgated on the same day (October 28,
1965), the Declaration on the Relationship of the Church to Non-
Christian Religions (*Nostra Aetate*): "The Catholic Church rejects nothing which is true and holy in these religions" (NA 2).

In its Decree on the Missionary Activity of the Church (*Ad Gentes*)
the council naturally considers appropriate ways of teaching and studying theology in situations where Christians may be still only a new and
relatively small minority. In those countries seminarians, "in their philosophical and theological studies," should "consider the points of contact
between the traditions and religion of their homeland and the Christian
religion." Thus they will be "duly prepared for fraternal dialogue with
non-Christians" (AG 16). A later article of *Ad Gentes* encourages "theological investigation" to draw on the customs, traditions and learning of
various peoples. Without prejudicing its foundation in Christian revelation, theology can "seek for understanding" through "the philosophy
and wisdom" of each culture (AG 22).

Since it devotes considerable attention to the relationship between
Christians and Jews, *Nostra Aetate* recommends, among other things,
"biblical and theological studies" which can help to produce "mutual
understanding and respect." The great "spiritual patrimony common to
Christians and Jews" demands this (NA 4).

10) When *Ad Gentes* talks of "the philosophy and wisdom" of various cultures, this leads us to the council's endorsement of the necessary
contribution that philosophy makes to theology.

Optatam Totius requires the study of philosophy as an essential part
of the program for priestly formation and expects "a better integration
of philosophy and theology" (OT 14). Without explaining what these
connections mean in detail, the decree simply asks that "students should
be helped to see the connections between philosophical argument and
the mysteries of salvation," which theology treats "under the superior
light of faith" (OT 15). At least one thing is clear here. The council does
not encourage a separation of (theological) faith and (philosophical)
reason, as if the former were totally revealed and supernatural and the
latter merely rational and natural.[9]

11) Philosophy plays its part in helping theologians in their pastoral
task of understanding, clarifying and *communicating* more successfully
the divine revelation. *Optatam Totius* hopes that students of theology
will learn to communicate "eternal truths in a manner appropriate to the

people of today" (OT 16). But it is *Gaudium et Spes* that has more to say about philosophy and the role of theologians as communicators.

The Constitution on the Church in the Modern World notes how "from the beginning of her history" the church "has learned to express the message of Christ with the help of the ideas and terminology of various peoples, and has tried to *clarify it with the wisdom of philosophers*" (GS 44, italics mine). If this was the past, the council stresses the present work of bishops and theologians

> in hearing, distinguishing and interpreting the many voices of our age, and judging them in the light of the divine word. In this way, revealed truth can always be more deeply penetrated, better understood and set forth to greater advantage (GS 44).

The ecclesial nature of theologians' work obviously includes their role as communicators (see 6 above). But the call of *Gaudium et Spes* suggests highlighting this role in a special way. The council invites theologians, "while adhering to the methods and requirements proper" to their discipline, to play their part in reformulating and communicating more effectively revealed truth to the people of our time (GS 62).[10]

12) Finally, a word about the various theological disciplines. *Optatam Totius* lists "the study of sacred scripture," dogmatic theology, patristics, church history, liturgy, moral theology and canon law (OT 16). Pastoral theory and practice should also figure in the program of priestly formation (OT 19–21; see GS 62). *Sacrosanctum Concilium* speaks explicitly of "spiritual and pastoral theology," and the need to teach the relationship between these subjects and the liturgy (SC 16). Fundamental theology is missing from the council's list of disciplines, even if this subject's major tasks and themes are to be found in the conciliar documents—above all in *Dei Verbum* and *Gaudium et Spes*.[11]

Leaving aside the question of specific theological disciplines, let me sum up the council's vision of theology. It is 1) a sacred science, based on revelation and on 2) the Christ-centered history of salvation. It should be 3) deeply biblical, 4) founded in tradition, 5) guided by the magisterium, 6) ecclesial, 7) liturgical and 8) ecumenical in its concerns, 9) informed about and respectful toward other religions, 10) aided in particular by philosophy, and 11) working toward more effective communication.

This vision of theology touches on some things, endorses or at least presupposes other things, and leaves some other items quite out of the picture.

In stressing the place of liturgy in theology (see 7 above) and recognizing the liturgical and spiritual traditions of eastern Christianity (UR 14 and 15), the council indicates how "spirituality and liturgy" can stamp a whole tradition of theology (UR 17). The conciliar documents do speak of "spiritual theology" (SC 16) and the need for students to "nourish their spiritual lives" with "Catholic doctrine" drawn from "divine revelation" (OT 16). But one might have expected more on the deep interplay between a) theology and b) the spiritual life, in particular, the public liturgy, personal prayer and popular religiosity, which includes devotions (see SC 13) and pilgrimages.

Eastern Christianity gives the name of "the theologian" to St John the Evangelist (commonly identified there, as in the west, with the beloved disciple who appears in John's gospel [13:23] at Jesus' side and then turns up repeatedly in that gospel right through to the last chapter). Evagrius Ponticus (346–399), a key figure in the growth of eastern spirituality, wrote: "The Lord's breast is the knowledge of God, and whoever leans on it will be a theologian."[12] In *On Prayer,* a work attributed to Nilus Ancyra but probably by Evagrius, we read: "If you are a theologian, you will truly pray; and if you truly pray, you are a theologian."[13] This "third" style of theology (see the previous chapter) might have figured more strongly in what the Second Vatican Council had to say about theological teaching and learning.

Without ever stating them explicitly, the conciliar documents encourage several new ways of "doing" theology. Let me pick out three important developments in theological method, practiced and implicitly recommended by the council. The first is the shift from the First Vatican Council's language about revealed and divine "mysteries" (in the plural) to "the mystery" (in the singular) or "the mystery of Christ" (DV 24; see 2–4, 14–17). While not totally avoiding talk of "mysteries" (see UR 11; OT 16),[14] the Second Vatican Council preferred to speak of "the mystery" of the tripersonal God, revealed in the history of salvation and inviting human beings into a new relationship of eternal love. The council's terminology supports a theology which attends to the heart of the tripersonal God's saving self-communication in Christ (UR 12)—what Rahner calls the *"reductio in mysterium."*[15]

Along with "the mystery of the incarnation" and "the paschal mystery," the council addresses "the mystery of the human being" (GS 22). Not only in *Gaudium et Spes* (for example, GS 3–10) but also elsewhere (for example, NA 1), the conciliar documents reflect "the anthropological turn" that has characterized much modern theology. Various forms of existentialist, personalist and transcendental philosophies have shown how a truly usable theology must take account of the conditions which make men and women hearers of God's word and recipients of divine grace. Properly understood, this "anthropological turn" in no way displaces the centrality and priority of the divine self-communication in Christ. Anthropocentrism and christocentrism are complementary and not necessarily mutually exclusive. Although it does not in so many words recommend to theologians a "turn" to the human subject, *Gaudium et Spes* certainly practices it.

This "anthropological turn" shades into another feature of modern theology: an inductive approach "from below" that complements classical deductive approaches "from above." Once again the conciliar documents never explicitly endorse the need for theologians to be inductive as well as deductive. Nevertheless, the council's concern to state accurately the facts of the present human condition (*Gaudium et Spes* passim) and of the world religious situation (for example, *Unitatis Redintegratio* and *Nostra Aetate*) certainly exemplifies an inductive approach which a one-sided deductive approach neglects at its peril.

Finally, some things are missing in the council's vision of theology. First, our radical incapacity to understand the mystery of God, a central theme of apophatic theology and a guideline from the First Vatican Council (DS 3016), hardly figures in the teaching of the Second Vatican Council. The theme turns up once (DV 6)—in a quotation from the First Vatican Council (DS 3005).

Second, we saw how the "third" style of theology, with its stress on prayer and spirituality, does not show up strongly in the conciliar documents. What does not show up at all is the "second style," a style deeply concerned with both justice and the whole interplay between theological theory and practice. It would be anachronistic to make too much of this "omission." With Jürgen Moltmann's *Theology of Hope* first published in 1964, the theology of hope was hardly underway when the council ended in 1965. Johann Baptist Metz began lecturing and writing on political theology only after the council closed. The very last conciliar document, *Gaudium et Spes,* and then the Second General Conference of Latin American Bishops (which met in 1968 at Medellín in Columbia), opened the way for Gustavo Gutiérrez and others to develop liberation theology.[16] In the 1970s and 1980s further practical movements emerged that can properly be classified under the "second style" of theology. By describing in a pastoral way the church's relationship to and mission in the world, *Gaudium et Spes* can be seen as preparing the ground for various types of "second style" theologies. At the same time, however, one does not find this style represented in what the council said about theology, its procedures and methods.

After the Council. Since the close of the Second Vatican Council, a number of official documents have affirmed or at least implied things about the nature of the theology and its tasks. At this point I would like to list and reflect on some of these statements. Set against the twelve points gleaned above from the council, these subsequent documents show change and gain in their overall vision of theology and the work of theologians.

In chronological order the first document to be considered is *Normae Quaedam* (for ecclesiastical studies) issued by the Sacred Congregation for Catholic Education (May 20, 1968).[17] All the themes that shaped the council's vision of theological learning and teaching are faithfully reflected either in the General Norms (art. 1) of this 1968 document or in its Plan of Studies (art. 29, 31–33, 35, 44). Like *Optatam Totius* it fails to list fundamental theology among the particular theological dimensions and/or disciplines (see Plan of Studies 29 and 30 with its long footnote 12). Like *Optatam Totius* it expresses very clearly the need for theological teachers to bring out the "unity" of their work in the one "mystery of Christ and history of salvation" (Plan of Studies 30, with its footnote 12).[18]

In its Declaration on Christian Education (*Gravissimum Educationis*), although not explicitly mentioning theology in this context, the council had recognized a double role for "faculties of sacred sciences": not only their useful work for the mission of the church but also their "responsibility" to "explore more profoundly the various areas of the sacred disciplines so that day by day a deeper understanding of sacred revelation will be developed" (GE 11).[19] *Normae Quaedam* endorsed this double purpose for "faculties of ecclesiastical studies" (General Norms art. 1). In his first encyclical (of 1979), John Paul II was to call explicitly on theologians to fulfill their double role by not only collaborating closely with the church's "mission of teaching truth" but also dedicating "their studies and labors to ever deeper understanding" of divine truth which has "in God its one supreme source" (*Redemptor Hominis* 19). The Apostolic Constitution *Sapientia Christiana* (also of 1979), which was to supersede *Normae Quaedam,* recognizes a similar double purpose for ecclesiastical faculties and the work of theologians (see paragraph 3 of the Foreword and article 3 of the General Norms).

The responsibility of theologians to explore and expound more deeply divine revelation obviously raises the questions of a) their freedom to inquire and express themselves, and b) their relationship to the magisterium—that is to say, to the official teaching of the bishops and the pope. The Second Vatican Council, as we saw above, spoke briefly of the magisterium's watchful guidance (DV 23; OT 16) and of theologians' responsible freedom (GS 62). It singled out bishops and theologians as having a particular duty, "with the help of the Holy Spirit," to "hear, distinguish and interpret the many voices of our age, and to judge them in the light of the divine word" (GS 44). Given the remarkable collaboration between bishops and theologians at the council, it is not surprising that the conciliar documents almost took this situation for granted and had little to say about magisterial guidance and theological freedom. As its second opening principle, *Normae Quaedam* briefly describes the nature of this "just freedom" and speaks of the "mission" which teachers receive from the magisterium.

On this point *Sapientia Christiana* was to reproduce substantially what *Normae Quaedam* had laid down. I postpone treatment of the issue until we reach *Sapientia Christiana*. Before we do so, three other official documents merit attention.

In a particular way the Sacred Congregation for the Doctrine of the Faith addressed to theologians its 1973 declaration *Mysterium Ecclesiae,* encouraging them to explore "more and more the mystery of the church." In terms that recalled *Normae Quaedam* and anticipated *Sapientia Christiana,* the document reminded theologians that their freedom

> must always be limited by the word of God, as it is faithfully
> preserved and explained in the church, and taught and ex-
> plained by the living magisterium of the pastors and especially
> by the pastor of the entire people of God (6).

Unlike the Second Vatican Council but like the First Vatican Council (DS 3016), *Mysterium Ecclesiae* underlined the fact that the "hidden mysteries of God," even when revealed, transcend our human intellect (5). It was in another area that this 1973 document introduced a new element. We saw above (under 8) how the council acknowledged different but complementary formulations of doctrine (UR 17). *Mysterium Ecclesiae* added that dogmatic expressions of revealed truth are historically conditioned by the language in which they were couched (5). Admittedly *Gaudium et Spes,* echoing Pope John XIII's address at the opening of the council, invited theologians to

> seek continually for more suitable ways of communicating doc-
> trine to the people of their times. For the deposit of faith or
> revealed truths are one thing; the manner in which they are
> formulated without violence to their meaning and significance
> is another (GS 62).

Mysterium Ecclesiae, however, made it clear that the manner of formulating revealed truths is historically conditioned by the concepts and language of any given period. It is this historical conditioning which obliges theologians (and others in the church) to "seek continually for more suitable ways of communicating doctrine."

On February 22, 1976 the Sacred Congregation for Catholic Education published a document on the "Theological Formation of Future Priests."[20] At greater length than in its *Normae Quaedam* of 1968, the congregation here considers the relationship of theologians to the magisterium, their role of "research and critical reflection" and the share they receive in the church's teaching mission (44–47). It spells out the contribution of philosophy to theological studies (48–53). (On January 20, 1972 the same congregation had issued a document on the "Study of Philosophy in Seminaries."[21]) The congregation introduces three fresh elements in its 1976 document. First, fundamental theology is recognized as enjoying a necessary part in any adequate program of theological studies (107–13; see also 82–83). Second, while urging a number of appropriate safeguards, the congregation accepts a new theological pluralism which arises from "the diversity of methods employed, the variety of philosophies followed, the different terminologies used, and basic outlooks adopted" (65; see 64–68). Third, in a section on the function of theology the document contains echoes of political theology and the theology of liberation.

> There are problems of the new solidarity between social classes and peoples, the *liberation* of man from exploitation and alienation, sharing in the life of the state and of international society, the conquest of hunger, disease and illiteracy, elimination of war as a means of solving quarrels between peoples, and the creation of more effective means of preserving peace. In this sense, *theology* has a *"political"* function that is original and unique, because it throws light on problems and directs *action* in man's various occupations, according to the indications and precepts of God's word (28; italics mine).

A footnote directs the reader to *Gaudium et Spes* and several papal documents such as Pope John XXIII's encyclical *Pacem in Terris.* Beyond question, those magisterial texts helped to bring about the emergence of political theology and liberation theology. But my point here is rather this. The 1976 statement on the "Theological Formation of Future Priests" seems to be the first time an official church document acknowledges among the proper functions of *theology* something approximating to what I identified as "the second style" in the previous chapter of this book.

The first encyclical of John Paul II, *Redemptor Hominis* (March 4, 1979), reflected major theological principles that we noted in the documents of the Second Vatican Council, especially in *Gaudium et Spes*. Right through this document the pope speaks, for example, of the one saving mystery of Christ, rather than of revealed and saving mysteries (in the plural), exemplifying the *reductio in mysterium* (singular) that marks recent magisterial teaching and theological thinking.[22] This christocentrism goes hand in hand with the "anthropological turn" and inductive method, repeatedly found in the encyclical.

When explicitly addressing the mission of theologians in a section of article 19, the pope expects them to "serve" and "collaborate" with the magisterium—a collaborative service placed within the wider ecclesial context. This brief section mentions six times the "church" to which theologians should offer their "service" in their "apostolic commitment" to the "whole people of God." In the same brief section the pope adds two further points which as such the council did not apply to the theological ministry. First, theologians, along with the pastors of the church, enable the people of God to "share creatively and fruitfully in Christ's mission as prophet." The encyclical thus associates theologians with the prophetic office of Christ. Second, in the light of the enormous advances in human learning, knowledge and methodology, the pope recognizes that "a certain pluralism of methodology" is "permissible and even desirable" in theology. This last point states more briefly the second (new) item we noted in the 1976 document from the Congregation for Catholic Education.

On April 15, 1979 John Paul II promulgated an Apostolic Constitution on Ecclesiastical Universities and Faculties (*Sapientia Christiana*).[23] Articles 66–70 on a "Faculty of Sacred Theology," taken together with articles 50–51 of the special norms of application added by the Sacred Congregation for Catholic Education, draw together excellently all the thirteen points about theology we found in the documents of the Second Vatican Council. Article 51 of the special norms of application makes up for a conciliar omission by listing fundamental theology among the obligatory theological disciplines.

As regards the relationship of theologians to the bishops, the constitution calls for collaboration and communion (General Norms 3 and 26). It lays down that those who teach theology in ecclesiastical universities and faculties need to receive "a canonical mission" from the appropriate authority (General Norms 27). At slightly greater length than *Normae Quaedam* it treats the nature of "true freedom" in theological research and teaching. This freedom is understood to be affected and limited not only by "the pastoral needs of the people of God" but also, and more profoundly, by "firm adherence to God's word and deference to the church's magisterium, whose duty it is to interpret authentically the word of God" (General Norms 30).[24]

This last item about the limits of freedom reminds us that the essential "given" of theology comes from revelation and makes this discipline a *sacred* science. Hence the most radical issue about theological freedom goes beyond possible or actual tensions and even conflicts between bishops and theologians on the pastoral level to the question: Is theology so limited and conditioned by God-given revelation that it cannot be considered a true science? Clearly *Sapientia Christiana* does not consider that the revealed "given" stops theology from being a genuinely scientific discipline. Its foreword refers to "the sacred sciences" (twice in par. 3) and "the theological sciences" (par. 5). Ecclesiastical faculties should be places of "scientific research" (General Norms 3) and their teachers proven to be suitable also through their published "scientific research" (General Norms 25). Article 66 of the Special Norms speaks of "the scientific method proper" to sacred theology. In short, *Sapientia Christiana* clearly maintains that dependence on divine revelation does not disqualify theology as a genuinely scientific discipline.[25]

By the end of the middle ages theology was firmly established as "the queen of the sciences," providing a unity and synthesis for all other academic disciplines. Centers of theological learning played a key role in giving rise to the medieval universities of Europe and through them, eventually, to innumerable universities around the world. Nowadays, when "science" is often understood to be above all the experimental, "natural" sciences (flanked by the "human" sciences), many academics ask: a) Is theology a genuine science? b) Does it deserve a place among the faculties on the university campus?

Some notable theologians of our century, while answering question b) affirmatively and themselves teaching for a university faculty of theology, respond negatively to question a). They separate theology completely from science. Theological faith is seen as totally independent of natural knowledge and scientific reason (which investigate and draw their conclusions from the data of nature and history). The Neo-Orthodox school, inspired and headed by Karl Barth (1886–1968), exemplifies classically this refusal to associate theology with other sciences. For all his differences with Barth, Rudolf Bultmann (1884–1976) through his existentialist approach to faith keeps theology away from history, physics and the other sciences. Christian faith and its theology are discontinuous with and simply independent of any findings and conclusions coming from scientific research into history and nature.[26]

Over against those theologians and others who deny it this status, *Sapientia Christiana* rightly presents Christian theology as a properly scientific or academic discipline. It has its own distinctive "object," God revealed in Jesus Christ. It has its methods, shaped somewhat differently according to the three styles presented in the opening chapter. It should and can use terms and concepts with clarity and consistency. It can also be consistent in appealing to data, interpreting texts and applying its criteria to build up a systematic body of theological knowledge. No less than their colleagues in other disciplines, theologians can be aware of and test their assumptions and expectations. These considerations justify recognizing theology and its various specializations as a discipline or science with its own identity. In the last century John Henry Newman rightly argued for the place of theology among the university faculties.[27] More recently Wolfhart Pannenberg has championed the scientific status of theology and the right of this discipline to have its academic place alongside the human and natural sciences.[28]

At the end of the day, one justifies the academic and scientific status of theology by interpreting this discipline, as Newman did, within a broader vision of the nature and objectives of higher education. John Paul II's Apostolic Constitution on Catholic Universities (August 15, 1990) does just that by presenting theology within a total picture of a university's research, teaching and mission (19,29). In that way this document on Catholic universities offers the larger vision that was not to be found in *Sapientia Christiana,* an apostolic constitution for ecclesiastical faculties and universities.

In this account of postconciliar documents let us pick up the trail after *Sapientia Christiana* (promulgated on April 15, 1979).

I detected above some (very brief) official teaching on "the second style" of theology emerging in a 1976 document from the Congregation for Catholic Education. This official attention to such a style of theology is manifested much more fully in two documents from the Congregation for the Doctrine of the Faith: its "Instruction on Certain Aspects of the 'Theology of Liberation' " (August 6, 1984) and "Instruction on Christian Liberty and Liberation" (March 22, 1986). The first instruction acknowledges "theology of liberation" as "a thoroughly valid term: it designates a theological reflection based on the biblical theme of liberation and freedom and on the urgency of its practical realization" (III,4). The serious criticisms this document makes against some forms of theology of liberation do not stop it from acknowledging the valid and valuable connection between theological reflection and praxis (XI,13; see also the end of X,3) and the possibilities for an "authentic theology of liberation" (VI,7). The subsequent 1986 instruction upholds as the "noble ecclesial task" of the theologian to help the faith of the poor "to express itself with clarity and be translated into life" (98). In a major way both instructions broke new ground in recognizing and even encouraging what I have called "the second style" of theology.

On March 19, 1985 the Congregation for Catholic Education published its "Basic Plan (*Ratio Fundamentalis*) for Priestly Formation," an updated version of its 1970 basic plan. The section on theological studies (76–81) is preceded by a section on philosophical studies (70–75) and like the 1970 document it calls fundamental theology "apologetics" (79). Unlike the 1970 basic plan, but like *Normae Quaedam* (1968), the "Theological Formation of Future Priests" (1976) and *Sapientia Christiana* (1979), the 1985 basic plan expects professors of the "ecclesiastical sciences" to have an official "mission" to teach and to use their "just freedom" in collaboration with an obedience to the magisterium (87–88).

An "Instruction on the Ecclesial Vocation of the Theologian," issued by the Congregation for the Doctrine of the Faith on May 24, 1990, dedicated most of its attention to the magisterium and the relationship of theologians to the magisterium (13–41 = 29 out of a total of 42 articles). This instruction picked up a theme enunciated in John Paul II's first encyclical, *Redemptor Hominis* (1979): the prophetic function or vocation of theologians (see 5 and the beginning of 6). But where *Redemptor Hominis* associated this prophetic function with Christ's prophetic office, the 1990 instruction sees this function as a special grace given and awakened by the Holy Spirit. This instruction struck a fresh note among the postconciliar documents which have dealt with theology by introducing the theme of prayer: "The theologian is called to deepen his own life of faith and continuously unite his scientific research with *prayer*" (8, italics mine). We saw above how little this "third style" of theology turned up even in the documents of the Second Vatican Council.[29]

A full-scale account of what official documents (of varying degrees of authority) have said from 1965 to 1990 about the nature of theology and its tasks should include many further items: for example, the "Instruction on the Study of Fathers of the Church in the Formation of Priests," issued by the Congregation for Catholic Education on November 10, 1989; various addresses to theologians by John Paul II; addresses made to the International Theological Commission by Paul VI and John Paul II; and, for that matter, the documents issued by the International Theological Commission (hereafter ITC).[30]

That commission was appointed and met for the first time in October 1969. The first fourteen texts that it has published (1969–1985), like the two subsequent ones, reflect important topics that have emerged for reflection and debate in the postconciliar years. Its text of 1972 on the "Unity of Faith and Theological Pluralism" anticipated what we saw above in 1976 document on the "Theological Formation of Future Priests" and in Pope John Paul's first encyclical *Redemptor Hominis* (1979). The ITC documents show an officially appointed body "doing" theology together. Its only text that deals directly with the nature and function of theology appeared in 1975, "Theses on the Relationship Between the Ecclesiastical Magisterium and Theology."[31] That this was the topic treated in the single statement which the ITC has so far issued on theology mirrors one central theme of postconciliar developments.

How should one sum up all the developments in postconciliar official teaching on Catholic theology, its nature and tasks? First, some documents (for example, *Normae Quaedam* of 1968 and *Sapientia Christiana* of 1979) provided a true summary of the council's explicit vision of theology. Second, the spiritual and prayerful character of theology (my "third style"), touched on by the council, turned up briefly in the "Instruction on the Ecclesial Vocation of the Theologian" of 1990. Third, the council's *reductio in mysterium* and christocentrism figured strongly in *Normae Quaedam,* as they did in *Redemptor Hominis* (1979). That papal encyclical, like many subsequent texts coming from John Paul II, also followed the conciliar lead by practicing an "anthropological turn" and introducing an inductive style alongside the more deductive style of theology of earlier, manualist theology.

The council's silence about fundamental theology was remedied by the "Theological Formation of Future Priests" (1976) and *Sapientia Christiana.* The two versions of the "Basic Plan for Priestly Formation" (1970 and 1985) spoke rather of the need for "apologetics." The "Theological Formation of Future Priests" (1976) edged beyond the council by acknowledging a practical and "active" function of theology, a "second style" of theology which emerged massively in the 1984 and 1986 documents on liberation theology.

The 1973 declaration *Mysterium Ecclesiae* broke new ground by recognizing how the concepts and language used to express revealed truths are historically conditioned. Three years later the "Theological Formation of Future Priests" made room for the new theological pluralism which within proper limits can be legitimately followed. Besides recognizing the "permissible and even desirable" nature of "a certain pluralism in methodology," in *Redemptor Hominis* Pope John Paul II associated theologians with the *prophetic* mission of the church, as did the 1990 instruction from the Congregation for the Doctrine of the Faith.

Along with the legitimation of a practical or second style of theology, the most striking development has concerned the issue of theologians' relation to the magisterium and their mission in and for the church. Since *Normae Quaedam* in 1969, every document we have listed and commented on, with the sole exception of the 1970 version of the "Basic Plan for Priestly Formation," has had something to say about theological freedom, its limits and its relationship to the magisterium. The fact that the ITC's only statement about theology as such (1975) concerns just this topic faithfully represents postconciliar developments.[32]

As regards this last theme, the 1990 "Instruction on the Ecclesial Vocation of the Theologian" in one paragraph mentioned three times the "tensions" that "may arise between theologians and the magisterium. Significantly the document added that, given proper "collaboration," such tensions can "become a dynamic factor, a stimulus to both the magisterium and theologians to fulfill their respective roles while practicing dialogue" (25). In other words, far from being an unfortunate or merely negative factor, such tensions can play a thoroughly positive role in the life of the church.

Theologians on Theology. Thus far this chapter has directed its attention to magisterial teaching on theology coming from the First Vatican Council, the Second Vatican Council and subsequent official documents (down to 1990). In the second half of the twentieth century many theologians have been reflecting critically on their own professional work, its principles and its methods. I think here of articles and books on theology that have come from Yves Congar, Avery Dulles, Gerhard Ebeling, Claude Geffré, Bernard Lonergan, John Macquarrie, Jürgen Moltmann, Wolfhart Pannenberg, Karl Rahner, Juan Luis Segundo, Paul Tillich, David Tracy and others.[33] I myself have already written something on the procedures and factors that characterize theology.[34] Some readers may want to go back to those pages. Here and now I want to take them forward toward three questions which seem significant for the 1990s. I do this, recognizing the way my education and life-setting has made me, in terms of the previous chapter, a theologian of the first style. At the same time I hope to enlist help from the second and third styles in reflecting on theology and its methods.

a) *The Place of Theology.* What comes out quickly in most theological writings is the influence of the writer's context. *Where* we do our thinking, teaching and writing leaves a characteristic mark on the product. The deepest difference comes from doing theology in and for (and not outside or merely alongside) the believing community. As the title of Karl Barth's monumental *Church Dogmatics* (1932–67) suggests, theology is or should be essentially ecclesial in its context and aim. As a service undertaken within the church and for the church, it reflects on the community's official faith, aims to promote the common practice of justice and serves the community's public worship. In the broadest sense the "where" of theology is determined by doing one's theological work within the circle of faith and for the church community (see points 5 and 6 above from the Second Vatican Council).

The "place" of theology is, however, both broader and narrower than the entire believing community. It is broader in the sense of being always located within historical, human cultures. Whether it is a matter of theology, philosophy or some other discipline, the broader cultural and social setting will always affect how one understands, interprets and communicates. At the same time, however, we may not absolutize the context and its importance. The revealed and salvific "given" that is biblically recorded and interpreted (see points 1–3 above) is *the text* which both "reads" off and at times challenges the broader context.

The "place" of theology can also prove to be narrower than the whole believing community. The setting and audience for whom a particular theologian teaches and writes may be some university, monastery or seminary. It might even be a tiny circle of friends and relatives as in the case of Thomas More, Dietrich Bonhoeffer and other theologians who did some of their finest writing as prisoners in jail before their executions.

The predominant style of theology has its impact here. The first style makes the "place" of theology an institution for learning and research, a community of scholars set on teaching and training other competent professionals. In their desire to serve and liberate the poor and oppressed, those who have developed the second style turn their centers into places for training people ready to analyze society critically and change history. They engage in theological research, but their places of research are geared to transform society in the light of the gospel. Theological centers of the third style cherish above all the worship of God and train their students according to the spiritual, liturgical traditions of the east.

The different "places" of theology can then be characterized, respectively, by the (academic) *koinonia* of the first style, the *diakonia* of the second and the *leitourgia* of the third.

b) *Motivation.* But why should one take time out to engage in theology? We might re-express the question in terms of my three styles of theology. Why should we spend time thinking clearly and coherently about the God revealed in Jesus Christ (first style)? Why should we as Christian believers act self-critically (second style) or give ourselves to prayer and to reflecting on the implications of worship (third style)? To echo and adapt what Paul says about the spirit and "compulsion" of faith (2 Cor 4:13), we believe and therefore we must theologize in and through thought, action and prayer.

The passage of time and the state of the world offer strong reasons for giving serious attention to theology. Nearly two thousand years have gone by since the church began. As Christians we believe that God's self-revelation reached its climax in the life, death and resurrection of Jesus. But why and how should something that happened so long ago continue to determine our thinking, acting and praying? How can we and why must we still think, act and worship in a Christian fashion today?

If the passage of time may seem to turn the origins of Christianity into something irretrievably remote, the present state of the world makes the fundamental questions of theology (about God and the human condition) as urgent as ever. Extermination camps may have disappeared, but violence and the ruthless denial of basic human rights are as alive as ever. What is the point and purpose of our common existence when millions go hungry and medically deprived, while a privileged minority continues to enjoy hitherto unimaginable wealth and services? The technological age does not satisfactorily answer any radical questions about the meaning of human existence. Even at the material level it has initiated, as more and more experts admit, a trend toward the massive, long-run deterioration of our environment.

c) *Method.* We saw above how the Second Vatican Council maintained a traditional term in calling theology a "sacred science." As a *sacred* science the discipline deals with the mystery, the revealing and saving self-communication of the tripersonal God. Any claims that theology makes about the divine truth, justice and beauty remain provisional and contestable until the end comes and we see "face to face" (1 Cor 13:12).

As a sacred *science,* theology and its methods will be affected by the choice of basic style. Nevertheless practitioners of any of the styles must be ready to explain under what conditions and by what criteria their theological claims are, respectively, true, just (and liberating), or open to God's praise in prayer. The two major elements that shape these conditions and criteria are history and philosophy—a combination prefigured somewhat by the association of the historical (and prophetic) books with the wisdom literature in the Old Testament.

First, all three styles of theology appeal to historical considerations which may be drawn from the whole sinful and saved condition of the human race, the biblical record and the mediation of Christianity through church teaching and the wider tradition of God's people. In brief, theologians appeal to and use human history, biblical history and church history. Undoubtedly history will be assessed and evaluated somewhat differently. But it is impossible to imagine any truly Christian theology that would not be essentially shaped by history.

Second, right from the second century down to the present, philosophy has proved to be a clarifying and cohesive factor in the making of Christian theologies. Since the first style looks for God through truth, the second through justice, and the third through beauty, all three must give some account of what they mean, respectively, by truth, justice and beauty. One cannot engage in the analysis of meaning without raising philosophical questions (for example, about i) criteria used in establishing meaning and ii) the very meaning of meaning). To be sure, philosophical reflections bulk larger in the first style which reaches back through St. Thomas Aquinas to the patrimony of Plato and Aristotle. Nevertheless, a non-philosophical theology is not to be found among the representatives of the other two styles. The second style aims at analyzing the political, cultural and economic milieu and reflecting critically on praxis—in the light of the biblical promise of God's liberation for the oppressed. It is impossible to engage in such analysis and reflection at any depth without raising philosophical issues. The third style of theology, exemplified classically in eastern Christianity, is derived from and dedicated to public worship which is fed by tradition and the inspired scriptures. Eastern tradition draws much of its shape from a) the early councils with their trinitarian and christological definitions and b) a deep appreciation of how the Holy Spirit helps human beings to participate through grace in the divine life. Any serious reflection on a) and b) brings up such philosophical concepts and questions as nature (divine and human), personhood and the quality of human participation in God's life.

No matter what particular notions and systems are adopted, all three styles of theology involve some use of philosophy.[35] Here one expects some clarity of concepts and criteria for verifying the specific claims that are made.

To the extent that theologians attempt to be clear and critical in their use of history and philosophy, to that extent they are presenting theology as a public discipline, a "science" alongside other "sciences."

Having spent two chapters reflecting on theology in general, we turn next to the particular area of the discipline that shapes this book—fundamental theology.

3. FUNDAMENTAL THEOLOGY

To fix this book clearly in one direction I need to take a position on the specific identity, content and tasks of fundamental theology. The first two chapters aimed at plotting the actual "styles" of contemporary theology (Chapter 1) and then going back to see the directives which the Second Vatican Council and official postconciliar documents offered to theologians (Chapter 2). But, as I indicated in the Introduction, this book is meant to guide the argument steadily toward fundamental theology. So before lingering on particular conciliar and postconciliar themes, I need to state my convictions about my central focus: fundamental theology.[1]

Without tracing the history of the discipline and the origin of the term "fundamental theology" (and how it came to replace "apologetics" in Catholic theological vocabulary), I want to begin with several assertions. These will be explained and nuanced later in the chapter. First, fundamental theology (hereafter FT) is that discipline which in the light of faith reflects critically on the foundations of theology and basic theological issues. Second, FT is to be distinguished from the philosophy of religion. The philosophy of religion, when it investigates religious beliefs, conduct and cult, does so by the light of reason alone. As such it reflects from "the outside," without taking up any believing or confessional stance. FT, however, does its work from "the inside," as an exercise of faith seeking understanding, justice and prayer.

Third, its "basic" interests distinguish FT from dogmatic theology. Of course, over some points dogmatic theology raises fundamental questions. In sacramental theology, for example, one must examine the basic nature of signs and symbols before going on to consider the particular sacraments. But in general the various areas of dogmatic theology dedicate most of their attention to specific issues and/or revealed truths (such as various models for interpreting the Trinity, the union of two natures in the one person of Christ and grace as the divine indwelling). FT characteristically takes up only very general or basic questions, such as the nature of revelation, without going much into details or examining at depth particular revealed truths. In that sense FT is typically a formal study.

The "object" which gives FT its own identity can be stated as follows: 1) the self-revelation of the tripersonal God in Jesus Christ, 2) the credibility of that revelation, and 3) its transmission and interpretation. Let us now take up in turn those three major themes of FT.

1) *God's Self-Revelation.* FT finds its first major project in critically reflecting on the self-disclosure of the tripersonal God. This saving revelation, which reached its definitive climax with the resurrection of the crucified Jesus and the coming of the Holy Spirit, constitutes the basic religious reality for Christians and the primary object for their faith. This revelation forms the absolutely fundamental principle and foundation for theology in all its particular sectors. FT makes its appropriate contribution by seeking to understand and interpret the fact and essential structures of the divine self-revelation, leaving it to the other theological specializations (above all, dogmatic theology) to reflect systematically on the various truths that we know through this revelation.

FT's work here involves examining the profoundly personal nature of divine revelation, its means, its mediators and its specific characteristics (as being, for example, historical, salvific and sacramental). In particular, those engaged in FT must grapple with the way revelation is simultaneously both event and mystery. Progressing through the historical events of the Old Testament and the life of Jesus, revelation reached its climax with his death, resurrection and the sending of the Holy Spirit. There is much here to investigate historically: for example, the story of Israel, the preaching of Jesus, his post-Easter appearances, and the church's foundation and mission. FT invites us to scrutinize carefully the historical dimensions of revelation in a wide range of events through the Old and New Testaments. At the same time we are faced with the mystery of God's definitive self-revelation in Christ—a "strange" thing to handle in our words. FT must come to terms with the fact that through a particular set of events and a particular person the complete, final and unsurpassable revelation of God has taken place. Such a thoroughly perceptible and historical event as Jesus' crucifixion manifested a special presence of God that has carried consequences which are universal (= for all) and definitive (= for all times). Historical events can and did manifest eternal salvation.

Other basic issues about revelation should be mentioned. One takes up the "when?" of revelation and another its "where?" The former question concerns the difference between the apostolic experience of revelation's culmination in Christ and the experience of revelation enjoyed by all subsequent generations of Christians. The distinction between the normative, apostolic, "foundational" experience and the later, "dependent" experience of revelation will resurface in a later chapter. The latter question, the "where" of revelation, arises from the obvious fact that only some people (a minority of the world's population) have experienced and aligned themselves with the "special" history of revelation. How should we understand and interpret the knowledge of God and the whole religious experience of all those who have lived and live "outside" this "special" history—in what may be called the "general" history of revelation and salvation? This question too will also return later in this book.

2) *The Credibility of Revelation.* Some people have no trouble in describing their faith in God's revelation as a sheer decision, a blind leap in the dark. Admittedly believers "walk by faith, not by sight" (2 Cor 5:7). Nevertheless, nothing in the Christian scriptures and tradition justifies going to the extreme of interpreting faith as an unmotivated act of intellectual suicide. In fact, such a position proves self-contradictory, as soon as one begins offering reasons in its support. Here I simply want to affirm something I have argued for elsewhere—that, while not being simply the result of human argumentation, faith in divine revelation is reasonable and should offer some kind of verification.[2] It is not enough to declare in whom/what we believe; others can rightly expect to hear *why* we believe this revelation (see 1 Pet 3:15).

To some extent our method for explaining why the Judeo-Christian revelation is credible will be determined by our audience. While all of them are contemporaries, some will already be believers (often maintaining their faith in the face of serious difficulties). Others will be non-believers, interested enough to hear the message of revelation and perhaps already on the road to accepting it.

Attention to our audience is not only desirable but also indispensable in FT. What we summarized above under 1) represents the "objective" pole for FT. But there is also the "subjective" pole, those to whom the divine self-revelation is believable or not (yet) believable. Where 1) expresses the "dogmatic" principle in FT, 2) expresses its "apologetic" thrust. How our apologetic case will develop depends somewhat on the challenges it must face.

The characteristic challenge in the North Atlantic world comes either from post-enlightenment intellectuals or from an increasingly secularized society which often endorses a secularism that explains everything positively and exclusively in this-worldly terms. It looks for scientific explanations of past history and present experience, and rules out otherworldly, religious values and causes as distracting illusions which prevent us from seeking a free and fruitful existence.

In the third world the major challenge for the apologetic work of FT is caused by hunger, violence, lack of basic medical (and other) services, and the systematic denial of universal human rights—in short, by deep and widespread social, economic, political and religious injustice. Finally, FT faces the challenge arising from Christianity's dialogue with other religions (and cultures), especially but not exclusively in Asia and Africa. How can FT show the way to validate (and inculturate) the message of Christian revelation in and through the religious experiences of millions of Asians and Africans?

These then are three major challenges that should shape somewhat differently apologetic for FT. They correspond obviously to the three (general) styles of theology I identified in the opening chapter. First, the North Atlantic world typically wants witnesses and evidence that attest divine revelation in past history and present experience. What are the signs of God and the divine transcendence in the whole story of Jesus and in the present life of the church that witness to the other-worldly realities, truths and values? Why believe the apostolic witnesses when they proclaim certain events as God's final, redemptive self-manifestation in human history? Second, what kind of practical engagement for justice coming from believers can validate the saving revelation proclaimed by Christianity? What forms of liberating apologetic should the practitioners of FT inspire or at least endorse in a world that condemns millions to a non-human existence? Third, FT needs a contemplative, prayerful and liturgical apologetic if it is to be effective for those who value profound religious experience.[3]

Having acknowledged three appropriate shapes for FT's apologetic, we can, however, rephrase the issue of credibility at a deeper level. Who is the subject who through faith accepts the divine self-revelation? What creates the conditions for the possibility of hearing in faith and receiving God's revelation? What is the primordial human condition that makes us open to revelation? Where 1) above attends to the divine "object" who is revealed and known, 2) the credibility of revelation involves FT in offering some account of the human condition which makes us capable of receiving and even welcoming revelation.

One could fill a small library with valuable publications on the human condition. It has been described primarily in terms of our primordial questions (*homo interrogans*) about such matters as the origin, meaning and destiny of our life. Human beings can be interpreted through their communicative and symbolic nature (*homo communicans et simbolicus*). One of the richest versions of human existence is in terms of suffering and hope (*homo dolens et sperans*). We flee from death, absurdity and hatred/isolation and seek life, meaning and love. The death, absurdity and hatred/isolation that threaten us can assume a thousand forms. Life, for example, can be menaced not only by disease, drugs, and environmental pollution but also by such things as the frenetic pace of our existence ("I don't have any more time to read, to listen, to pray and to live properly").

The divine revelation "answers" the primordial orientation and needs of our human condition. *Homo interrogans* finds in that revelation the answer to the basic questions. God's saving revelation, as we shall see in a later chapter, "responds" to our symbolic, communicative nature. Through accepting God's self-manifestation *homo sperans* can hope for the fullness of life, a totality of meaning and an utterly satisfying love.

In short, the quest for credibility involves FT in developing a solidly-based version of human existence that allows us to see how it correlates with God's salvific self-revelation. Some discernible correlation between the human question and the divine answer lends an obvious credibility to claims for a divine revelation.[4] Such correlation cannot, however, purport to be "perfect." The divine response goes beyond human questions and expectations (1 Cor 2:9).

Lastly, any adequate account of credibility will include some reflection on the nature and structure of human faith. Revelation reaches its goal when accepted in faith. We can distinguish but not separate revelation from faith as it accepts and expresses revelation. Hence FT needs to give some version of faith if it is to give a full picture of what God's self-revelation entails and what its perceived credibility leads to.[5]

3) *The Transmission of Revelation.* The third major theme for FT concerns the handing on through the community of the experience of God's revelation. As the visible bearer of tradition the community of believers transmits their collective experience. FT needs to study the originators and inheritors of the church's tradition, reflecting also on the Holy Spirit as *the* invisible agent of tradition.[6]

As well as scrutinizing tradition, FT also examines the product of Old Testament and New Testament tradition, the inspired scriptures. The nature of biblical inspiration, its connection with revelation, its major consequence (in particular, the saving truth of the sacred scriptures) and the basic theological issues involved in forming the canon are all items that belong on the agenda of FT.[7]

Understanding and interpreting the scriptures and the other texts

and "monuments" of tradition are likewise challenges for FT. Here too
FT should maintain a broad vision of its hermeneutical task. Understanding and interpreting the normative biblical witness entails more than
actualizing the scriptures merely at the level of church teaching and
theological reflection. Hermeneutics also comes into play at the "practical" level where, for example, the effective love displayed by saintly
men and women towards those in need lives out in a powerful fashion
the meaning of the biblical record. Third, the public worship and personal prayer of innumerable Christians, fed from the beginning by the
scriptural texts, also constantly actualize what the understanding and
interpretation of the Bible mean.[8]

4) *Further Agenda for FT.* This rapid sketch of the three main themes
that establish a specific identity for FT intends to be inclusive, rather
than exclusive. Other basic questions can rightly call for attention from
the practitioners of FT.

The nature, functions, methods and scientific status of theology
filled the pages of the first two chapters of this book. All those items,
involving as they do basic and fundamental issues, belong in a program
of FT. So too do questions of a) theological language and b) criteriology.
John Macquarrie's *God-Talk* and other such works on theological language are essays in FT rather than dogmatic theology.[9] As regards theological criteriology, FT examines the principles and methods invoked,
while dogmatic theology will systematically clarify and develop the conclusions reached. Take, for instance, the claim that Jesus Christ was the
founder of the church. FT looks into the meaning and truth of this
statement. What does "found" mean here? What criteria need to be
fulfilled for one to recognize a "founder"? Once the meaning is clarified,
how can we appropriately verify, both historically and theologically, that
Jesus Christ "founded" the church? In this way FT takes up the conditions and criteria for clarifying and verifying basic theological claims.

Before closing this chapter it could be useful to make some observations about the actual state of the discipline. The *Handbuch der Fundamentaltheologie* has updated a classical approach to FT: first, a "religious
demonstration" (= questions about God), then a "Christian demonstration" (= questions about Christ) and finally a "Catholic demonstration"
(= questions about the church). This model of FT which moves from
verifying belief in God to verifying belief in Christ and his (Catholic)
church has the advantage of implying a trinitarian structure—from God
(the Father) and the incarnate Son through to the Holy Spirit which
fashions, indwells and guides the church. Such other contributors to FT as
Eugen Biser and Claude Geffré have developed the discipline in the key

of interpretation. Alongside such versions of FT that highlight hermeneutics, others have taken experience and symbolism as their leitmotifs.

In terms of the three challenges that call for an appropriate "apologetic," one might classify René Latourelle as having responded to the North Atlantic, post-enlightenment challenge. Johann Baptist Metz's *Faith in History and Society* offers a "practical" liberating apologetic. Hans Waldenfels has developed a fundamental theology at least partly in the context of world religions and the challenge of their experiences of God.

What we still lack is an approach to FT formed and fashioned in the key of the liturgy. To round off this chapter I want to sketch some aspects and advantages of a liturgical FT. An initial advantage comes from its rootage in the earliest Christian traditions and their Old Testament background. The New Testament incorporates here and there liturgical hymns (for example, Phil 2:6–11), confessions probably made on the occasion of baptism (for example, Rom 10:9) and acclamations (for example, 1 Cor 12:3; Gal 1:1) which antedate our first Christian writer (Paul) and go back to the very origins of Christianity. Both prior to the birth of Christianity and right down to our own day, it has been through the liturgical feasts (above all, the Passover) that Jewish faith and theology has remained alive and been transmitted. Thus a liturgically fashioned FT would take its cue from the oldest texts of Christianity and ancient Jewish feasts.

The liturgy illuminates strikingly the three major themes of FT. First, as we shall see in Chapter 5, the church's liturgy is now the primary place of revelation for us. The liturgical words and gestures create a disclosure situation dependent upon and analogous to that created by the words and deeds of Jesus (see next chapter). I observed above the intertwining of (historical) event and (divine) mystery in the communication of God's revelation. Through *anamnesis* the liturgical actions, above all the eucharist, bring to mind certain historical events which conveyed the revealing and saving interventions of God. The faithful assembled for worship are invited to recall and appropriate for themselves God's salvific manifestation which Christ brought to a definitive climax for all and once and for all. For every new generation the liturgy re-presents *the* redemptive revelation that was the paschal mystery.

The analogical approach to an understanding of the divine mysteries recommended by the First Vatican Council (see Chapter 2) can easily remain a merely cerebral game. The lived and celebrated analogies of the liturgy let the transcendent God and the divine word come through. When water is poured and bread is broken, worshipers can know God and hear the word.

Those lived analogies have repeatedly brought to non-believers or half-believers the revelation of Christ and his powerful presence in the liturgy. In all its richness the liturgy has proved itself over and over again the great and convincing sign of Christian *credibility*. Under that second special theme of FT, I considered the human condition and our faith that accepts God's revelation. A liturgical frame of mind would encourage us to interpret the human person as one called to pray and bless God (*homo orans et benedicens*). Such a "prayerful" and "doxological" account of human existence obviously has little difficulty in correlating who we essentially are with what we accept from the self-communication of God. This version of the human condition can happily incorporate major elements from other versions. The sufferings of *homo dolens* can be brought to the liturgy and there find their transformation. In the church's year no other ceremony expresses more vividly this acceptance and transformation of human suffering than the liturgy of Good Friday. At the same time, the liturgy orients and strengthens hopes of *homo sperans* toward the fullness of life, meaning and love that through worship we experience in anticipation.

Along with the human condition the liturgy focuses our faith in the self-revealing God. In an earlier work I followed St. Paul's lead by presenting faith in terms of confession, commitment and confidence. The liturgy throws new light on these three dimensions of faith. At the Easter vigil, at every Sunday mass and on other occasions the faithful renew together their confession of faith. Our public worship, especially the eucharist, is *the* source from which comes the strength for faith's commitment (SC 10). Third, our confident expectation of future life in heaven is fed by the present, "earthly liturgy" (SC 80). In short, it is at our peril in FT that we forget the church's liturgy when reflecting on the confession, commitment and confidence that characterize our Christian faith.

Finally, *Dei Verbum* itself reminds us how it is through "her teaching, life and *worship*" that the church "perpetuates and hands on to all generations all that she herself is, all that she believes" (DV 8; italics mine). Even if the liturgy is not the only place and means for transmitting, interpreting and actualizing the whole church tradition, its role remains essential. No study of the third major theme of FT, tradition in all its fullness (including the liturgical use of scriptures), can afford to ignore the church's public worship.

This chapter ends thus with a wish and dream—that someone may develop a full-scale FT in the key of the liturgy, so as to enrich and complete the wide range of studies we already possess in that discipline.

4. *DEI VERBUM*

The opening chapters of this book have been looking for directions: about theology in general (Chapters 1 and 2) and about fundamental theology in particular (Chapter 3). This chapter takes us to the heart of the book, the Second Vatican Council's Dogmatic Constitution on Divine Revelation, *Dei Verbum* (promulgated on November 18, 1965).

Clearly a piece of church teaching that primarily reflects and encourages the first style of theology (see Chapter 1 above), *Dei Verbum* contains, nevertheless, hints of the third and even the second style of theology. In its closing chapter the document hopes for a spiritually renewed church in which theologians, no less than others, let their lives and work become more deeply nourished by the scriptures, public worship and personal prayer (DV 21, 23-25). Earlier chapters of *Dei Verbum* contain brief points which also converge toward a third style of theology: the reference to the "wonderful treasury of prayers" to be found in the Old Testament (DV 15) and the reference to the "worship" through which the "believing and praying" church hands on her tradition (DV 8). There are references also to the Old Testament's "sound wisdom about human life" (DV 15) and the church's own "practice and life" (DV 8) which edge us a little in the direction of the practical, second style of theology. But the dominant style remains the first.

Normally the commentaries have found much to praise in *Dei Verbum*.[1] Acknowledging clearly the divine initiative, the document interprets revelation as the personal self-revelation of the triune God who invites human beings to enter freely into a dialogue of love, so that through their response of integral faith they may receive salvation. *Dei Verbum* has been evaluated as thoroughly christocentric, since it recognizes the climax of revelation and its signs in the death and resurrection of God's incarnate Son—with their outcome in the sending of Christ's Holy Spirit through whom the revelation given once and for all remains a present reality. Commentators frequently speak of the sacramental and historical approach, which understands revelation to be a living event communicated through deeds and words functioning together in the course of salvation history. The tone of *Dei Verbum* has been seen to be pastoral and non-polemical, and its ecumenical spirit is unmistakable. Many heirs of the Protestant reformation like the title of the constitution ("Word of God") and its recognition that the church's official teachers are not above the word of God but serve it (DV 10). The secondary literature has singled out various other merits and achievements of *Dei Verbum:* the way in which the presentation of revelation as primarily an encounter with the self-disclosing God puts into a new context the whole debate about the relationship between tradition and sacred scripture; the emphasis on the unity between tradition and scripture in the transmission and reactualization of revelation; the endorsement of scientific biblical scholarship; the interpretation of biblical truth as salvific; the stress on the role of scripture for theology; and the stimulus given to the use of the Bible in every area of the church's life.

In the preconciliar situation and in the conciliar debates which led to the final text, three points proved particularly difficult: a) the precise relationship between scripture and tradition, b) the nature of biblical truth, and c) the historical reliability of the gospels.[2] What *Dei Verbum* eventually taught on these points (in DV 9, 11 and 19, respectively) calls for some comment before this chapter examines some aspects of the document's teaching on revelation. A later chapter will take up the directives on biblical interpretation.

1) *Three Debated Points.* a) In 1546 the Council of Trent declared "the gospel" to be "the source of all saving truth and rule of conduct," adding that "this truth and rule of conduct are contained in the written books [of the Bible] and unwritten [apostolic] traditions" (DS 1501). Despite Trent's language about the gospel being "the source" (in the singular), there emerged in Catholic theology the so-called "two-source" theory of revelation, according to which scripture and tradition are two distinct sources for revealed truths. Tradition could and does supply some truths which were not to be found in scripture. In other words, scripture is not merely "formally insufficient" (= needing to be interpreted and actualized) but also "materially insufficient" (= not containing all revealed truth). This view of things obviously privileged a propositional view of revelation: namely, the model of revelation as the communication of truths which would otherwise remain hidden in God. Although *Dei Verbum* did not rule out the "two-source" theory, that theory is certainly much more difficult to maintain in the face of the council's understanding of divine revelation (as being primarily God's self-revelation) and its stress on the unity between scripture and tradition (DV 9).[3]

b) On the question of biblical truth *Dei Verbum* began by following the lead of the First Vatican Council and Pope Leo XIII in his encyclical *Providentissimus Deus* (1893) by distinguishing between biblical inspiration and biblical truth or inerrancy (DS 3006, 3292), which is a major corollary of the special guidance from the Holy Spirit given to the sacred authors. Second, in the same article *Dei Verbum,* while recognizing that the books of scripture teach "without error," stressed their positive function as teaching "that truth which God, for the sake of our salvation," wanted to be recorded by the Bible (DV 11). Beyond question, talk about salvific *truth* implies that we can first determine something about the *meaning* of the scriptures. Questions of meaning normally take precedence over questions of truth. Hence Chapter Three of *Dei Verbum* deals not only with the divine inspiration and the consequent salvific truth of the scriptures but also with their *interpretation and meaning* (DV 12). In a later chapter we return to the issue of biblical interpretation.[4]

c) The development of form criticism after the First World War and of redaction criticism after the Second World War raises the question of our access to the Jesus of history. Does the redactional work of the gospel writers at the third stage and the various forms of oral or written tradition at the second stage (that is to say, from the 30s through to the 60s when Mark's gospel was written) make it extremely difficult if not impossible to say anything about the first stage: the actual deeds, words and public history of Jesus?

Is our historical knowledge of Jesus blocked by a holy iconostasis at the third stage (the gospel writers' work) or at least at the second stage (the creative traditions in the early church)? *Dei Verbum,* while acknowledging modifications and additions coming both from the evangelists (stage three) and the community (stage two), insists that the gospels do tell us "the honest truth about Jesus" (DV 19). The religious character of the gospels does not stop them from providing a substantially reliable account of the last years of Jesus' life.[5]

d) It seemed important to mention, at least summarily, three major issues which lay behind the final making of *Dei Verbum*. That helps to explain why, despite the announced intention to "set forth the true doctrine on divine revelation and its transmission" (DV 1), the document pays much more attention to the transmission of revelation through tradition and scripture (five chapters out of six). What *Dei Verbum* says about divine revelation (and human faith) in its opening chapter was conceived as an introduction to all that follows about tradition and scripture. As it was not planned to be a full treatment of revelation and faith, Chapter One of *Dei Verbum* has little or nothing to offer about such important themes as the human condition (or the human person open to the message of revelation), the signs of credibility, the social nature of faith, the signs of the times, and the knowledge of God in other religions (or in the general history of revelation and salvation). The next chapter will show, among other things, how the other conciliar documents shed light on these issues. Let us now turn to some major thrusts in the teaching of *Dei Verbum* on revelation.

2) *The Biblical Orientation.* Unlike *Dei Filius,* the First Vatican Council's Constitution on Faith (1870), *Dei Verbum* is profoundly biblical in its language and mentality. The document makes seventy-three references to scripture and quotes three passages from the Bible.

Chapter One of *Dei Verbum* sets the tone for the rest of the document by choosing three classical biblical texts on revelation. The prologue cites 1 John 1:2–3, verses which indicate the personal character of the divine self-revelation, its salvific aim and its apostolic, ecclesial nature (DV 1). Chapter One begins with a reference to Ephesians 1:9, a classic passage on God revealing "the mystery" of the divine will— namely, the saving plan for all humanity now revealed in Christ. The opening verses of Hebrews are cited in part by our document (DV 4): "In many and various ways God spoke of old to our fathers by the prophets. But in these last days he has spoken to us by a Son" (Heb 1:1– 2). *Dei Verbum* has already made it clear that not merely words ("God spoke") but also events ("works performed by God") are integral to revelation (DV 2). By having already named the patriarchs and Moses (DV 3), our document recognizes that "the prophets" of Hebrews 1:1 should be understood more broadly as all those Old Testament figures through whom God spoke and not merely as those who gave their names to the prophetic literature.

Chapter Two, among the new ways of "doing" theology encouraged by the council, mentioned the *reductio in mysterium,* that tendency to highlight *the* mystery of the tripersonal God revealed through Christ in the history of salvation and inviting human beings to share in a new communion of love. As we have just seen, this language is based on the Pauline letters (see not only Eph 1:9 but also, for example, Eph 3:4,9; 6:19; Col 1:27; 4:3; Rom 16:25-26). Talk of "the mystery" forms a major *leitmotif* in *Dei Verbum;* five times this constitution speaks of "mystery" in the singular (DV 2, 15, 17, 24 and 26) and never of "mysteries" in the plural. The same tendency shows up in the other texts promulgated by the Second Vatican Council: the sixteen documents use "mystery" in the singular one hundred and fourteen times and "mysteries" in the plural only fourteen times. For that matter, right from his first encyclical John Paul II has exemplified the same tendency. *Redemptor Hominis* (1979) speaks fifty-nine times of "the mystery of redemption," "the paschal mystery," "the mystery of Christ," "the mystery of the divine 'economy' " and so forth, without ever using the term "mystery" in the plural.[6]

The examples just given should suffice to establish the profoundly biblical orientation of *Dei Verbum*. It comes as no surprise to find the document inviting theologians to make the study of scriptures "the very soul" of their work (DV 24), a recommendation taken from *Providentissimus Deus* of Leo XIII (1893) who in turn drew it from a long-standing Jesuit tradition.[7] The Second Vatican Council nowhere says that the scriptures should be "the very soul of the magisterium." Nevertheless, the nature of magisterial teaching exemplified by the conciliar documents and, in particular, by *Dei Verbum* (see DV 10) clearly implies that the church's official teaching should find its "soul" in the inspired scriptures.

3) *The Divine Self-Communication.* Right from its opening article *Dei Verbum* presents revelation as primarily being God's self-disclosure. As we shall see in an excursus at the end of this chapter, the theme of divine *self*-revelation entered the making of *Dei Verbum* three years before the council promulgated the definitive text. The theme turns up repeatedly in that final text (see, for example DV 1–6, 14, 17).

What is normally overlooked, however, is the way *Dei Verbum* introduces the notion of the divine "self-communication," a notion that has its background in Kierkegaard, Barth and Rahner (in particular, his theology of grace).[8] In doing so, our document echoes here some words from *Dei Filius,* the only passage where the First Vatican Council presented revelation as the divine *self*-revelation: "It pleased his [God's] wisdom and goodness to reveal himself and his eternal decrees" (DS 3004). In *Dei Verbum* this becomes: "By divine revelation God wished to manifest and communicate himself and the eternal decrees of his will concerning the salvation of human beings" (DV 6). (See also the clear echo of *Dei Filius* in DV 2: "It pleased God, in his goodness and wisdom, to reveal himself and make known the mystery of his will.") Various comments could be made on the development that emerges here. But my point is simply this. Where *Dei Filius* spoke of "revealing," this verb gets doubled in *Dei Verbum* to become "manifest and *communicate.*" The immediate background to this development is as follows.

In April 1964 Pieter Smulders completed a draft of what became Chapter One of *Dei Verbum*. Number five of that draft began:

> Divine revelation is concerned with those things which God
> wished to communicate about himself and the decrees of his
> eternal will for the salvation of human beings and [their] partici-

pation in the divine life. (*Divina revelatio agit quidem de eis, quae de seipso ac de aeternae voluntatis suae decretis circa hominum salutem divinaeque vitae participationem Deus communicare voluit.*)[9]

By the time the Smulders' draft was presented for discussion at the council's general session on September 30, 1964, the above sentence had been modified in a revised text of July 1964 to read:

> By divine revelation are manifested those things which God wished to communicate about himself and the eternal decrees of his will for the salvation of human beings and [their] participation in the divine life. (*Divina revelatione manifestantur ea, quae Deus de seipso ac de aeternis voluntatis suae decretis circa hominum salutem divinaeque vitae participationem, communicare voluit.*)[10]

From the fourteen-page draft and report prepared by Smulders in April 1964 one sees that in the light of a written proposal from Abbot Christopher Butler, Smulders had composed the sentence we are examining.[11] Butler, however, had used only the verb "manifest." Smulders, as we see above, substituted the verb "communicate."

In the form debated by the council in September and October 1964 (see above) "manifest" was back in the text, but separated from "communicate." In the definitive version of *Dei Verbum* (which corresponds to a revised text of November 20, 1964) the verbs stand together: "manifest and communicate" (*manifestare ac communicare*) with "God" as both subject and object (DV 6).

It is obvious from Smulders' report of April 1964 that it was only in the context of the object of revelation that he introduced the language of God's "communication." He was not thinking explicitly of Rahner's theology of grace, still less of Kierkegaard's philosophy. Nevertheless, by accident or providence through Smulders the language of the divine "communication" and eventually God's "self-communication" entered official Catholic teaching.[12] It was later used by John Paul II in a 1980 encyclical, *Dives in Misericordia* (7) and then repeatedly in a 1986 encyclical on the Holy Spirit, *Dominum et Vivificantem* (13 [twice], 14, 23, 50 [four times], 51 [twice] and 58 [twice]). The peculiar value of the term comes from the way it can hold together God's self-*revelation* and self-*giving* through saving grace. God's communication is not merely cognitive but constitutes a *real* self-communication of God which not only makes salvation known but actually brings it in person.

Right from its prologue *Dei Verbum* indicates how God's revelation and offer of salvation coincide. The council wanted to "set forth the true doctrine on divine revelation," because it wanted "the whole world to hear the summons to salvation" (DV 1). The plan or "economy of revelation" is synonymous with "the history of salvation" (DV 2). Repeatedly without hesitation the document passes from the language of revelation to that of salvation and then back to revelation (see, for example, DV 3, 4, 6, 7, 14–15, 17, 21), thereby recognizing that we are dealing with two inseparable, if distinguishable, realities. Talk of the "divine self-communication" is as good a way as any for acknowledging that God's revealing word necessarily offers saving life. In Johannine terms, if Jesus is *the* truth in person he is also *the* life in person.[13]

The sacramental language of *Dei Verbum* applies equally to the "economy of revelation" and "the history of salvation." As with the administration of the sacraments, the words and deeds of persons interact to communicate God's revelation and salvation (DV 2, 4, 14). Above all in the case of Jesus himself, the words and deeds of a person convey the saving self-manifestation of God (DV 17).

This "sacramental" way of presenting God's saving and revealing self-communication does not appear to have an ecumenical origin. It is not that *Dei Verbum* combined the language of a) word-of-God theologians like Karl Barth and Rudolf Bultmann with b) that favored by Oscar Cullmann, Wolfhart Pannenberg, and George Ernest Wright about God's revealing and/or saving acts in history. A year before the promulgation of *Dei Verbum,* the council's Dogmatic Constitution on the Church (*Lumen Gentium*) recalled Jesus' proclamation of God's kingdom: "This kingdom shone out before men in the word, in the works and in the presence of Christ" (LG 5). But two years before that, in November 1962, the language of "word(s)" and "works" had already entered the making of *Dei Verbum* through Pieter Smulders (see the excursus that follows this chapter).

Already one of the world's experts on St. Hilary of Poitiers, Smulders, when drafting what was to become Chapter Four of *Dei Verbum,* unconsciously (?) echoed the language of Hilary. In the opening article of his *Tractatus Mysteriorum* Hilary wrote of the biblical "words" (*dicta*) and "facts" (*facta*) that "announce" (*nuntiare*) and "reveal" (*exprimere*) the coming of Christ. Of course, one can interpret *Dei Verbum* as a Catholic text which welcomes and joins together themes favored by two opposed schools of Protestant theologians. Nevertheless, through Smulders the scheme of "words *and* deeds" as the vehicle of revelation goes back rather to St. Hilary.

4) *The Content of Revelation.* The opening chapter of *Dei Verbum* makes it abundantly clear that revelation means *primarily* God's personal self-revelation (DV 1–4). *Secondarily,* however, the divine revelation discloses something about God and human beings. The interpersonal "dia-logue" which is God's saving self-communication says and communicates something. A word or "logos" comes through to the human partner of the divinely initiated dialogue.

Hence the second chapter of *Dei Verbum* opens as follows: "God graciously arranged that *the things he had once revealed* for the salvation of all people should remain in their entirety, throughout the ages, and be transmitted to all generations" (DV 7; italics mine). Since it deals with the transmission of revelation, that same chapter naturally speaks of "all revealed truths" (DV 9) and goes on to use a classic term for the content of the definitive revelation communicated through Christ and his apostles: "All that it [the magisterium] proposes for belief as being divinely revealed is drawn from this single *deposit of faith*" (DV 10; italics mine). At the end *Dei Verbum* talks of "the treasure of revelation entrusted to the church" (DV 26) which is to be faithfully preserved and proclaimed.

To speak of the deposit of *faith* or its equivalent, the treasure of *revelation,* brings us to the issue of fidelity to and continuity with the revelation which reached its definitive and unsurpassable climax with Christ's resurrection from the dead and the sending of the Holy Spirit. How does our faith in God's self-revelation remain essentially identical with the apostolic faith which responded to the divine self-communication in and through Christ? What allows us to believe the same "things" or "truths" that God "once revealed for the salvation of all people"—or, in other words, to profess and live by the same "treasure of revelation" communicated to the apostolic Church?

Chapter Two of *Dei Verbum* names the three factors that collaborate in assuring the essential continuity with "the things" God long ago revealed in Christ: the Holy Spirit, the inspired scriptures, and the whole people of God with their entire tradition and under the leadership of the bishops. It is not my intention here to take up in detail this issue of continuity. One point, however, calls for comment.

After treating the transmission of divine revelation, the council begins the very next chapter by talking of "the divinely revealed realities, which are *contained* and presented in the text of sacred scripture" (DV 11). Here we come up against the limits of the verb "contain" and the noun I have used for the title of this section, "content." Strictly speaking, revelation, inasmuch as it is an interpersonal event of God's self-communication, cannot be "contained" in or by anything, not even the inspired and sacred scripture.

Primarily, revelation does not consist in "things" but in God's own self-manifestation. Secondarily, one can and should speak of revelation's "content," which is recorded by the Bible. A later chapter will discuss in detail the relationship between revelation and the inspired scriptures.

5) *Concluding Remarks.* To round out this chapter in which I have presupposed reflections on *Dei Verbum* which I have published elsewhere,[14] I wish to add two points: the first concerns the Holy Spirit and the second the Blessed Virgin Mary.

Dei Verbum refers twenty-three times to the Holy Spirit. Nevertheless, the document remains very christocentric. Despite the statistics, it illustrates a Latin tendency to subordinate the work of the Spirit to that of the Son. The chapter on the Old Testament (DV 14–16), for example, is oriented toward Christ but says nothing about the Holy Spirit. On October 5, 1964, during a debate on the revised text of *De Divina Revelatione* that was to become *Dei Verbum,* an eastern archbishop, Néophytos Edelby, in a remarkable speech indicated the need to recognize more fully the role of the Spirit in revelation and its transmission through scripture and tradition. (For the first time, an English translation of this speech is available; see the Appendix below.) Unfortunately Edelby's intervention came too late and hardly affected the final shape of *Dei Verbum.*

If the Second Vatican Council had met in the 1990s the Holy Spirit would have bulked larger in *Dei Verbum.* Since the 1960s the Catholic Church and its leaders, especially those of the Latin rite which makes up the overwhelming majority, have become much more sensitive to the role of the Holy Spirit. The charismatic renewal within the western church and westerners' increased contacts with eastern Christianity have helped to bring about the change. The space dedicated to the Holy Spirit in John Paul II's encyclical on the church's missionary mandate, *Redemptoris Missio* (1990), is emblematic of this increased sensitivity (see, for example, 21–30).

Second, *Dei Verbum* enters a scheme of parallels in recent (Catholic) church history which has a strong providential look to it. In 1854, Pius IX solemnly proclaimed as a divinely revealed truth the immaculate conception of the Virgin Mary. Fifteen years later the First Vatican Council opened, and in one of its two documents (*Dei Filius*) it dealt with questions of revelation and faith. In 1950, Pius XII solemnly proclaimed as a divinely revealed truth the bodily assumption of the Virgin Mary. Twelve years later the Second Vatican Council opened, and one of its sixteen documents was *Dei Verbum* which dealt with divine revelation and its transmission. In both cases the definition of a Marian dogma by a pope was followed by a general council which made revelation one of its major themes. The proclamation of a particular revealed truth led to conciliar teaching on the doctrine of revelation in general. A focus on Christ's mother preceded a focus on mother church gathered in an ecumenical council.

Beyond question the parallels and contrasts between the events of a) 1854 and 1869/70 and b) 1950 and 1962/65 call for much more examination and reflection. But there is a providential look to the way the theme of Mary and revelation repeats itself in the events of a) and b).

EXCURSUS: AT THE ORIGINS OF *DEI VERBUM*

In the history of Christianity *Dei Verbum* was the first conciliar document on God's self-revelation. Even if it also considered revelation, the First Vatican Council's *Dei Filius* (1870) was as such a constitution on faith. Many commentators have described the making of *Dei Verbum*—from the severe criticism of the preliminary text in November 1962 down to the practically unanimous acceptance of the definitive draft in the fourth and final session of the council. In this excursus I want to add further information on the historical genesis of *Dei Verbum* by presenting and evaluating a decisive contribution made by an archbishop and a theologian.

In November 1962 many council fathers strongly criticized the preliminary "schema" *De Fontibus Revelationis,* and a majority voted to have the document returned to the Theological Commission for rewriting. Pope John XXIII intervened to confirm the majority view and set up a new joint commission to handle the work of revision. The members of this "mixed commission" were drawn from the Secretariat for Christian Unity and from the Theological Commission itself.

The "mixed commission" first met on the evening of November 24, 1962. Johannes Feiner reports that a bishop from the Theological Commission was given the task of "drafting a *Prooemium* for the next meeting."[15] The bishop in fact was Alfredo Vicente (later Cardinal) Scherer of Porto Alegre in Brazil. In Rome he was staying in the same house as Father Pieter Smulders, who had been invited by the bishops of Indonesia to advise them at the council. Smulders would be an official *peritus* for the second, third and fourth sessions of the council (1963–65). Around ten in the evening Scherer visited Smulders and asked him to prepare by three thirty p.m. the following day a draft on revelation and the Old Testament. In fact, Scherer did not say that he was charged with preparing a *Prooemium,* but rather that he had been appointed to a subcommission on the Old Testament. As he expected the curial members of this subcommission to present a draft in their style (which in the event happened), he wanted to be able to submit another draft.

After consulting with Father Ernst Vogt and with the help of Father Luis Alonso Schökel (both at the Pontifical Biblical Institute), Smulders had a one-page text (hereafter SD) ready for Scherer the next afternoon.[16] In his diary Smulders noted a German and Dutch proverb (about the use of flour mills) which Scherer suggested to him: "The one who comes first grinds best" (= first come, first served).

Apropos of SD but without identifying its authorship, Feiner remarks:

> It was a matter of a statement on revelation in the history of salvation, a statement the essential items of which were to be found again in the definitive text of the Constitution. . . . Basing itself above all on the whole Christ event, that text [= SD] declared that revelation consists also of deeds.[17]

SD clearly contained the three themes mentioned by Feiner: the history of salvation as the medium of revelation, the central place of Christ, and the role of deeds (*gesta*) in revelation. Apropos of the first point made by Feiner, it is worth remarking that Smulders' paper used the term "history" (*historia*) for the whole "event of revelation" (*eventus revelationis*) which reached its climax with the coming of Christ. The final text of *Dei Verbum* preferred the term "economy" (*oeconomia*).[18] In Chapter One (which Smulders was to draft in 1964) *Dei Verbum* did, however, speak (DV 2) of "the history of salvation" (*historia salutis*).

Over and above the three points noted by Feiner, SD included a number of other themes which would find their place in the definitive text of *Dei Verbum:* 1) revelation as being primarily divine self-revelation (*"Deus . . . seipsum . . . revelavit"*); 2) the central significance in salvation history of the covenants made with Abraham and Moses; 3) the place of the prophets in the story of revelation; 4) the people's experience of God in the Old Testament; 5) the coming of God's Son as the fullness of revelation (*"plenitudo revelationis"*) to complete the divine self-revelation through his person, deeds and words (*"persona, gestis, verbis suis revelationem consummantis"*); 6) the theme of "the word of God" (*"verbum Dei"* occurs twice); 7) the knowledge of God and human beings yielded by the Old Testament scriptures (*"Cognitionem Dei et hominis praebent"*; *"docent quibus mirabilibus modis Deus cum hominibus agat"*) 8) Romans 15:4 as indicating the permanent value of the divinely inspired Old Testament scriptures; 9) an approach to scriptures as the product of revelation ("*eventus revelationis fit Scriptura*"). Apropos of this last point, *Dei Verbum* itself was also to express the (temporal, logical and theological) priority of revelation over the inspired books of the Bible—not least by using the same device as SD: the scriptures were treated only after the nature of the whole historical self-revelation of God had been outlined.

All of these items (1–9) were maintained in what was to become Chapter Four of *Dei Verbum*. Some of these themes (especially 1, 2, 3 and 5) were to find a place also in Chapter One of *Dei Verbum*. Theme 6 was to provide the document with its opening words, a title which would also be echoed in its closing phrase about "the word of God which remains forever" (*verbi Dei quod manet in aeternum;* DV 26). The notion of human beings experiencing a perennial "witness" to God in nature (supported by a reference to Acts 14:17), a tenth theme, did not move from the opening sentence of SD into Chapter Four but turned up in Chapter One of *Dei Verbum* (DV 3), now supported by Romans 1:19–20.

As regards point 5 above, it should be noted that on November 21, 1962 (that is to say, several days before Smulders was asked by Scherer to draft his paper) Bishop Emile Guano had proposed to the council that the "exordium" of the new *schema* on revelation should state that "God speaks to men through . . . his Word made flesh." Christ "speaks to men, to begin with, through his words (*dicta*), but also . . . through his works (*facta*) and deeds (*gesta*), indeed through his very person."[19] In the end the final text of *Dei Verbum* was to talk repeatedly of revelation being communicated "by deeds and words."[20] As terms which suggest somewhat better the personal nature of revelation, "*gesta*" (twice) and "*opera*" (twice) rather than "*facta*" (only once) were used in the definitive draft of the constitution.

What I have summarily listed above as (7) and (8) merit further discussion. a) SD spoke of "a number of things . . . which belonged exclusively to the time of preparation" and which "were abrogated by the new law (*plura . . . quae tempori praeparationis exclusive conveniebant. Nova Lege abrogata sunt*)." In a slightly more positive way *Dei Verbum* was to express similar sentiments: "These books [of the Old Testament], though they also contain some things which are incomplete and temporary, nevertheless show us true divine pedagogy" (DV 15). b) *Dei Verbum* called God "the inspirer and author of the books of both Testament" (DV 16), a statement with precedents which reach back to the church's rejection of Marcion in the second century. SD acknowledged that the books of the Old Testament remained the "word of God" for the church, because they had been written under divine inspiration

("*Deo inspirante*"). It was obviously implied that this was true also for the writing of the New Testament scriptures.

c) SD recognized in the Old Testament scriptures an "apologetic, dogmatic and moral value" (*valor apologeticus, dogmaticus, moralis*). At this point *Dei Verbum* was eventually to maintain only a little of the original terminology: "*Dei et hominis cognitionem ac modos quibus Deus . . . cum hominibus agit . . . manifestant* ([the books of the Old Testament] . . . disclose a knowledge of God and man and the ways in which God . . . acts with human beings)" (DV 15). Nevertheless, *Dei Verbum* kept something of the same order of the "apologetic, dogmatic and moral" values—especially in the case of the "dogmatic" and "moral" values. DV 15 moved from the preparation for and prophetic announcement of the coming of Christ and his messianic kingdom (= apologetic value?), through the revelation of a "knowledge of God and of man" and "a store of sublime teaching about God" to be found in the Old Testament scriptures (= dogmatic value), to the "sound wisdom about human life" and "wonderful treasury of prayers" contained in those scriptures (= moral value). SD had expressed this "moral" value in terms of "the way man should behave toward God and neighbors" (*quo modo se homo ad Deum ac proximos gerere debeat*).

d) Finally, DV 16 preserved the link of *meaning* between the two Testaments which SD had already sketched. That draft noted that many things in the Old Testament books had been "incorporated into the Christian revelation" (*revelationi Christianae incorporata*). Thus they "acquire and show forth a fuller sense" (*profundiorem sensum acquirunt et ostendunt*). A text from Augustine's *De Catechizandis Rudibus* was used to support the claim that the Old Testament, "just as it is fully opened up from the New Testament (Lk 24:37), so on the other hand it has greatly contributed to our richer understanding and relish of the New Testament" (*sicut . . . Vetus Testamentum ex Novo plene aperitur* [Lc 24:32], *ita ex altera parte ad sapidam ac ditiorem Novi Testamenti intellectum summopere confert*. *Dei Verbum* was to maintain the same stance on the reciprocal hermeneutical link between the two Testaments: "God . . . arranged that the New Testament be hidden in the Old and the Old be made manifest in the New . . . the books of the Old Testament . . . caught up into the proclamation of the gospel, acquire and show forth their complete meaning in the New Testament . . . and in turn shed light on it and explain it" (DV 16). Instead of quoting from the *De Catechizandis Rudibus* the sentence, "*in Veteri Testamento est occultatio Novi, in Novo Testamento est manifestatio Veteris* (in the Old Testament the New is hidden, in the New Testament the Old is revealed)," *Dei Verbum* referred in footnote 42 to the *Quaestionum in*

Heptateuchum (2,73; PL 34,623), where Augustine made the same point.

Thus far I have been concerned to illustrate the links between SD (the Smulders' paper of November 1962) and the definitive text of *Dei Verbum*. A fairly straight line led from that paper to Chapter Four of the constitution. There are also many echoes of the thirteen points found in SD (three noted by Feiner and ten further ones noted by myself) in *other* chapters of *Dei Verbum,* particularly in Chapter One. I should add that SD was (a) a little reticent about the link between revelation and salvation, and b) more explicitly incarnation-centered rather than oriented toward the dying and rising of Christ. Right from its preface, *Dei Verbum* (a) firmly associated revelation and salvation as the two sides of the one divine "self-communication" (DV 1,6). (b) It presented Christ's death, resurrection and sending of the Holy Spirit as the full climax of the work of revelation and salvation (DV 4). As regards (b), it is understandable that both SD and the final text of Chapter Four thematized matters in terms of the incarnation. After all the chapter deals with the Old Testament and its history which reached its climax with the birth of Christ (Gal 4:4).

In describing the genesis of *Dei Verbum*, Gregory Baum[21] evaluated in the following terms the April 1963 draft, *De Divina Revelatione,* produced by the "mixed commission" and sent to the council fathers in May 1963.

> The corrected chapter 3, on the Old Testament,[22] is the place where a deeper concept of revelation is first inserted into the conciliar document. This concept will be developed in the later drafts in a special chapter [= Chapter I of *Dei Verbum*]. Chapter 3 distinguishes clearly between God's self-revelation in His action and word in Israel and the Spirit-inspired record of these events in the writings of the Old Testament. This attempt to overcome the concept of revelation as teaching in favor of a concept of revelation as personal self-communication in history represents the important turning point in the development of the Dogmatic Constitution on Divine Revelation.[23]

Chapter Three of this April 1963 text (which would become Chapter Four in *Dei Verbum*) was, in fact, largely based on SD. It had added to that paper a strong opening statement about God's salvific purposes for the whole human race and, in particular, for the chosen people. Reference was made to the three divisions of Old Testament scriptures, the prophetic, historical and wisdom books, which, respectively, "foretold, recounted and explained" God's saving dealings with the chosen people. (One must observe that it is a little forced to sum up the prophetic literature as "foretelling" and the wisdom literature as "explaining" God's saving dealings with the people.) Chapter Three of *De Divina Revelatione* also appealed to 1 Corinthians 10:11 in maintaining a typological link between the two Testaments. A little more than SD, this chapter stressed the perennial value of the books of the Old Testament which present "the true word of God" (*verum Verbum Dei*) and which the church "reverently acknowledges as her own scriptures" (*ut suas Scripturas reverenter agnoscit*). But the changes and additions were minor.

What is more, we know from Kerrigan's commentary that these changes and additions had already been made months earlier, when a group (Ahern, Baum, Kerrigan and Smulders) delegated by the subcommission met on December 2, 1962. Their draft, a reworking of SD, was approved "with some small amendments" by the mixed commission at "one of its plenary sessions held in December 1962."[24] A copy of this draft from December 2, 1962 preserved in Smulders' archives establishes the same point. It shows too that the "small amendments" were only stylistic improvements. With a few small changes and additions (like the reference to the "divine pedagogy" in DV 15), Chapter Three of *De Divina Revelatione* was to emerge as Chapter Four in the final conciliar text.

To sum up this history: The paper drafted by Smulders on November 25, 1962 moved fairly intact through the revision of December 2, 1962 (made by himself and three others as delegates for the subcommission of the mixed commission), and through the slight retouches from the mixed commission (later that December) which produced *De Divina Revelatione* in April 1963, on through the revised version of *De Divina Revelatione* (debated by the council in 1964) to become Chapter Four of *Dei Verbum* in November 1965. As we saw above, the thirteen points one can isolate in SD were echoed in other chapters of that constitution, particularly in Chapter One. In the making of *Dei Verbum* the proverb cited by Archbishop Scherer proved its truth: "The one who comes first grinds best."[25]

5. THE "OTHER" DOCUMENTS ON REVELATION

Recognized by Catholics as the twenty-first ecumenical council in the history of Christianity, the Second Vatican Council published sixteen documents, thereby contributing nearly one-third of all the texts promulgated by those general councils of the church.[1] Sheer quantity should not be allowed to cloak the high quality of nearly all the documents promulgated by the Second Vatican Council.

For fundamental theology's central theme of revelation, *Dei Verbum* is beyond question *the* document. Nevertheless, it is at our peril that we neglect the other fifteen texts from the council. In differing ways they not only repeat and amplify the teaching from *Dei Verbum* on revelation, but at times they also add new and important points.

Regrettably, translations, commentaries and other literature on the council have normally ignored or played down the valuable teaching on revelation available in the "other" documents. The index for the standard English translations of the council's documents, edited by W.M. Abbott and A. Flannery under the headword "revelation" offers a mere four (Abbott) or five (Flannery) references to those "other" documents. In a fifteen page account of revelation according to the Second Vatican Council, H. Waldenfels does not make a single reference to any of the "other" documents. He limits himself entirely to the text of *Dei Verbum*.[2] H. Pfeiffer, in a substantial study on the understanding of revelation in the First and Second Vatican Councils, does consider how the "other" documents fill out the council's doctrine of revelation.[3] However, two serious limitations show up in his section on those documents (pp. 154–78). First, Pfeiffer is so concerned to establish thoroughly that Second Vatican Council also allows for an intelligible and statable expression of revelation, that he overlooks other valuable points in the council's teaching. For instance, on p. 162 he interprets within the perspective of religion (rather than that of revelation) the list of basic human questions and needs which rounds off the preface of the Declaration on the Relation of the Church to Non-Christian Religions (*Nostra Aetate*).

This is to miss the way God's self-revelation comes as the divine answer to the primordial questions which affect all human beings. Reflection on such questions *also* belongs to a full doctrine of revelation (see GS 10, 13 and 41). In studying the use of the term *fides* in the Second Vatican Council, Pfeiffer briefly mentions what *Dignitatis Humanae* says on the freedom involved in the act of Christian faith (p. 231). Yet in his main treatment of that Declaration on Religious Liberty he passes over what the document indicates about divine revelation respecting and not restricting human freedom (pp. 168–69). He is so engrossed with one important issue (the personal self-revelation of God ruling in rather than ruling out the objective truth of revelation) that he does not pick up other contributions from the council toward a complete theology of revelation. A further example: Pfeiffer's restricted perspective leads him to omit completely the reflections from *Gaudium et Spes* (4 and 11) and other council documents on reading and interpreting the signs of the times. This is to leave out of consideration one important way revelation functions as a present reality.

The second limitation in Pfeiffer's approach to the documents from the Second Vatican Council other than *Dei Verbum* comes from his concentration on the terminology *revelare, revelatio,* and various synonyms. As the word *revelatio* only occurs once in *Nostra Aetate,* this encourages him to argue that the declaration does not offer much on the theme of revelation (p. 161). Likewise the fact that neither *revelatio* nor *revelare* occurs in the Constitution on the Sacred Liturgy means that Pfeiffer decides not to study *Sacrosanctum Concilium* in detail (p. 154). This is to miss its valuable article on the revealing and saving presence of Christ in liturgical celebrations: "Christ . . . is present in his word, since it is he himself who *speaks* when the holy scriptures are read in the church" (SC 7; italics mine). Pfeiffer is aware of this passage (p. 298, fn. 17), but he does not appreciate what it adds to the full teaching of the council on revelation.

I have dwelt of Pfeiffer's book for two reasons. On the one hand, it has the merit of attending to what the "other" documents from the Second Vatican Council contribute to church teaching on revelation. On the other hand, however, Pfeiffer reduces the value of his contribution by several self-imposed restrictions: in particular, in the area of terminology. Such terminological limitations would have dramatically strange results if applied to key books of our Christian heritage. If we were to judge the value of John's gospel for a doctrine of revelation by its use of the verbs "reveal" (*apokaluptein*) and "disclose" (*phaneroun*), we would not find much to report (Jn 2:11; 3:21; 7:4; 9:3; 12:38; 17:6; 21:1; 21:14).

But when we enlarge our net to include such terms as "glory," "glorify," "light," "signs," "truth," "witness" (as noun and verb) and "word," we see how richly revelational the Johannine vocabulary and theology really are.

This chapter aims to encourage an adequate reception of the Second Vatican Council's integral teaching on revelation by moving beyond *Dei Verbum* to consider many of the other fifteen documents. But let me first introduce some necessary methodological considerations.

Reading the Sixteen Documents. From December 1963 to December 1965 the council promulgated sixteen documents, the first being the Constitution on the Sacred Liturgy (*Sacrosanctum Concilium*) and the last being the Pastoral Constitution on the Church in the Modern World (*Gaudium et Spes*). One does not need to be ingenious to see something providential about this journey from the liturgy to the contemporary world. Unfortunately not all translations and editions of the conciliar documents respect the chronological order of their appearance. Some (for example, the Abbott translation) rearrange the documents according to their status: first, the four "constitutions," then the nine "decrees," and finally the three "declarations."

Among other effects, such a rearrangement obscures the way the later documents of the council refer to ones already promulgated. For instance, the Decree on the Appropriate Renewal of Religious Life (*Perfectae Caritatis*), promulgated on October 28, 1965, refers in its opening paragraph to the Dogmatic Constitution on the Church (*Lumen Gentium*) which had appeared the year before. The Decree on the Bishops' Pastoral Office in the Church (*Christus Dominus*), also promulgated on October 28, 1965, refers to *Lumen Gentium* four times in its opening paragraph and five times in its second paragraph. The Decree on the Apostolate of the Laity (*Apostolicam Actuositatem*) which appeared on November 18, 1965 refers in its first paragraph not only to *Lumen Gentium* but also to six of the other conciliar documents that had already been promulgated. A final example: The Decree on the Church's Missionary Activity (*Ad Gentes*), promulgated on December 7, 1965, right in its opening sentence makes its first of many references to *Lumen Gentium*.

These four examples encourage a diachronic reading of the council's documents. The explicit references later texts make to those that appeared earlier invite the readers to understand and interpret the later documents in the light of the earlier ones. We miss some, or perhaps much, of the meaning of the later (and for that matter the earlier) texts if we read them in isolation, or, for that matter, in an order that we have arranged for ourselves.

One could speak here of a "canonical" meaning to be drawn from the sixteen conciliar texts. In the case of the seventy-two books of the Bible, questions of the canonical meaning arise because the church recognizes these books as divinely inspired, publishes them together in the one canon and uses them together in the liturgy. The books of the Bible complete and illuminate each other; we can see this at once from several examples.

a) One biblical work can deal with the same theme as others, but in a somewhat different way. Chapter 11 of this book will illustrate the point by showing how various parts of the Bible handle the notion of faith analogously. b) Some books of the Bible can introduce a theme like the resurrection of the dead which we do not find in other books. c) The order in which the biblical canon has arranged the books yields much meaning: see, for example, the way the New Testament canon moves from Matthew (with an opening genealogy that reaches back to Abraham) to Revelation and its closing prayer, "Come, Lord Jesus" (Rev 22:20). To alter this traditional order by, for example, putting Mark or 1 Thessalonians at the head of the New Testament canon would tamper with the spectacular way Matthew's gospel functions as a bridge to the Old Testament canon.

We can apply similar, although not identical, considerations to the council's "canon" of sixteen documents. While not written under a special inspiration of the Holy Spirit as were the books of the Bible, the conciliar texts came from the church and her leaders being guided by the Holy Spirit. a) These sixteen documents may deal with the same theme but in different ways. b) Some texts will add points of teaching not found in others. c) The "canonical" order, created by their date of promulgation, can, as we have already seen, prove illuminating.

Attention to the "canonical" meaning of these sixteen texts will lead us to the integral teaching of the council. Before reading the conciliar texts diachronically on the theme of revelation, I should add that this is not simply an attempt to recapture the meanings present in the minds of the authors (in this case, the bishops and their advisors). As we shall recall in Chapter 12, the meaning of a text is by no means to be limited to the explicit intentions of the original authors. It can go beyond what they consciously intended to communicate. In particular, the passage of time can produce new perspectives and bring out implications that were previously imperceptible. Reading the conciliar texts thirty years later in our new context, we can creatively draw out fresh meaning. Chapter 12, in dealing with biblical interpretation, will provide a justification for what I wish to do with the conciliar texts first diachronically and then synchronically.

Revelation Diachronically. 1) Our first conciliar document, *Sacrosanctum Concilium* (December 4, 1963), gave us what is now a classic passage on the variety of Christ's revealing and saving presence.

> Christ is always present in his church, especially in her liturgical celebrations. He is present in the sacrifice of the mass not only in the person of his minister . . . but especially in the eucharistic species. By his power he is present in the sacraments so that when anybody baptizes it is really Christ himself who baptizes. He is present in his word since it is he himself who speaks when the holy scriptures are read in the church. Lastly, he is present when the church prays and sings (SC 7).

This is an eloquent list of the liturgical places, signs, means and persons who mediate the crucified and risen Christ's self-communication. Obviously we are not faced with a silent presence or a voice from the past that is echoed by others or merely recorded in a text. His liturgical presence is that of a living and revelatory voice: "In the liturgy God speaks to his people, and Christ is still proclaiming his gospel" (SC 33).[4]

In this Constitution on the Sacred Liturgy the council makes an inclusive, rather an exclusive, statement. In other words it recalls the range of Christ's liturgical presences without denying that he is also present both non-liturgically and beyond the visible community of Christians: for example, in all those who suffer and need our practical love (Mt 25:31–46). The constitution does *not* say, "Christ is present only in his church"; still less does it say, "Christ is present only in her liturgical celebrations."

This passage from *Sacrosanctum Concilium* could encourage us to develop a theology of revelation in the key of Christ's self-communicative and salvific presence. This would entail putting together and developing the themes of a) divine self-communication (see Chapter Four) and b) presence. As regards a), German philosophy and theology (in particular, that of Rahner) has much to offer. As regards b), we would have to cope with the difficulty that the whole western philosophical tradition does not have a great deal to offer on the theme of presence and the different qualities of presence. However it turns out, a theology of revelation in this key would work together *Dei Verbum* (the divine *self-communication*) and *Sacrosanctum Concilium* (Christ's living *presence*). Chapter 8 of this book will attempt something along these lines, adding a third element (*symbolism*) to explore revelation as the symbolic self-communication of the divine presence.

A major item is missing from the list in *Sacrosanctum Concilium* 7, inasmuch as it does not say that "Christ is present when the word is preached." This omission, however, is made up, in SC 33, as we have seen, and in a later conciliar document, as we shall see.

2) A doctoral dissertation should be written about the teaching on revelation to be found in *Lumen Gentium* (November 21, 1964). Let me sample some of the points such a dissertation should explore.

Dealing with the earthly ministry of Jesus and his preaching of the kingdom this Dogmatic Constitution on the Church states: "This kingdom shines out (*elucescit*) before men in the word, the works and presence of Christ." "Principally," it adds, "the kingdom is revealed (*manifestatur*) in the person of Christ himself" (LG 5). On the one hand, the present tense of "shines out" and "is revealed" is an historic present and refers to the past ministry of Jesus which is over and done with. On the other hand, the use here of the historic present suggests how Jesus' preaching and revelation of the kingdom remain a reality here and now. Then we already see also that sacramental understanding of revelation ("word, works and presence/person") which will turn up the following year (1965) in *Dei Verbum*. *Lumen Gentium* rightly dedicates a whole article here to the kingdom of God (LG 5), a central theme of the synoptic gospels and a key to the salvific revelation mediated through the ministry of Christ. *Dei Verbum,* in its opening chapter on revelation, unfortunately says nothing about the kingdom, merely mentioning it along with other themes in its first article on the New Testament (DV 17).

The central topic of *Lumen Gentium* is the church. The first chapter of the constitution, dedicated to the mystery of the church, ends by declaring her purpose: she is to "reveal [*revelet*] faithfully in the world" the mystery of her Lord, "until at the end it [the mystery of Christ] will be revealed [*manifestabitur*] in full splendor" (LG 8). This definition of the church in terms of her revelatory mission also invokes an essential theme of revelation to which we shall return shortly: its eschatological nature.

In treating the teaching office of the bishops *Lumen Gentium* naturally introduces points about the transmission of revelation:

> Among the more important duties of bishops that of preaching
> the gospel has pride of place. For the bishops are heralds of the
> faith. . . . Under the light of the Holy Spirit they make that

faith shine forth (*illustrant*), drawing from the treasure of revelation (*ex thesauro revelationis*) things new and old (LG 25).

"Preaching the gospel" amounts to proclaiming the definitive revelation
communicated through Jesus Christ, announcing what Chapter 8 of this
book will call foundational revelation. Those who cherish the centrality
of revelation in Christian theology read with satisfaction the way in
which the Second Vatican Council recognized how the bishops' ministry
in "preaching the gospel" takes precedence over their duty to administer
the sacraments and give pastoral leadership (LG 26-27).

As LG 25 centers on the *transmission* of revelation through the
bishops' ministry of the word, the *content* of revelation comes naturally
to the fore: "the gospel," "the faith" (= the *fides quae* or faith that we
confess) and "the treasure of revelation." Like public heralds, the bishops announce God's revelation which the light of the Holy Spirit illuminates and makes credible. The external word of the bishops and the
interior word of the Holy Spirit "conspire" in witnessing to God's self-
revelation and evoking faith.

A synonym for the more classical "deposit of faith" (DV 10), the
"treasure of revelation" expresses slightly more directly the full and
definitive self-communication of God in Christ. Like *Dei Verbum* this
paragraph from *Lumen Gentium* recalls the strict link between the bishops' authoritative teaching (or magisterium) and God's self-revelation
given in salvation history (see DV 9, 10). The exercise of the bishops'
magisterium depends on and draws from God's revealed word. Like the
"scribe trained for the kingdom of heaven" (= the first evangelist?), the
bishops should teach the whole of revelation, "drawing from the treasure of revelation new things and old" (see Mt 13:52).

Lumen Gentium, while highlighting the bishops' role as present
mediators of revelation, in no way suggests any episcopal monopoly
here. Referring to persons of heroic sanctity, the constitution remarks:

God shows (*manifestat*) to men, in a vivid way, his presence
and his face in the lives of those companions of ours in the
human condition who are more perfectly transformed into the
image of Christ (LG 50).

It is worth unpacking in detail this rich and dense claim. Unlike
bishops, priests, deacons, catechists and other "official" mediators of
and witnesses to God's revelation in Christ, saints cannot produce a
document to prove that they have received such a commission. Like

prophets, saints show themselves to be such mediators and witnesses through the impact on others of their personal gifts and generosity. They do so incessantly in "ordinary" life, communicating vividly in extra-liturgical settings the "presence" and "face" of God. Here the tense of "shows" (*manifestat*) highlights present (or what I call dependent) revelation: the divine self-communication to us here and now. The constitution underlines its concern with the present nature of revelation by adding that in the saints God "speaks to us" and "offers us" both "a sign" of "the kingdom" and "a witness to the truth of the gospel" (LG 50). A footnote (fn. 12) directs us to the First Vatican Council (DS 3013) and a biblical reference to 2 Corinthians 3:18. The link with *Dei Filius* serves to suggest a difference between the two councils. For the First Vatican Council eminent holiness works as one of the signs or "notes" that establish the credibility of the Catholic Church and show that she was instituted by Christ. *Lumen Gentium,* however, interprets outstanding sanctity as primarily a sign of God, Christ, the divine kingdom and "the truth of the gospel." The reference to 2 Corinthians 3:18 proves more valuable. That particular passage portrays holiness as a progressive transformation into the image of Christ. Furthermore, the whole of 2 Corinthians is one of the richest books of the New Testament for the doctrine of revelation. It features repeatedly in *Dei Verbum* (DV 5, 7, 16; Ch. 1, fn. 2). By appealing to that letter in the context of revelation, *Lumen Gentium* prepares the way for the fuller use of 2 Corinthians to be found in *Dei Verbum.*

The last passage I have chosen from *Lumen Gentium* looks beyond the present life of the church to the future revelation at the end: "The pilgrim church . . . herself lives among the creatures which still groan in travail and await the revelation of the sons of God (cf. Rom 8:19–22)." At the end of the same paragraph the constitution adds: "Strong in faith we expect the blessed hope and the advent of the glory [= glorious coming] of our great God and Savior Jesus Christ" (LG 48).[5] *Dei Verbum* says substantially the same thing about the final revelation, albeit negatively: "No new public revelation is to be expected before the glorious manifestation of our Lord, Jesus Christ (cf. 1 Tim 6:14 and Tit 2:13)" (DV 4). *Dei Verbum* wishes here to maintain the definitive nature of the divine revelation which reached its climax with Christ. Before his second coming, no so-called "private revelations" can add anything to the content of God's revelation in Jesus Christ. *Lumen Gentium* quotes Titus 2:13; *Dei Verbum* merely refers to it. Unlike *Lumen Gentium,* it does not use Romans 8:19–22, a splendid passage about the consummation of salvation and revelation to come at the end of time. Even more than *Dei Verbum, Lumen Gentium* brings out that God's self-revelation will, in the full and proper sense, be completed only at the eschaton. Here *Lumen Gentium* shows itself more sensitive to the language of the New Testament which often speaks of "revelation" in terms of the end (for example, 1 Pet 1:5, 7, 13; 4:14; 5:4).

3) As we saw above, the Declaration on the Relation of the Church to Non-Christian Religions (*Nostra Aetate*) of October 28, 1965 speaks only once of "revelation." It does so in reference to the Old Testament revelation (NA 4). Nevertheless, explicit terminology can be misleading here. The document summarizes those basic questions about life, the meaning of life, suffering, happiness, existence after death and the other primordial issues which open up human beings to religious responses (NA 1). (Less than two months later *Gaudium et Spes* was to develop at greater length a similar list of questions which illustrate the method of correlation between the essential human questions and the divine answers offered by God's saving self-revelation which we briefly noticed in Chapter 3.) Then, *Nostra Aetate* speaks of the divine will to save all people and let them share in the same final revelation, that "day when the elect are gathered together in the holy city which is *illuminated* by the *glory* of God, in whose *splendor* all peoples will walk (NA 1; see Rev 21:23–24; 22:5; italics mine). Further, NA recognizes how here and now a true knowledge of God is found among the adherents of non-Christian religions, ranging from "a certain awareness of a hidden power that lies behind the course of nature and the events of human life," through Hinduism, Buddhism and Islam (NA 2–3) to the revelation communicated to God's chosen people (NA 4). The next chapter will take up in detail the council's teaching on the elements of religious truth and salvation to be found outside Christianity (and Judaism). Here let me simply note how three times NA 2 acknowledges how Hinduism, Buddhism and other such world religions contain at least some true teaching. Echoing John 1:9, the declaration states that they "often reflect a ray of that truth which enlightens all human beings" (*ibid.*). Given the different scope of the two documents, NA tends to be more positive than the next document we consider in acknowledging the role of non-Christian religions in mediating a saving knowledge of God.

4) Inevitably the Decree on the Church's Missionary Activity (*Ad Gentes*) of December 7, 1965 has a good deal to say about revelation. Let me sample some passages to establish that conclusion.

So far from being something alien to the human condition and its hopes, God's self-revelation in Christ stands in correlation with them:

Missionary activity is intimately bound up with human nature and its aspirations. In manifesting (*manifestando*) Christ, the

church reveals (*revelat*) to human beings their true situation
and calling (AG 8).

Like *Gaudium et Spes,* as we shall see, AG here understands the revelation of Christ to be simultaneously the revelation of the nature and
destiny of men and women. The divine and human mystery are bound
together. This passage also illustrates a point to which I shall return in
Chapter 7: in the conciliar terminology (and beyond) "reveal" and
"manifest" come across as synonymous. We would not alter the meaning
by switching the verbs to make the second sentence read as follows: "In
revealing Christ, the church manifests to human beings their true situation and calling."

Lastly, the text exemplifies something we would expect in a decree
on missionary activity: revelation happens here and now through such
activity. Two paragraphs later the decree makes the same point. It emphasizes that the church "has been sent by Christ to reveal and communicate the love of God" to all (AG 10).

The church's role in mediating present (or "dependent") revelation
also turns up in the following passage: "Missionary activity is nothing
else, and nothing less, than the manifestation (*manifestatio*) of God's
plan, its epiphany and realization in the world and in history" (AG 9).
What this passage also indicates is that, so far from merely appearing
and communicating to us a new knowledge, the revelation of God's
saving plan entails its efficacious realization in world history. The divine
self-communication is both informative *and* effective.

Some remarks on the missionary obligations of Christians include
several important points about the mediation, the sacramental nature
and the "object" of revelation.

All Christians by the example of their lives and the witness of
the word have an obligation to manifest (*manifestare*) the new
man which they put on in baptism, and the power of the Holy
Spirit by whom they were strengthened at confirmation, so that
others, seeing their good works, might glorify the Father . . .
and more perfectly perceive the true meaning of human life
and the universal solidarity of mankind (AG 11).

Here *all* baptized and confirmed Christians, by the simple fact of their
baptism and confirmation, are seen as at least potential mediators of
revelation, called to manifest who they are so that others might "perceive the true meaning of human life." Talk of "the example" of Christian lives and "the witness of the word" serving to convey this disclosure

to others recall the sacramental version of revelation coming through "deeds/events and words" endorsed by *Dei Verbum*. Finally, the council once again holds together the divine and human mystery: manifesting God means manifesting the meaning of all human existence.

A rich passage on love reinforces some observations we have already made and adds a fresh point:

> Human beings are aided in attaining salvation by love toward God and one's neighbor; the mystery of Christ begins to shine out (*elucere*), that mystery in which has appeared the new man created in the likeness of God . . . and in which the charity of God is revealed (*revelatur*) (AG 12).

In helping the exercise of love that is "vertical" (toward God) and "horizontal" (toward other human beings), the church's missionary activity effects here and now the revelation of the mystery of Christ. The use of the singular "mystery" rather than "mysteries" runs in the groove of what we saw to be the characteristic usage of *Dei Verbum* (in Chapter Four). The genitive "the mystery *of* Christ" (*mysterium Christi*) is best understood as a genitive of identity or definition: the mystery which is Christ. This passage, like *Dei Verbum*, links salvation and revelation, the two inseparable dimensions of God's self-communication, in passing from present revelation ("begins to shine out") to past (or foundational) revelation ("has appeared") and back to present (or dependent) revelation ("is revealed"). At least as emphatically as *Dei Verbum* (see DV 2), *Ad Gentes* here presents the heart of revelation as the disclosure of the love of God. Revelation discloses not only the mystery of redemption ("the new man created in the likeness of God") but also the mystery of God who is love (see 1 Jn 4:8, 16).

Finally, where *Nostra Aetate* declares that "the Catholic Church rejects nothing of what is true [= revelation] and holy [= redemption]" in non-Christian religions, *Ad Gentes* speaks of missionary activity "purging of evil associations those elements of truth [= revelation] and grace [= redemption] which are found among peoples" (AG 9). The two documents differ in purpose and stress. We take up these matters in the next chapter.

5) The last and longest document from the Second Vatican Council, the Pastoral Constitution on the Church in the Modern World (*Gaudium et Spes*) of December 7, 1965, even if it does not fill out all the details, has many illuminating things to say about revelation. Any serious sampling of the document can easily substantiate that assertion.

In an early paragraph GS recognizes the correlation between divine revelation and human experience.

> What revelation makes known to us agrees with our own experi-
> ence. For when man looks into his own heart he finds that he is
> drawn toward what is wrong and sunk in many evils which
> cannot come from his good creator. . . . Both the high calling
> and the deep misery which human beings experience find their
> final explanation in the light of this revelation (GS 13).[6]

What the council says here about foundational revelation finds its counterpart in what the same chapter of GS goes on to propose about the
dependent revelation mediated here and now. "The church knows full
well that her message is in harmony with the most secret desires of the
human heart" (GS 21). Although GS does not specify here whether this
harmony is partial or complete, it maintains some measure of correlation between the central message of the church and the deepest human
desires, or between "the light of revelation" and human "experience"
(GS 33).

Being a pastoral document for the contemporary world, GS lives
comfortably with the reality of present (dependent) revelation. It understands "the function of the church" to be that of "rendering God the
Father and his incarnate Son present and as it were visible" (GS 21).
Subsequent paragraphs reiterate this conviction about the revelatory
role of the church here and now:

> The Church is entrusted with the task of disclosing (*mani-
> festare*) to man the mystery of God, who is the last end of man;
> in doing so it opens up to him the meaning of his own exis-
> tence, the innermost truth about himself (GS 41).[7]

At the same time, GS does not ignore the way sinful failures can hamper
and hinder this present mediation of the divine self-revelation. The
constitution cites *Lumen Gentium* in stating:

> Guided by the Holy Spirit the church ceaselessly "exhorts her
> children to purification and renewal so that the sign of Christ
> may shine more brightly over the face of the Church" (GS 43;
> see LG 15).

Like *Lumen Gentium,* and for that matter like *Dei Verbum,* GS appreciates that the church's mediatorial role involves both manifesting and
actualizing God's saving love for us:

> Every benefit the people of God can confer on humankind during its earthly pilgrimage is rooted in the church's being "the universal sacrament of salvation," at once manifesting and actualizing (*manifestans simul et operans*) the mystery of God's love for human beings (GS 45; see LG 48).[8]

Present revelation is automatically present salvation. Here, as elsewhere, the history of revelation and the history of salvation are distinguishable but inseparable.

On other counts GS parallels and fills out the teaching on revelation from *Dei Verbum*. First, where DV speaks of God providing constant self-witness in created realities (DV 3; see 6), GS affirms that "believers, no matter what their religion, have always recognized the voice and disclosure (*manifestationem*) of God in the language of creatures" (GS 36). Both passages highlight not so much our human search for God, but rather the divine self-witness and "voice." Not only in the special history of God's self-communication recorded in the Old Testament and the New Testament but also in the general history of that self-communication the divine initiative comes to the forefront. In an analogous form, the Augustinian principle holds good even in and through the created order: we would not search for God unless God had first "found" us.[9] Second, GS repeats several themes from *Dei Verbum* about revelation as primarily God's self-revelation, as directed first and foremost to the whole people of God (rather than to individuals), as reaching its definitive fullness in Christ and being mediated progressively and according to a divine pedagogy. The constitution affirms that "in his self-revelation (*sese revelans*) to his people culminating in the fullness of manifestation (*manifestationem*) in his incarnate Son, God spoke according to the culture proper to each age" (GS 58; on these themes see DV 2–5, 14–15).

New themes on revelation turn up in GS which include and go beyond the method of correlation that we have already seen above. First, there is anthropology or a vision of the human condition. Aligning itself with a tradition that goes back to St. Paul (Rom 7:13–25), GS presents the human being as a radically questioning animal (*homo interrogans*): "Man will ever be anxious to know, if only in a vague way, what is the meaning of his life, his activity and his death" (GS 41; see GS 10). The divine revelation stands in correlation not only with our experiences but also with our related questions: "The most perfect answer to these questionings is to be found in God alone, who created man in his own image and redeemed him from sin; and this answer is given in the revelation in Christ his Son who became man" (GS 41). Revelation matches the reality and need of human beings as essentially questioners.[10]

Second, its closeness to life leads GS to highlight the signs of the times. The council speaks, on the one hand, of these signs as "out there" and requiring to be interpreted "in the light of the gospel" (GS 4). On the other hand, "in the events, needs and longings" of our time there can be "genuine signs of the presence or purpose of God" (GS 11). In other words, the signs of the times, whether positive or negative, may reveal to us something about *where* God is present in a special way and *what* God aims to bring about in our world. A later paragraph draws together what we find in GS 4 and 11, by spelling out the responsibility of discerning the "voices of our times," so that the reality of revelation might be more powerfully deployed.

> With the help of the Holy Spirit, it is the task of the whole people of God, particularly of its pastors and theologians, to listen to and distinguish the many voices of our times and to interpret them in the light of the divine word, in order that the revealed truth may be more deeply penetrated, better understood, and more suitably presented (GS 44).

To read the signs of yesterday is comparatively easy. To read the signs of the present can pose great difficulties, but is a task that may not be shirked. Discerning the special presence and purpose of God today belongs to an integral Christian openness to God's revelatory and redemptive self-communication.

My diachronic reading of the doctrine on revelation to be discovered in the conciliar texts other than *Dei Verbum* has selected and commented on passages from only five documents. The further ten documents have their points to add. Although *Dei Verbum* did not neglect the freedom of faith in responding to divine revelation (DV 5), *Dignitatis Humanae,* the Declaration on Religious Liberty of December 7, 1965, has much more to say (DH 9–12). The declaration addresses itself primarily to the question of the common human right to exercise public religious liberty. But it cannot assert this public right without also underlining our inner, personal freedom to respond freely in faith to God's self-communication. Besides attending to those further ten documents, a full-scale examination would also deal with other items on revelation in the five documents I selected. The contrast, for example, drawn between "the truths of faith" and "the manner of expressing them" (GS 62) could obviously be rephrased in terms of revelation. Revealed truths are one thing, the manner of expressing and communicating them is quite another.

Revelation Synchronically. But it is time to shift from a diachronic reading of the conciliar documents to a synchronic reading. We can do that by seeing (1) where the other documents parallel points to be found in *Dei Verbum,* (2) where they develop themes of *Die Verbum* and (3) where they introduce new points on revelation.

1) Among the first major points the other documents have in common with *Dei Verbum* comes the conviction that revelation, while primarily a matter of God's self-revelation (LG 50; AG 12), involves secondarily a content or "deposit of faith" (LG 25; GS 13, 44). Like DV the other documents speak of the disclosure of mystery—whether the mystery of God and the divine love (GS 41, 45), that of Christ (AG 12) or of human beings' nature and destiny (GS 10). God's love or God as love constitutes the heart of revelation (AG 12; GS 45). Essentially salvific (AG 9, 12; GS 45), revelation has a sacramental structure (LG 5; AG 11). God speaks not only through the events of salvation history but also through created realities (GS 36). The consummation of revelation will come at the end of history (LG 48). Lastly, faced with God's self-revelation, human beings are called to respond freely in faith (DH 9–11).

2) For at least two points, the other documents come up with new material, or at least develop these points well beyond where *Dei Verbum* leaves them. The first is the church's role in mediating revelation; the second is divine self-revelation simultaneously bringing the revelation of human beings. First, DV introduces some items about the ecclesial communication of revelation (DS 7–10, 12, 21–26). Nevertheless, we can range over against this many details about the church's mediation of the divine self-disclosure: through her liturgy (SC 7, 33), missionary and pastoral activity (LG 15, 48; AG 8, 9, 11, 12; GS 10, 11, 41, 45) and through the lives of her truly saintly members (LG 50). It is not surprising that these documents frequently attend to God's saving revelation being actualized here and now. They deal with present activities: the liturgy (SC), the church in herself (LG) and in her pastoral relation to the contemporary world (GS), and her missionary activity (AG). Second, *Dei Verbum* does remark that in Christ "the most intimate truth" about human salvation also "shines forth" (DV 2). But it is left for other documents (AG 11; GS 10, 22, 41) to state quite clearly that the revelation of the divine mystery also discloses the human mystery.

3) Lastly, the fifteen conciliar documents other than *Dei Verbum* introduce several new and valuable points about revelation. They set themselves to show the correlation between the human condition and the salvific self-disclosure of God in Christ (NA 1; AG 8; GS 10, 13). Then *Lumen Gentium* finds room for that central theme from the gospels, the revelation of the divine rule or kingdom (LG 5, 50). *Dei Verbum* touches on this theme but not in its chapter on revelation (DV 17). Third, the other documents point to one major avenue of potential

revelation here and now which *Dei Verbum* passes over in silence: the signs of the times (GS 4, 11, 44; see also SC 43; PO 9; DH 15; AA 14; UR 4). Fourth, the other documents add a further significant item by recognizing the true knowledge of God available in varying degrees beyond the Judaeo-Christian revelation (NA 2–3; AG 9, 11; GS 36; see also LG 16).

This chapter has aimed at encouraging an adequate reception of the Second Vatican Council's integral teaching on revelation. The next chapter sets itself to spell out one theme from that integral teaching: the saving knowledge of God mediated through non-Christian religions.

6. SAVING REVELATION FOR ALL PEOPLES

In his commentary on *Dei Verbum* Eduard Stakemeier expressed disappointment at finding practically nothing on the knowledge of God provided by various religions and religious philosophies. In passing he referred to LG 16, GS 22 and 45 and, globally, to *Nostra Aetate*.[1] This was to ignore *Ad Gentes* and many other relevant texts from the Second Vatican Council. We should face the way those other texts show how God is not the God of Jews and Christians only, but is "also the God of Gentiles" (Rom 3:29).

To carry this retrieval of the conciliar teaching on revelation through to completion, we need to take up what the "other" fifteen documents indicate about God's saving self-communication being available for all people on earth. *Dei Verbum* attends almost exclusively to the "special" history of revelation and salvation, the story of God's redemptive self-disclosure through the Old and New Testaments and the subsequent history of Christianity. The other conciliar texts, without using the technical language of the "general" history of revelation and salvation,[2] state much about the situation before God of those who are neither Jews nor Christians. Do they and how do they participate in the knowledge and grace of God mediated definitively through Jesus Christ? To adapt Paul's words once again, this chapter sets itself to show how the council conceived Christ to be Savior and revealer to "Gentiles also."

This chapter will proceed thematically and synchronically to deal with five items from the conciliar teaching: 1) the general situation before God of all human beings; 2) the council's language of truth and grace; 3) its view of the change in those non-Christians who come to Christian faith; 4) the presence of Christ to non-Christians; 5) the action of the Holy Spirit.

1) *The General Situation*. Ontologically and epistemologically all human beings are directed toward God. Let me explain this comment on the council.

Whether they realize it sooner or later, all men and women come from God and are going to God. They are made in the divine image and God is the creator and Father of all (NA 1, 5). God has called them all home to the same glorious destiny (NA 1). The cross of Christ, even when it is not yet known and accepted, is "the sign of God's universal love" (NA 4). The God who is creator of all "never ceases to pour out" the divine "goodness to bring about the salvation of all people (AG 2–3; see GS 22).

This is the ontological situation of all people: they have the same origin and final destiny in God. Their basic questions also direct them toward God: "What is the meaning and purpose of life? What is upright behavior and what is sinful? Where does suffering originate, and what end does it serve? How can genuine happiness be found? What happens at death?" (NA 1; see GS 10, 21). These and further profound questions sum up our common search for ultimate meaning and truth. It is, finally, a search for "the ultimate mystery, beyond human explanation, which embraces our entire existence, from which we take our origin and to-ward which we tend" (NA 1). The primordial questions that sooner or later we allow to surface summarize humanity's deepest epistemological quest for meaning and truth. We will return to this a little later.

2) *Truth and Grace.* The council characteristically uses a double-sided terminology when reflecting on the religious condition of non-Christians: true/holy, true/good, truth/grace and light/life. These dyads reflect the two distinguishable but inseparable dimensions of the divine self-communication: revelation and salvation.

In his first encyclical Pope Paul VI wrote of what is "true and good" in the Moslem worship of God.[3] Within a few months similar language surfaced in *Lumen Gentium:* "The one mediator, Christ, established and ever sustains here on earth his holy church . . . as a visible organization through which he communicates *truth and grace* to all men" (LG 8, italics mine). Some paragraphs later the constitution applied a parallel dyad, not to what is communicated through the visible church, but to what the church finds among

> those who, without fault of theirs, have not yet arrived at an explicit knowledge of God, and who, not without grace, strive to lead a good life. Whatever is *good or true* to be found amongst them is considered by the church to be a preparation for the gospel and given by him who *enlightens* all people that they may at length have *life* (LG 16; italics mine).

The Johannine language of revelation and salvation (in that order: "enlightens" and "life" [Jn 1:4, 9]) alternates with the recognition of elements of salvation and revelation (in that order: "whatever is good or true") to be found among upright non-believers.

The documents from the last session of the council included similar "double" terminology. Implying that other religions, even often, can exhibit elements of truth and holiness, *Nostra Aetate* declared:

> The Catholic Church rejects nothing of what is *true and holy* in these religions. She has a high regard for the manner of life and conduct, the precepts and doctrines which, although differing in many ways from her own teaching, nevertheless often reflect a *ray of that truth which enlightens* all people (NA 2).

Once again echoing John's gospel, the council here combined the terms in the usual order of revelation and salvation ("true and holy"). Six weeks later it followed that same order, while being more critical in the way it thought about other religions: "Missionary activity . . . purges of evil associations every element of *truth and grace* which are found among peoples" (AG 9; italics mine).

In their different ways *Nostra Aetate* and *Ad Gentes* depend on *Lumen Gentium* 16 and 17. Besides the terminology we have already seen, these two paragraphs of LG deploy a variety of terms to indicate the *revelatory* dimension ("the gospel," the good "sown in the minds of human beings" and a "knowing" of God that leads to "faith") and the *salvific* dimension ("salvation," "grace" and the good "sown in the hearts of human beings") of God's self-communication.

To remark on this double-sided terminology may seem to border on the banal. However, this persistent usage in the conciliar documents has two lessons for us. We may not raise the question of salvation without raising that of revelation, and vice versa. When interpreting anyone's situation before God, we need to recall the two inseparable dimensions of the divine self-communication. Second, the conciliar terminology indirectly bears witness to the way Christ's mediatorship entails his being universal revealer as well as universal Savior. He cannot be accepted as Savior of all without being accepted as revealer for all, "the true light that enlightens everyone coming into the world" (Jn 1:9).[4]

3) *The Move to Faith.* What the council says about those who come to embrace Christian faith opens a window on the conciliar view of non-Christians.

Those who accept the gospel undergo a revelatory and salvific process of being "enlightened and corrected" (AG 3). For their part, Christ's disciples, while respecting "the riches which a generous God has distributed among the nations," should "try to illuminate these riches with the *light* of the gospel, *set them free,* and bring them once more under the dominion of God *the Savior*" (AG 11; italics mine). Despite the cultural and religious "riches" already distributed to them by a "generous" God, non-Christians need the illumination of revelation and the liberation of salvation.

Lumen Gentium uses three schemas to interpret the change in those who accept faith. They move from an implicit to an "explicit knowledge," from "shadows and images" to light and from a state of "preparation for the gospel" to "full maturity" (LG 16–17; see AG 3). In all cases there is no question of starting from zero. Implicit knowledge, while not yet a "full and conscious" acceptance (AG 7), is still some kind of knowledge; shadows and images rise above mere formless darkness; a preparation already sets us in movement toward a goal.

Three verbs also help to shape the conciliar vision of those who do not yet accept the gospel. Their condition leaves them somehow wounded, at a lower level and imperfect. The effect of the church's missionary work is that

> whatever good is found sown in the human heart and mind in
> the rites and cultures of peoples, so far from being lost, is
> *healed, raised to a higher level,* and *perfected* for the glory of
> God (LG 17; italics mine).

The key verbs in *Lumen Gentium* (*sanare, elevare* and *consummare*) were repeated in *Ad Gentes*.

> Every element of goodness found present in the human heart
> and mind or in the particular customs and cultures of peoples,
> far from being lost, is *healed, raised to a higher level* and *per-
> fected* for the glory of God (AG 9; italics mine).[5]

Both passages emphasize the salvific impact of conversion to Christianity. But the reference to the goodness already found in the human *mind* can be seen as reference to the divine revelation already communicated and known prior to accepting the gospel. Non-Christians who become Christians bring with them elements of revelation and salvation. All is not lost or discarded. The process of healing, elevating and perfecting obviously bespeaks some measure of continuity.[6]

4) *Christ Beyond Christianity*. So far we have let the conciliar documents frame the question of non-Christians in terms of revelation and salvation. They also shape the issue in the name of Christ and his revealing and saving activity before and beyond Christianity. In tackling the issue we can distinguish the orders of creation and redemption.

a) A footnote to *Ad Gentes* quotes from St. Irenaeus a splendid passage about "the Word existing with God, through whom everything was made and who was always present to the human race." Then it adds a further passage from St. Irenaeus: "From the beginning, the Son, being present in his creation, reveals the Father to all whom the Father desires, at the time and in the manner desired by the Father" (AG 3, fn. 2). These lines from Irenaeus, endorsed by the Second Vatican Council, call for detailed comment as they have much to say about the situation before God of non-Christians.

Ad Gentes aligns itself with Irenaeus in acknowledging the christological character of creation. In a Johannine way the passage recognizes the Word as the agent of all creation (Jn 1:1–3, 10; see 1 Cor 8:6; Col 1:16; Heb 1:2). Consequently the Word has "always" been "present to the human race," and not just to certain groups or nations. St. Athanasius of Alexandria makes a similar remark in his *On the Incarnation of the Word*.

> The Word of God, incorporeal, incorruptible and immaterial,
> came down to our world. Not that he had been far off before,
> since no part of creation was ever without him. Together with
> his Father he filled all things (n. 8).

Since the second century this real but hidden presence of the Word *in* the created world and *to* the human race has gone under the name of "the seeds of the Word" (AG 11), a term picked up by John Paul II in his first encyclical (RH 11, fn. 67).

Granted the christological origin and character of creation, right "from the beginning" of human history the Son has been "revealing" the Father to human beings. The conciliar documents never apply the noun "revelation" to the knowledge of God mediated through the created world, and it is only here that the verb "reveal" (*revelare*) is used in this connection. Clearly this revelation of God through creation and "ordinary" human history allows for endless variety, as the Son "reveals the Father to all whom the Father desires at the time and in the manner desired by the Father." In contemporary terms, Irenaeus was speaking of the "general" history of revelation (and salvation). From the beginning of the human story, under the divine initiative the Son has been revealing not himself, but the Father in that "general" history of revelation. The divine agent of creation has also been, for all human beings, the revealer through creation.

b) Alongside the hidden presence and activity of Christ in virtue of his being the Word "through whom everything was made," *Ad Gentes* speaks of his presence mediated to non-Christians through the church and her redemptive activity. Even when "there is no possibility of directly and immediately preaching the gospel," missionaries "can and ought at least bear witness to the love and kindness of Christ, preparing thus a way for the Lord and in some way *making him present*" (AG 6; italics mine). Where Christ can be preached and the sacraments celebrated, in his salvific role he is present for and among all peoples.

> Through the word of preaching and the celebration of the sacraments, of which the most holy eucharist is the center and summit, missionary activity makes Christ present, he who is the author of salvation (AG 9).[7]

Lastly, the church can be "a perfect sign of Christ" to others where "there is a genuine laity existing and working alongside the hierarchy" (AG 21).

As regards the order of redemption, *Gadium et Spes* recalls that "in a certain way"—presumably with a revelatory and salvific impact—by the sheer fact of his incarnation the Son of God has "united himself" with every human being (GS 22). *Ad Gentes,* however, ties the redemptive (and revelatory) presence of Christ closely to the missionary activity of the church.

All in all, the conciliar documents do not yield very much explicitly on Christ's revelatory and salvific activity beyond and before Christianity. At least they point the way toward understanding that activity in terms of the order of creation and that of redemption. The eternal and incarnate Son of God is present to all human beings "protologically" (by virtue of his being the mediator of creation) and also eschatologically (in that his work as "author of salvation" will be consummated at the end.

In the light of *Gaudium et Spes* one might also speak of Christ's "epistemological" presence—in the human quest for meaning and truth. *Gaudium et Spes* portrays human beings as essentially questioners (GS 4, 10, 21) in search of meaning. (The document speaks thirty-six times of "meaning" [*sensus*].) In Christ we find "new meaning" and the human mystery becomes "truly clear" (GS 22). Admittedly *Gaudium et Spes* does not develop this theme. But its stress on the universal human quest for meaning allows us to speak of Christ as "epistemologically" present to all people in their search for enlightenment about the ultimate meaning and truth of things (see also LG 16; NA 2).

5) *The Action of the Holy Spirit.* In retrieving the conciliar teaching on God's saving revelation reaching all people, we need to be alert to several passages on the Holy Spirit in *Ad Gentes* and *Gaudium et Spes*. Neither here nor elsewhere do we have to choose between Christ and the Spirit—between a christological or a pneumatological response to an issue. The pneumatological material fills out what we have already seen.

Recalling God's "universal plan for the salvation of the human race," *Ad Gentes* observes that this plan "is not carried out exclusively in people's souls, with a kind of secrecy" (AG 3). In the next paragraph the document notes that "the Holy Spirit was at work in the world *before* Christ was glorified," and bases itself on several passages in Acts (Acts 10:44–47; 11:15; 15:8) to acknowledge that the Holy Spirit "at times *visibly* anticipates apostolic action" (AG 4; italics mine). Such visible interventions of the Spirit exemplify what *Ad Gentes* has previously stated about the divine plan for the salvation of all not being carried out merely in the secrecy of people's minds and hearts. In his first encyclical (of 1979) John Paul II offers contemporary evidence for recognizing "the Spirit of truth operating beyond the visible bounds of the mystical body": the "firm faith shown by followers of non-Christian religions which at times can embarrass Christians themselves" (RH 6).

The classic conciliar statement on the Holy Spirit's universal function in the order of redemption emphasizes, however, the invisible ("known only as God") impact of "grace" or, putting matters more personally, the mysterious working of the Holy Spirit. The council acknowledges that "grace is active invisibly" in the hearts of "all people of good will," and adds:

> Since Christ died for all, and since all human beings are in fact called to one and the same destiny, which is divine, we must hold that the Holy Spirit offers to all the possibility of being made partners, in a way known to God, in the paschal mystery (GS 22).

The constitution focuses here on salvation rather than revelation—on human "hearts" rather than minds. It recalls both Christ dying in the *past* for "all" (and not just for those "of good will") and the *future* common destiny for all people, and draws a conclusion. Here and now the Holy Spirit, in some way or another, makes it possible for all to share the paschal mystery—that is to say, in the life and light which comes from the crucified and risen Christ. The document does not spell out the exact details. Nevertheless, sharing in the paschal mystery cannot be restricted just to redemption; it must somehow include sharing in the revelation of God that reached its definitive climax with Christ's dying and rising (DV 4).

Stakemeier's negative judgment that led off this chapter was possible only because he ignored what I have called the "canonical" meaning of the sixteen conciliar texts. What *Dei Verbum* "fails" to offer about non-Christians and non-Christian religions can, in part, be found elsewhere— in *Nostra Aetate, Ad Gentes, Gaudium et Spes* and *Lumen Gentium* 16– 17. I say "in part" because the council never speaks of such matters as the founders of other religions or their sacred writings.

All in all, when reflecting on the situation of those "outside" Christianity, the council follows a long-standing tradition of attending more to the issue of their salvation.[8] However, the place given both to the essential questions about the nature and destiny of human beings and to the frequent double-sided terminology of life *and light* helps to revise somewhat that judgment. The conciliar documents alert us to the fact that God's self-communication has both a salvific *and revelatory* dimension.

The council reads the situation of non-Christians in the key of two "missions": the mission of the Son of God and that of the Holy Spirit. The christological interpretation of the divine concern for all humanity is balanced by a pneumatological interpretation. In the decades that have followed the council both official teaching and theological reflection have developed christological and pneumatological lines of approach to the situation before God of non-Christians.[9]

Chapters 5 and 6 have exploited the "other" documents to retrieve the full scope of the conciliar teaching on revelation. We turn next to an issue raised by the language of *Dei Verbum:* How can we reconcile claims about revelation as completed in the past with those about revelation occurring now?

7. REVELATION PAST AND PRESENT

The question to be faced in this chapter emerges from the fact that *Dei Verbum* speaks of the divine self-disclosure in both the past and the present tense. On the one hand, Jesus

> completed and perfected revelation and confirmed it with divine guarantees. He did this by the total fact of his presence and self-manifestation—by words and works, signs and miracles, but above all by his death and glorious resurrection from the dead, and finally by sending the Spirit of truth (DV 4).

On the other hand, *Dei Verbum* also portrays revelation as a present event which invites human faith: " 'The obedience of faith' (Rom 16:26; cf. Rom 1:5; 2 Cor 10:5–6) must be given to God as he reveals himself" (DV 5). The constitution associates revelation as it happened then and as it happens now (in the church) in these terms: "God, who spoke in the past, continues to converse with the spouse of his beloved Son" (DV 8).

Other documents of the council likewise use both the present and the past tense in talking of the divine self-revelation. In preaching the gospel bishops draw "from the storehouse of revelation" (LG 25)—that is to say, from the "deposit of faith" or the definitive revelation of God given once and for all through Christ and entrusted to the church to be proclaimed and preserved with fidelity. *Gaudium et Spes* notes the cultural pedagogy in God's revelation which reached (past tense) its complete climax with Christ: "In his self-revelation to his people culminating in the fullness of manifestation in his incarnate Son, God spoke according to the culture proper to each age" (GS 58).

At the same time, those other documents from the Second Vatican Council also recognize the divine revelation to be a *present* reality. Apropos of the various liturgical presences of Christ, the Constitution on the Sacred Liturgy acknowledges that "it is he himself who speaks when the holy scriptures are read in the church" (SC 7). In the context of the community's worship "Christ is still proclaiming his gospel" (*ibid.* 33). The Decree on the Church's Missionary Activity properly highlights the actual nature of revelation: "In manifesting Christ, the church reveals to human beings their true situation and calling" (AG 8). In the mystery of Christ "the charity of God is revealed" (AG 12). Finally, *Gaudium et Spes* describes the church as "the universal sacrament of salvation" which is both "manifesting and actualizing the mystery of God's love for man" (GS 45). The same document also acknowledges the shadow side of things. By their deficiencies Christians may here and now "conceal" rather than"reveal the true nature of God and religion" (GS 19).

The same approach to revelation as being both a past and present reality turns up in the teaching of John Paul II. In his 1979 Apostolic Exhortation on Catechesis in Our Time (*Catechesi Tradendae*) the pope wrote of

> the revelation that God has given of himself to humanity in Christ Jesus, a revelation stored in the depths of the church's memory and in sacred scripture, and constantly communicated from one generation to the next by a living active *traditio* (22).

A "simple revelation of a good and provident Father" is something, however, which happens now when "the very young child receives the first elements of catechesis from its parents and the family surroundings" (36). In a telling passage about catechesis for the young, Pope John Paul II presents divine revelation as something which has happened and which should continue to happen:

> In our pastoral concern we ask ourselves: How are we to reveal Jesus Christ, God made man, to this multitude of children and young people, reveal him not just in the fascination of a first fleeting encounter but through an acquaintance, growing deeper and clearer daily, with him, his message, the plan of God that he has revealed, the call he addresses to each person, and the kingdom that he wishes to establish in this world . . . (35)?

In 1980 the pope published *Dives in Misericordia,* an encyclical which took as its theme "the revelation of the mystery of the Father and his love" (1). The language of this document repeatedly recalls the central theme. Over eighty times the pope uses the verb or the noun "reveal" and "revelation." Other revelational terms like "manifest," "sign" and "proclaim" turn up constantly. If the 1979 encyclical *Redemptor Hominis* explored the human condition, *Dives in Misericordia* highlights the revelation of the divine mercy which "responds" to our primordial needs. No other document published by John Paul II has more to say on the theme of revelation.[1] He begins by portraying the divine revelation as something completed in the past: "It is 'God who is rich in mercy' whom Jesus Christ has revealed to us as Father: it is his very Son who, in himself, has manifested him and made him known to us" (*ibid*). Yet the same encyclical repeatedly proclaims the present nature of this revelation: "The cross . . . speaks and never ceases to speak of God the Father" (7); "the genuine face of mercy has to be ever revealed anew" (6). John Paul II names the reason for the church's ongoing existence as being "to reveal God, that Father who allows us to 'see' him in Christ" (15). Through Mary the love of God "continues to be revealed in the history of the church and of humanity" (9). The pope himself prays that "the love which is in the Father may once again be revealed at this stage in history" (15).

To sum up this sketch of recent church teaching: Both in the documents of the Second Vatican Council and in important postconciliar statements, revelation is understood to have been a complete, definitive and unrepeatable self-communication of God through Jesus Christ. Almost in the same breath, however, this official church teaching also calls revelation a present reality which is repeatedly actualized here and now. How can we relate these two sets of affirmations which at first sight could seem to be mutually exclusive? If revelation was definitively completed in the past, how can it happen today? If revelation is a present event, how can we speak of it as having reached its final and perfect culmination two thousand years ago?

(1) *Some False Moves*. It could be tempting here to allege that present revelation is not revelation in the proper sense but only a growth in the collective understanding of biblical revelation completed and closed once and for all with Christ and his apostles. Undoubtedly such a growth in true understanding can and does take place. *Dei Verbum* takes up this theme:

> The tradition that comes from the apostles makes progress in the church, with the help of the Holy Spirit. There is a growth in insight into the realities and words that are being passed on. . . . Thus, as the centuries go by, the church is always advancing toward the plenitude of divine truth (DV 8).[2]

Nevertheless, we would not do justice to tradition if we credited it only with the development in understanding of a closed and past revelation, but denied that it brings about an actual revelation of God. *Dei Verbum* offers no such low version of tradition. It sees in the following terms the results of tradition as guided by the Holy Spirit:

> By means of the same tradition . . . the holy scriptures themselves are more thoroughly understood and constantly actualized. Thus God, who spoke in the past, continues to converse with the spouse of his beloved Son. And the Holy Spirit, through whom the living voice of the gospel rings out in the church—and through her in the world—leads believers to the full truth, and makes the Word of God dwell in them in all its richness (*ibid.*).

Here the council expresses its conviction that through the force of tradition, the divine self-revelation recorded by the scriptures is not only "more thoroughly understood" but also "actualized" as a living revelation of God to Christ's church and through her to the world.

To deny present revelation is to doubt the active power here and now of the Holy Spirit as guiding the tradition and mediating the presence of the risen Christ. In effect this also means reducing faith to the acceptance of some revealed truths coming from the past rather than taking faith in its integral sense—as the full obedience given to God revealed here and now through the living voice of the gospel. In brief, to deny the present revelation of God is also to sell short its human correlative, faith.

Of course, if one persists in thinking that revelation entails *primarily* the communication of revealed truths, it becomes easier to relegate revelation to the past. As soon as the whole set of revealed doctrines is complete, revelation ends or is "closed." For this way of thinking later believers cannot immediately and directly experience revelation. All they can do is remember, interpret and apply truths revealed long ago to the apostolic church.

Dei Verbum and the other conciliar and postconciliar documents do, of course, describe revelation as something which reached its full and definitive climax in the past—through "the total fact" of Christ's "presence and self-manifestation" (DV 4). There was content to this personal revelation, so that *Dei Verbum* could refer to "the things he [God] had once revealed for the salvation of all peoples" (DV 7), "the divinely revealed realities" (DV 11) and the "deposit of faith" entrusted to the church at the beginning and to be maintained faithfully through the tradition (DV 10). Nevertheless, these official church documents do not hesitate to portray the divine self-revelation as something happening now through the liturgy (SC 7, 33), the prayerful reading of the scriptures (DV 25), missionary activity (AG 8), the signs of the times (GS 4, 11), the Christian education of very young children (*Catechesi Tradendae,* 36), the lives of saintly persons (LG 50), and so forth.

One could sum up this magisterial teaching on revelation as follows. Present revelation *actualizes* the living event of the divine self-manifestation but it *does not add* to the "content" of what was completely and fully revealed through Christ's life, death, resurrection and sending of the Holy Spirit. Revelation continues to be an actual encounter, but this living dialogue adds nothing to "the divinely revealed realities" (which essentially amount to Jesus Christ crucified and risen from the dead).

(2) *A Choice of Terminology.* The double "time-sign" of revelation leaves open the invitation to find an appropriate terminology for naming (i) revelation inasmuch as it reached an unsurpassable climax with Christ, and (ii) revelation inasmuch as it remains a living, interpersonal event. In one sense revelation is past; in another sense it is always present. How can we best describe (i) the history of revelation which found once and for all its perfect fulfillment with Christ, and (ii) the history of revelation which continues and will continue to the end of time?

(a) The National Catechetical Directory for Catholics of the United States, *Sharing the Light of Faith* (Washington, 1979), uses (i) "revelation" and (ii) "manifestation" or "communication" to contrast what happened *then* with Christ and what happens *now* in the church and the world (50). An earlier draft of the same directory had tried out another terminology: "Revelation" (upper case) then and "revelation" (lower case) now. After noting (42) the various "signs" of God's self-communication (for instance, biblical and liturgical signs), the final text contrasted the "revelation" which was concluded and completed nearly two thousand years ago with the self-manifestation of God which continues today (54–55). It insisted that this manifestation is a genuine, actual communication and not merely "the memory of something that happened long ago" (53).

This terminology of "revelation" *then* and "manifestation" *now* does not, however, serve too well for distinguishing the past and the present. In many contexts "revelation" (whether in upper or lower case), "manifestation" and "communication" prove synonymous or pratically synonymous. The same goes for the verbs "reveal," "manifest" and "communicate." In particular, the Second Vatican Council often enough uses these terms more or less interchangeably. For instance, *Ad Gentes* describes missionary activity as follows: "In manifesting (*manifestando*) Christ, the church reveals (*revelat*) to men their true situation and calling" (AG 8). The verbs could be switched without altering the meaning: "In revealing (*revelando*) Christ, the church manifests (*manifestat*) to men their true situation and calling." When translating *Lumen Gentium* the Flannery version in at least one place uses "is revealed" rather than "is manifested" or "is disclosed" to render *manifestatur:* ". . . the kingdom is revealed in the person of Christ himself" (LG 5).

Appealing to the Pauline notion of "the new man," *Ad Gentes* observes that all Christians "have an obligation to manifest (*manifestare*) the new man which they put on in baptism" (AG 11). A little later the same document presents "the mystery of Christ" in which "the new man created in the likeness of God has appeared . . . and in which the charity of God is revealed (*revelatur*)" (AG 12). In these two passages about the witness of Christian life we would hardly tamper with the sense if we made the first talk of the "obligation to reveal (*revelare*) the new man" and the second speak of "the mystery of Christ" in which "the charity of God is manifested (*manifestatur*)." Another example: Apropos of the gospel and various human cultures, *Gaudium et Spes* recalls the history of Old Testament revelation: "In his self-revelation (*sese revelans*) to his people culminating in the fullness of manifestation (*manifestationem*) in his incarnate Son, God spoke according to the culture proper to each age" (GS 58). No real alteration of meaning would occur if, instead of the given text, we were to read: "In his self-manifestation or self-disclosure (*sese manifestans*) to his people culminating in the fullness of revelation (*revelationem*) in his incarnate Son," etc. A final example, which involves "communicate": Toward the end of Chapter One, *Dei Verbum* sums up what has been stated about revelation: "By divine revelation (*divina revelatione*) God wished to manifest (*manifestare*) and communicate (*communicare*) both himself and the eternal decrees of his will concerning the salvation of mankind" (DV 6). Here "revelation," "self-manifestation" and "self-communication" largely coincide. In this context all three terms refer to what happened through the past history of God's people which climaxed with the events involving Jesus Christ. This passage would not support the linguistic decision to reserve "revelation" for the past and apply "self-manifestation" and "self-communication" to God's present activity.

To sum up: *Sharing the Light of Faith* wishes to contrast the "revelation" which happened back there and then with the divine "self-manifestation" and "self-communication" which continues now. The distinction does not seem very serviceable. In ordinary usage the three expressions seem to be largely synonymous. The documents of the Second Vatican Council in the examples given above seem to apply the terms interchangeably.

(b) In his *Revelation and Its Interpretation* (London, 1983) Aylward Shorter proposes to alter my terminology of "foundational" and "dependent" revelation (of which more shortly) by speaking of "foundational" and "participant" revelation (pp. 139–143). Shorter prefers "participant revelation" because of "the participatory character of all reality." In particular,

> our experience of Jesus Christ in the events and relationships of our own life really participates in the foundational revelation bestowed on the apostles and living on effectively in the tradition (p. 141).

The "participatory character of all reality" raises a problem, however, for Shorter's choice of terms. The apostles themselves participated in the final stage of Israel's history and in the events which climactically embodied God's self-revelation—the life, death and resurrection of Christ and the sending of the Holy Spirit. Hence one could properly talk of the participant revelation bestowed on the apostles. In these terms we participate in a participation. One might then contrast the "Participant" (upper case) revelation communicated at the time of Christ with the "participant" (lower case) revelation available now.

Ultimately, however, it is a question of explaining more fully the terminology I first suggested in the aftermath of the council: "foundational" and "dependent" revelation.[3] As regards God's self-communication, where the apostles participated in a foundational way, later Christians participate in a dependent way—that is to say, in dependence upon those apostolic witnesses.

(c) According to the letter to the Ephesians, "the household of God" is "built upon the foundation of the apostles and prophets, Christ Jesus himself being the cornerstone" (2:19–20). The book of Revelation's account of the new Jerusalem includes a similar image to describe the foundational role of the apostles: "The wall of the city had twelve foundations, and on them the twelve names of the twelve apostles of the Lamb" (21:14).

This foundational role of the apostles and the apostolic generation included the following functions. (i) The kerygmatic formulas recorded in Paul's letters (for example, 1 Cor 15:3–5), the Acts of the Apostles (2:22–24, 32–33, 36; 3:13–15; 4:10–12; 5:30–32) and elsewhere in the New Testament (for example, Lk 24:34) reflect a primary function of

Peter and the other apostles. Their basic message ("the crucified Jesus has been raised from the dead and of that we are witnesses") gathered the first Christians. Those who had not seen and yet believed (Jn 20:29) depended upon the testimony of the Easter witnesses for their faith in and experience of Jesus crucified and risen from the dead.[4] (ii) Believers entered the community through being baptized "into" Jesus' death and resurrection (Rom 6:3–11). Together they celebrated eucharistically the death of the risen Lord in the hope of his final coming (1 Cor 11:26). Thus the post-Easter apostolic proclamation initiated the essential liturgical life of the Christian church. (iii) The apostolic leaders made the normative decision not to impose on Gentile converts the observance of the Mosaic law (Acts 15:1–30; Gal 2:1–21). The resurrection of the crucified Jesus brought the new covenant which both confirmed God's promises to the chosen people (Rom 9:4; 11:29; 2 Cor 1:20) and liberated believers from the obligation of circumcision and other burdens of the law (Gal 5:1). (iv) The apostles and "others of the apostolic age" left in writing "the fourfold gospel" and the other New Testament writings (DV 18–20). Together these inspired books "stand as a perpetual and divine witness" to the definitive revelation of God in Christ and the origins of the church (DV 17).

In short, the apostles and others in the apostolic age shaped once and for all the essential sacramental (ii) and moral (iii) life of the church. Through the New Testament books (iv) they left for all subsequent ages of believers a divinely-inspired record of the definitive revelation and its reception in the first decades of Christianity. Right from the birth of Christianity, through their Easter kerygma (i) the apostles witnessed to the absolute climax of God's self-revelation which they had experienced in the crucified and risen Christ.

I sum up these apostolic functions by speaking of those who witnessed to that "foundational" revelation which took place normatively through a specific series of events and the experiences of a specific set of people. God's saving word came through the history of Israel, the prophets and then—in a definitive fashion—through Jesus of Nazareth and the experiences in which he and his first followers were immediately involved. Christians experience now God's self-communication, reaching them through preaching, sacraments, the scriptures and other things which recall and re-enact those past experiences and events. Thus the mediation of revelation (and grace) by means of the sacramental life, the scriptures, the preached word and other means essentially depends upon our acceptance of authoritative testimony about certain past acts of God on our behalf. In that sense revelation as we experience it and accept it now is "dependent" revelation. The adjective "dependent" expresses our permanent and living relationship to the apostolic witnesses, whose faith and proclamation of the gospel sprang from their special, immediate experience of Jesus during his lifetime and as risen from the dead. The apostolic witness to foundational revelation remains determinative for the post-apostolic history of Christians and their experience of God in Christ.

We saw how documents of the magisterium speak of the divine self-revelation in the past and the present tense. We may appropriately add that revelation in the past tense is "foundational" and revelation in the present tense is "dependent." The history of revelation goes on and will go on till the end of time, as God continues to speak and invite people to the life of faith. In equivalent terms *Dei Verbum* talks of "the Christian economy" which "will never pass away" while we wait for "the glorious manifestation of our Lord, Jesus Christ" (DV 4). But all this post-apostolic history of revelation takes place in dependence on that irrevocably valid revelation which reached its unsurpassable climax with Jesus Christ and his apostles.

(3) *The End of Foundational Revelation.* To complete this reflection on past (foundational) revelation and ongoing (dependent) revelation, it is worth asking: When did foundational revelation end and the period of dependent revelation begin?

Without using my terminology, one traditional response (a) has in effect stated that foundational revelation ended with the apostolic age— that is to say, around the close of the first century. Thus the anti-modernist decree of July 3, 1907, *Lamentabili,* condemned the proposition that "revelation, which constitutes the object of Catholic faith, was not completed with the apostles" (DS 3421). Obviously this document understood divine revelation primarily in terms of its content, the various truths or mysteries disclosed by God. Theological manuals often expressed the view of *Lamentabili* by declaring that revelation closed at the death of the last apostle.[5]

Karl Rahner and others have suggested that (foundational) revelation ended much earlier—with the resurrection of the crucified Christ, his appearances to the official witnesses, and the coming of the Holy Spirit. Rahner wrote:

> While textbook theology usually says that revelation was closed with the death of the last apostle, it would be better and more exact to say that revelation closed with the achievement of the death of Jesus, crucified and risen.[6]

This second view (b) highlights the revealing events themselves without paying much attention to the way the apostolic witnesses fully assimilated and expressed those events. It underplays the fact that, as a reciprocal affair, revelation is not properly there before being adequately accepted and lived out by the recipients.

Provided that it is adjusted to allow that revelation consists primarily in a personal encounter and then secondarily means some revealed "content," view (a) seems preferable. It can allow for the full reception of revelation by respecting the fact that the apostles' experience of Christ included also the phase of discernment, interpretation and expression of that experience. Peter, Paul and the other founding fathers and mothers of the church spent a lifetime expressing and proclaiming their experience of the crucified and risen Jesus. Collectively and personally they gave themselves to interpreting and applying the meaning, truth and value of their total experience of Jesus. That experience lodged itself profoundly in their memories to live on powerfully and productively till the end of their lives. They could not interpret once and for all what they had directly known of Jesus' ministry, death and resurrection, so as to be finished with their experience of those events.

Understood that way, the period of foundational revelation covered not merely the climactic events (the life, death and resurrection of Jesus and the gift of the Spirit) but also the decades when the apostles and their associates assimilated those events, fully founded the church for all peoples, and wrote the inspired books of the New Testament. During those years the apostles were not receiving new truths as if Christ had failed to complete revelation by all that he did, said and suffered. Rather they were being led by the Holy Spirit to express, interpret normatively and apply what they had directly experienced of the fullness of revelation in the person of Christ. In these terms the activity of the Spirit through the apostolic age also entered into foundational revelation—in its phase of immediate assimilation. Thus that age belonged to the revealing and redemptive Christ-event, and did so in a way which would not be true of any later stage of Christian history.

When the apostolic age closed—roughly speaking at the end of the first century—there would be no more founding of the church and writing of inspired scriptures. The final period of foundational revelation, in which the activity of the original witnesses brought about the visible church and completed the written word of God, was finished. The total experience (including its normative expression) of the apostolic believers, which coincides with what we also call the deposit of faith, was over and completed. Through the apostolic church and its scriptures, later generations could share dependently in the saving self-communication of God mediated through unrepeatable events surrounding Jesus and his apostles. As the prologue of *Dei Verbum* indicates by citing 1 John 1:2–3, till the end of time all later generations will be invited to accept the witness of those who could announce what they had personally experienced of the full divine revelation in Christ: "We proclaim to you the eternal life which was with the Father and was made manifest to us."

8. GOD'S SYMBOLIC SELF-COMMUNICATION

Those who study the best of preconciliar theology will appreciate how *Dei Verbum* marked a point of arrival. Its opening chapter, for example, officially received and incorporated such themes from Catholic (and other) theologians as revelation being primarily God's self-revelation, the history of revelation being inseparable from the history of salvation, and revelation being the greater reality which overshadows and interprets both tradition and biblical inspiration.

As well as being a point of arrival *Dei Verbum* has also proved a point of departure. In Chapter 4 we noted how the document registered the sacramental nature of revelation and incorporated the scheme of divine self-communication. Putting together these two schemes we can explore ways of expounding revelation as God's symbolic self-communication.[1] Theology may find here a helpful, contemporary synthesis—at least for the question of the means and mediators of revelation (=its how?). Can we usefully interpret God's revealing and saving self-communication as taking place through symbolic events, words, persons and things? Is this divine self-communication actually and even necessarily symbolic?

Homo Symbolicus. In Chapter 5 we saw how the Second Vatican Council, particularly in *Gaudium et Spes,* attached itself to a long tradition by presenting human beings in terms of their basic questions. There is much to commend in this view of the human person as a questioner *(homo interrogans).* But this anthropology cannot claim to be inevitably superior or even exclusive. After all one could muster much evidence to support an anthropology which finds its center in the suffering human person *(homo dolens).* We might also describe the human person as essentially symbolic *(homo symbolicus),* a being that is both material and spiritual and hence constantly expresses itself in symbolic acts. Human beings reveal themselves to others (and to themselves) when they perform properly human acts which are always symbolic: speaking, working, dressing, eating, love-making, traveling, worshiping, being sick and dying. The divine self-communication "corresponds" to our symbolic nature. If God wishes to communicate with *homo symbolicus,* this revelation must take a symbolic form and road. God the revealer is necessarily God the symbolizer. But it is high time I declared my hand and set down what I understand by symbols.

Symbols. A working account of a symbol could run as follows: (a) something (or someone) perceptible that (b) represents dynamically something (or someone) else, especially something invisible or abstract.[2] First, (a) the "something perceptible" may be a gospel story we hear, a group of people we see united for prayer, a body we touch, the perfume we smell or the wine we taste. It is through our senses that we perceive and grasp a symbol. (b) Whatever it may be, a symbol always reveals, represents, or, better, "re-presents" (in the sense of somehow making actually present) what is symbolized. A letter, a portrait or the tombstone of my deceased mother can symbolize her, mediating and realizing for me her presence. These symbols represent a person whom death has made invisible. The incarnate and visible Word of God symbolized and represented the invisible Father. In John's language, "he who has seen me has seen the Father" (Jn 14:9). Paul speaks of Christ as the image or icon of (the invisible) God the Father (2 Cor 4:4; see Col 1:15). He is "the radiance" of the Father's glory, the "perfect copy of his being" (Heb 1:3). Symbolic language can also express such "abstractions" as the qualities of prudence and simplicity: "I send you out as sheep in the midst of wolves; so be wise as serpents and innocent as doves" (Mt 10:16).

We need to dwell on the way a symbol makes present and in some sense even perceptible what is symbolized. What is the relationship between the symbol and the reality it symbolizes? The link may be conventional (as is the case with a flag that symbolizes a particular nation), or else may be thoroughly natural and rooted in reality (as is the case with my body that symbolizes me). In the latter case the symbol is not truly separate or different from what is symbolized. Yet even here, although the reality symbolized ("I") is present and appears in the symbol (my body), it is not fully expressed by this appearance. My body never captures my full reality.

One can go to two extremes when assessing the relationship between a symbol and what is symbolized. On the one hand, one could merge the symbol with what is symbolized. On the other hand, one could separate them excessively. The former error might take the form of confusing the visible church with the invisible Christ (the result being some kind of ecclesiolatry), or of confusing some visual representation with God (the result being idolatry or image-worship). This is to forget that such symbols represent and transmit far more than they themselves are. The latter error might express itself in iconoclasm, a refusal to recognize in the symbol the real presence of the (heavenly) reality that is symbolized. This is the error of those who smash statues, take down religious paintings or deny any presence of Christ in his ongoing, visible symbol, the church.

Talk of extremes should not be allowed to cloak the fact that there is a whole range of possibilities for the link between the symbol and what it symbolizes. In the case of Christ, he is symbolized, with varying degrees of intensity, by icons, the gospels, men and women, ministers in his church and the celebration of the sacraments (especially the eucharist). These and other symbols express and realize his presence in qualitatively different ways.

Here, as elsewhere, symbolic self-communication always involves something kenotic. Even though the symbol really symbolizes and makes present what is symbolized, a certain self-emptying and resultant hiddenness arises inasmuch as what is symbolized takes the form of the symbol. To the extent that the symbol does not coincide with that which it symbolizes, a gap opens up and concealment (as well as revelation) becomes possible. The humanity of Jesus, for example, truly symbolized but did not simply coincide with the Logos or second person of the Trinity. Hence the humanity of Jesus concealed, as well as revealed, the Logos.[3]

This gap between the symbols themselves (for example, the humanity of Jesus and the sacraments) and what they symbolize (the fullness of divine life in the future vision of the tripersonal God) introduces the element of hope. Being by their nature limited, symbols cannot capture the full, future reality of what they symbolize. They invite us to look in hope for the plenitude, as yet invisible, of God's future self-communication (Rom 8:24–25; 1 Cor 2:9; Heb 11:1).

Before moving on from this working account of symbols, it is worth underlining one essential item implied by naming a symbol as "something or someone *perceptible*." Symbols belong to our world of space and time, and hence are always, at least in some sense, historical. Hence talk of symbols entails, rather than excludes, history. The symbolic nature of Jesus' cross and crucifixion in no way challenges the historicity of the events of the first Good Friday. An appreciation of the symbolic message communicated by the virginal conception should not foolishly be interpreted as rejection of its historical reality. It would be absurd to construe attention to the symbolic characteristics of Mehemet Ali Agca's attempt on the life of John Paul II as some kind of crypto-challenge to the factuality of the events that took place in St. Peter's Square on May 13, 1981. These and other such symbolic events, persons, words and things belong squarely to human history.

A major point that calls for clarification is the relation between signs and symbols. Although we must admit that the boundary between signs and symbols is not always clear and precise, we can recognize signs as the broader reality, at the heart of which comes that special class of signs called symbols. (a) Normally symbols differ from mere signs, in being more "natural" and corresponding more closely to the things symbolized. Signs can be utterly conventional like directions in an airport terminal, but may also be utterly "natural," the classic case being smoke (an effect) as a sign of fire (its cause). (b) By evoking a rich range of meaning rather than simply stating one clear message, symbols are generally more "significant" than mere signs. We know much, often everything, about signs, because we have made them and they conform to our conventions. Symbols, however, emerge mysteriously, are given to us and prove themselves richly open-ended in their significance. One finds such depth and range of meaning in the symbolic language of the fourth gospel: for instance, "I am the bread of life"; "I am the light of the world." (c) Symbols contain and make present the things symbolized.[4] Mere signs simply point to something else, without mediating its presence. (d) Mere signs, such as road signs or directions on bottles of medicine, can prove very useful, if not simply indispensable. But they normally lack the powerful impact on feelings and actions enjoyed by symbols. Burning a mere sign like a road sign would normally not excite the emotions or release the energies roused by burning a national symbol like the country's flag. People will die for a symbol, but it is hard to imagine someone dying for a mere sign. (e) Where such symbols as church ceremonies, national holidays and the presence of a prophet invite and facilitate participation in some activities, mere signs have a utilitarian function in conveying information. (f) Lastly, unlike *mere* signs, symbols often tend to be *living* persons or things. This point calls for a fuller discussion, especially in terms of the living symbols of the Bible.

From the book of Genesis on, God's communication often takes that form. After the flood, heaven and earth are linked by the sign of the rainbow, which reveals and guarantees God's grace and favor. The rainbow symbolizes God's undying friendship. Like a living thing a rainbow comes and goes in the sky. The manna in the desert is gathered fresh every morning; it cannot be stored up like dead produce. The classical prophets constantly reach for living signs and symbols to communicate their message from God: an almond tree in blossom, a woman in childbirth, hearts of flesh, people going into exile, potters busy at their work, shepherds with their sheep, vineyards promising a great yield of wine, fountains bubbling with water.

Obviously not all biblical signs and symbols are living. The great sign of God's saving presence, the temple, was built of stones and other dead materials. But often living symbols predominate: above all, such rich and sacred symbols as blood, which expresses deliverance, purification and pledged friendship. Eventually, even the temple becomes such a symbol when Paul and Peter write of the community of the baptized as God's temple of "living stones" that make up a "spiritual house" (Eph 2:19–22; 1 Pet 4:5).

It comes as no surprise, then, to read the angel's words to the shepherds: "This will be a sign for you; you will find a babe wrapped in swaddling clothes and lying in a manger" (Lk 2:12). The face, mouth, hands, and curled-up toes of that tiny baby are God's unique, non-verbal gesture to us. Mary's child is the living, visible symbol of the invisible God. That baby has made God present for us in a startlingly new way.

We might adapt here the prologue of John's gospel and say: "The Word became body language and dwelt amongst us." What began with body language in the manger at Bethlehem ended with body language when Jesus stretched out his hands and feet to be nailed to the cross.

It takes no great leap of the imagination to read as God's living signs the people who welcome the newborn Jesus. There are the shepherds roughing it at night and representing the poor of this world who receive God's special blessing. In Bethlehem the shepherds find Mary and Joseph, whose faith and love make them utterly and uniquely open to the divine will. In the temple the aged Simeon and Anna symbolize just what lifelong fidelity to God can mean. The wise men from the east signify the pilgrims of this world, who may travel for years before they find him "who was born king of the Jews" (Mt 2:2).

Intensely symbolic people fill up the Christmas story. Here, as elsewhere, the biblical narratives reveal a profound preference for living symbols.

The examples already given have provided a partial answer to the further question: What range of items can be grouped under the heading of symbols? Words, actions (or events), persons and things cover the possibilities. Symbols can take such linguistic forms as symbolic names like Jesus and Cephas (or Peter), oracles, parables, miracle stories (for instance, Jn 9), sacramental formulas and self-presentation ("I am the bread of life," "I am the good shepherd" and "I am the vine and you are the branches"—from John's gospel). Symbolic actions and events run from the Babylonian captivity, the liturgical feasts of the Israelites, the miracles of Jesus and his crucifixion, through the use of water in baptism and the sign of the cross made millions of times each day by Christians. Prophets (see Jer 16:1–21; Ez 24:15–25; Hos 1:1–8), parents and priests are obviously symbolic persons. But such examples in no way exhaust the possibilities here. Through what they do and suffer all men and women (and not least the sick and the old) present themselves as symbolic beings. This must be so if what we have claimed above is true—that every human being is through and through *homo symbolicus*. Finally, all created things are actually or potentially symbols, whether they are such natural objects as an eagle, a mountain, a stream and the sun, or such human artifacts as a church, a chalice, an icon or a printed copy of the Bible. Like human beings themselves, all other created objects can symbolize and make present what is invisible—in particular, the invisible things of God.

Among the examples just provided, some religious symbols originated thousands of years ago, entered the Judaeo-Christian tradition and maintain their power and potency (for instance, the Old Testament prophets, the Babylonian captivity, and the crucifixion). Other such symbols have emerged or continue to emerge in the course of history. Among these belong "the signs of the times," a major theme of the Second Vatican Council (see GS 4; PO 9; AA 14; UR 4), which are no mere signs but could well be called "the symbols of the times," as they are perceptible events of current history that "re-present" invisible realities and communicate religious meaning.

Self-Communication. The double-sided way the symbols of the times and other symbols function obviously makes them suitable vehicles for God's *revealing and saving* self-communication. Symbols have a cognitive content and always say something. The symbolic actions and events I listed above—from the Babylonian captivity through to the sign of the cross—all communicate some truth and transmit some information. At the same time, we can never hope to express conceptually once and for all the meaning and truth of these symbols. They have a multi-layered power to communicate. Not only symbolic language but also other kinds of symbols enjoy this plus-value—in particular, religious symbols with their overt connection with the infinite mystery of God. Where mere signs can be translated and completely explained, we cannot do this with symbols. They work elusively on the intuitive, instinctive level, and can never be fully grasped and rationally conceptualized. We experience and intuitively know more than we can express, when confronted with the mysterious, inexhaustible nature of Christ's nativity, crucifixion and empty tomb.

The *salvific* impact of symbols is inextricably bound together with their relevatory power. They affect the whole person in his or her mind, memory, feelings, imagination, hopes and fears. This total impact, which is obviously experienced with varying degrees of intensity, we see exemplified in a massive way by such sacred and secular ceremonies as the inauguration of a new president, a world soccer final, a funeral, a marriage or an ordination to the priesthood. Such major symbolic events write large what holds true of all symbols and, in particular, blatantly religious symbols. They enjoy a transformative, redemptive power. Symbols transmit and evoke meaning, and all meaning is transforming.

Symbols release energies, help us to act and participate in new ways. They can invite us to identify strongly with a story and live in a new kind of world. Every year parishes around the world experience this power as they welcome fresh members who have followed the Rite of Christian Initiation of Adults. These newly baptized persons have come to identify strongly with the biblical story that culminated in Jesus' life, death and resurrection, the gift of the Holy Spirit and the emergence of the church. As Christians, through the symbolic acts of the sacraments, they have freely accepted the challenge to live in a new kind of way.

"Participatory knowledge" serves to sum up the two inseparable but distinguishable dimensions of symbols and, specifically, religious symbols. God's self-communication through symbols entails not only meaning, knowledge and truth (= revelation) but also meaning/truth that transforms and knowledge that calls on us to participate in a new life (= redemption).

The total impact exercised by symbols helps to explain the anger felt by some or even many people over changes in familiar symbols and especially over their loss. People normally do not become very agitated by the change or destruction of mere signs. Alterations in the style of road-signs will usually go through easily, provided the new signs prove to be at least as clear and effective as the former ones. But to change or destroy a national flag will provoke deep dissent and anger. Important symbols, in particular religious ones, are cherished as untouchable.

Healing characterizes the salvific function of many symbols. In the church, political society and family life, tensions, divisions and contradictions emerge and often perdure. Feast days, flags and deeply loved national holidays play their part in bridging and to some extent reconciling antagonistic groups. Symbolism that attaches to spiritual leaders like bishops and popes can heal division and bring unity in the diocese or the church at large. Weddings, baptisms and funerals may function in the same way for divided families. Mere concepts and rational argument alone cannot resolve antagonisms and ease strong tensions. Such signs and symbols as the cross, the story of Christ's passion and the sacraments repeatedly show their saving power in making unbearable situations somehow bearable and even fruitful. Faced with tragic personal losses, Christians naturally reach for symbols rather than "rational" explanations.

When we focus on the two classic mysteries of salvation, apparent contradictions emerge which cannot be solved conceptually but only accepted and lived with the help of symbols. I refer first to the mystery of absurd evil and innocent suffering in the world. How can that continuing drama of human pain be reconciled with our faith in a God of infinite love, justice, mercy and power? Job's question finds its partial, provisional and symbolic answer at the foot of the cross. Second, the related mystery of the collaboration between divine grace and human freedom produced legendary debates between Dominicans and Jesuits but no real clarification. We would do better here to read the two symbolic stories that Jesus left side by side: one (the parable of the sower) evokes the varieties of human responses to the good grace of God (Mk 4:3–9); the other story (the parable of the seed that grows by itself [Mk 4:26–29]) evokes the power of the divine redemptive activity. To repeat these two stories is not to abandon professional integrity but to make the mystery symbolically bearable.

Before leaving the disclosive and salvific function of symbols, let me add a word about their shadow side. Both in the civil and religious spheres, the unscrupulous and devious manipulate symbols to conceal rather than reveal truth. In their hands symbols can prove oppressive and enslaving rather than healing, liberating and transforming. In such cases people will feel betrayed by the symbolic words, events and persons to whom they gave their loyalty as citizens and believers.

Credibility and Tradition. Thus far this chapter has sketched a way for understanding and interpreting God's self-revelation as taking place through symbolic events, words, persons and things. Through an indefinitely varied range of symbols, God, the symbolizer and the symbolized, is present and communicated.

Chapter 3 of this book recognized alongside divine revelation two further basic themes for fundamental theology: the credibility of God's self-manifestation and its transmission. Hence any outline of a symbolic approach to revelation should include something about credibility and tradition.

In the case of mere signs there is hardly a problem about credibility. We accept instantly from a road sign the direction and distance it indicates. But what makes symbols credible? How do we justify symbolic stories, actions and persons? Why believe symbols, whether secular or sacred?

To an extent historical evidence establishes some important points about the life, death and resurrection of Jesus. With a good degree of probability one can maintain various facts about his authoritative preaching of the kingdom, his miracles, his crucifixion, the Easter appearances, the spread of his community and so forth. Here, as elsewhere, the history of someone or some event is essential for determining the meaning and truth of some symbols. But finally it is personal experience that legitimates the symbolic realities, especially those which make up the Christian message and life. Lived symbols are believable symbols. By appropriating and entering into the central symbolic realities of Christianity, we allow them to "veri-fy" themselves or make themselves true. We validate experientially symbolic knowledge, in particular the symbolic knowledge of faith.

In the following chapter we reflect on experience—its evidence and authority. Here let me simply observe in advance how religious experience (and language) are not only essentially symbolic but also imaginative and emotional (in the sense of evoking feelings). Hence respecting the symbolic nature of God's self-communication also means respecting our imagination and emotions.

Two tendencies reduce the impact of symbols in making credible the central message of Christianity: a partial loss of symbols and their privatizing. Our symbolic nature guarantees that we can never totally lose a sense of symbolism. But the western world has experienced a profound impoverishment of central human and religious symbols, along with a (relative) triumph of trivial symbols. That diminishment of central symbols and the pursuit of trivial symbols has played its part in a certain loss of Christian plausibility. The privatizing of religion in the west has helped to produce a situation in which many symbols have lost their public hold. At the same time, some symbolic stories like that of Christmas still shape the collective life of Christians.[5] As elsewhere, symbols establish, intensify and maintain group identity. With this observation we arrive at the social and traditional function of symbols.

Our remembered and shared symbols identify and define the Christian community. They allow us to receive God's salvific self-communication, to communicate with each other and to hand on our faith in Christ to the next generation.

In brief, common symbols constitute the perceptible dimension of Christian tradition—not just "symbols" in the classical sense of ancient creeds but the full range of symbolic words, events, persons and things that we share. *Dei Verbum* speaks of the church "in her teaching, life and worship," handing on to all generations all that she herself is, all that she believes" (DV 8). The church's "teaching, life and worship" have through and through a symbolic structure and nature. Coming from symbolic persons who represent invisible realities (for example, bishops, catechists and parents), this teaching concerns symbolic words, events, persons and things. Among other things Christian life calls us to minister to those in need (Mt 25:31–46), visible men and women who symbolize and "re-present" the invisible Christ. The public worship of the church centers on the sacraments, perceptible symbols of God's invisible realities, both present and future.

To sum up: The teaching, life and worship of the church begins and ends in symbol. Her tradition, or remembering and handing on "all that she herself is, all that she believes," may be properly seen as handing on her Christian symbols. In doing this each generation invites the next to enter a symbolic history, share the same symbols and experience in hope the same life.

This chapter has suggested an appropriate line of response to the "how?" of the divine self-communication: revelatory and salvific symbolism. It has argued as well that symbolic words, actions (or events), persons and things also offer a clue to understanding the other two major themes of FT: the credibility of God's self-revelation and its transmission through tradition. We turn next to the appropriation of God's self-communication through human experience.

9. EXPERIENCE AND SYMBOLS

Human life is radically symbolic. Both among ourselves and before God, all that we do and experience begins and ends in symbols. The Old Testament prophets, Paul, Augustine, Teresa of Avila, innumerable other saints and above all Jesus himself have appealed to their own experience, special experiences and common human experiences as that which conveys God's revealing and saving activity. Human experience did and does that through its symbolic character. Signs and symbols disclose and communicate the divine mystery. Through symbols we experience the holy God. If "*symbolic* self-comunication" helps to describe, but not fully explain, divine revelation, our experience is the medium through which we encounter God's self-communication.[1]

Hence the choice and place of this chapter. Even those who do not find talk of God's *symbolic* self-communication very congenial should, nevertheless, look for some answers about divine revelation by reflecting on experience. The truth holds both for the foundational recipients of revelation in Old Testament and New Testament times and for later believers. God's self-manifestation either meets us in our experience or it does not meet us at all. Given the essentially personal and interpersonal character of revelation, non-experienced revelation would be a simple contradiction in terms.

That said, I need to recognize in passing a certain modern hesitancy to use the language of experience. John's gospel, the letters of St. Paul, the letters of St. Basil, the *Confessions* of St. Augustine and other classic works established and encouraged an experiential approach to understanding and interpreting the divine-human relationship. A long line of spiritual and mystical authorities examined this relationship in the key of experience. William of Saint-Thierry (1085–1148) is one of very many Christians who have explored in depth our spiritual experience. Nevertheless two modern documents of the Catholic magisterium, *Dei Filius* in 1870 and *Pascendi* in 1907, respectively, warned against denying that external signs could lend credibility to divine revelation, and against appealing only to the internal experience of individuals (DS 3033), making faith in God depend on the private experience of the individual and maintaining that interior, immediate experience of God prevails over rational arguments (DS 33484). This justified opposition to one-sided and partial versions of religious experience unfortunately encouraged the dangerous delusion that somehow we could encounter and accept the divine self-communication "outside" human experience.

In 1965 *Dei Verbum* helped to set the record straight, at least for those Roman Catholics who needed to have it set straight. Through their special history of revelation and salvation, the Israelites "experienced the ways of God" (DV 14). In the post-New Testament life of the church, so the council acknowledged, their "experience" of "spiritual realities" has helped believers contribute to the progress of tradition (DV 8). As normally happens in the texts from ecumenical councils and other magisterial authorities, terms get used without analysis and explanation. They are left up for examination by theologians.[2]

Thus far in this chapter I have been concerned to justify and account for the discussion of experience that follows. At the very least it can be seen as an extended commentary on the teaching from *Dei Verbum* about God's self-revelation and its transmission. At best it aims to complement on the *human* side what the last chapter offered about the *divine* self-communication through symbols. What do we mean by "experience" when we speak of our experience of God's symbolic self-communication?

In what comes next I will first introduce fourteen points to illuminate the reality of human experience in general and then add some items on religious experience in particular. From the outset one must observe how polyvalent the notion and reality of experience are. They defy reduction to a simple formula. My fourteen points range across the (inter-connected) orders of being, knowledge and language. The reader should be on the watch to notice whether I am speaking about "experience" ontologically, epistemologically or linguistically, or in all three ways.

General Characteristics of Experience. 1) The first point, which links up with what I have just written, is one often bandied about: the paradoxical status of experience. On the one hand, in what has frequently been called "the age of experience" many people search experientially for insight and explanation. Faced with the major questions of life, they look for answers in and through their experience. On the other hand, the concept of experience is "many-levelled and ambiguous."[3] Despite its popularity, it resists precise definition.

(2) In contemporary Indo-European languages we speak about ex-

perience in two related ways. It is a *process,* made up of a series of sub-experiences. Any tourist's experience of a new country or a new city would be a typical example. We also apply "experience" to the *condition* that results. Some observant, well-read and adventurous tourists reach the point of becoming genuine experts. Whatever the field—be it teaching, tourism, management, surgery or something else—an expert is one who has learned much through his or her experiences, and who now "has" the experience to cope well with new, surprising and difficult circumstances. Such people are thoroughly "experienced."

(3) My third point is also, at least initially, a linguistic one. Unlike English, French, Italian, Spanish, and some other modern languages, German enjoys not one but two nouns to express experience: *Erfahrung* (with its corresponding verb *erfahren*) and *Erlebnis* (with its corresponding verb *erleben*). *Er-fahren* suggests traveling, exploring and learning things through time and trouble. *Ein erfahrener Mensch* is a person who has learned much through a series of experiences. Often enough the language of *Erfahrung* highlights the realities we encounter and come to know, or the condition that objectively results from many experiences—in brief, the objective pole. *Er-leben,* on the other hand, points to life *(Leben)* which reveals itself in experiences. It suggests the feelings and emotions our experiences can arouse—in short, the subjective pole.

All that said, any distinction between *erfahren* and *erleben* should be based on and supplemented by further examples. Usage and context are decisive, rather than artificial attempts to exploit the fact that German offers a choice of terms not found in other languages. At the same time, some distinction between the objective and subjective poles of experience is very much in place—whether or not we explicate it with reference to the German *Erfahrung* and *Erlebnis.*

(4) The fourth observation closely follows on the third. Experience necessarily involves some direct contact between the subject experiencing and the object experienced. Somehow the object is or becomes present, so as to be immediately encountered. An indirect or second-hand experience by proxy is a contradiction in terms. Experiences are either first-hand and immediate or they are not there at all. One cannot experience marriage without actually getting married oneself.

This immediacy should not be misconstrued as if I meant to deny the presuppositions and prior conditioning involved in every experience. Every experience has its presuppositions. Our social, cultural and religious conditioning makes our experiences possible and intelligible. In various guises this point will recur in what follows. Here I simply wish to insist that acknowledging the immediate nature of experience in no way implies the assertion that we bring a clean, presuppositionless "state"—a kind of *tabula rasa*—to our experiences.

Nor should the immediacy of experience in the religious sphere be misunderstood as if we could encounter God alone rather than "in, with and under" other experiences. God deals immediately with human beings. We can and do experience God, and that means that we immediately experience God. Yet it is always through "other" experiences that God is symbolically communicated to us.

An important, "positive" consequence of the immediacy of experience is that every experience has its subjective and objective pole. In all experiences a subject comes somehow into contact with some kind of object. In given experiences the subject can be more prominent, in others the object. On some or even many occasions the subject may misinterpret the object or remain deeply puzzled by what it experiences. But we never have a "purely subjective" experience nor, for that matter, a "purely objective" one. In any experience a subject directly encounters an object. We must resist the temptation to speak of "purely subjective" experiences. They would be a contradiction in terms.

(5) Particularity characterizes all experiences. They are always concrete and specific, never general and universal. An experience means *this* specific reality at this time. Despite the phenomenon of the "professionally ill," people cannot be sick in general. They experience this or that specific health problem.

(6) All experiences show an *active* and a *passive* component. The subject not only acts but also undergoes something. The symbolic language of Jesus' parables invites their hearers not only to receive them but also to actively respond to this experience. (a) Admittedly some experiences put the subject in a much more active role: laboratory experiments, in which research scientists carefully set up the conditions for what will be experienced furnish the classic instance of such "active" experiences. (b) The experience of dying and death serves to exemplify the more passive experiences. Yet passive elements turn up in cases of (a): after all, the scientific experiment may turn out quite differently from what was planned. Cases of (b) do not exclude active involvement in what the subject experiences. John's gospel goes out of its way to stress the way Jesus actively participated in his death (Jn 19:30).

Before moving on from this sixth point, it could be worth noting two opposite tendencies in philosophy which respectively emphasize unilaterally the active and the passive dimensions of experience. On the one hand, idealism in its various forms highlights the activity of the human spirit. On the other hand, empirical strains of philosophy tend to underline onesidedly the passive aspects of human experience. Any balanced approach should refuse to follow either trend toward absolutizing either the active or the passive side of experience.

(7) Unlike the logical conclusions of some deductive argumentation, the evidence of experience simply imposes itself directly. What we experience is undeniable. The immediate "authority" of what we experience when we read biblical narratives or participate in the sacramental life of the church will not go away. These experienced symbols, precisely as experienced, present themselves directly.

Here, however, I am not claiming that we always read off correctly the immediate evidence of experience. Notoriously people have misinterpreted great biblical symbols, turning the creation story into a scientific account of the world's origins or the sign of the cross into a guarantee of worldly domination by Christians. We may get things wrong by forgetting that our experience is only partial. In fact, short of the *eschaton,* all experience remains partial and provisional. We can rush toward error when we absolutize some experience and refuse to remain open to the evidence of new experiences which may modify what we have already learned. In the biblical story the people are not summoned to ignore and forget the authority of their foundational experiences but to open themselves to new experiences: in the end, the incarnate symbol of God who came to live among them. Hence, while I would agree with C. S. Lewis that experience yields direct evidence and is not "trying" to deceive,[4] I would also insist on the need for discernment—a lesson inculcated by the very first Christian text (1 Thess 5:19–21). The multi-leveled nature of the central religious symbols we experience individually and collectively can mean that we misread what we see and misinterpret what we hear.

(8) Experiences easily invite categorization into good/bad, pleasant/ painful, enlightening/puzzling, or, more simply, positive/negative experiences. Obviously we are threatened here with a facile reductionism that assesses experiences according to a calculus of pleasure. In those terms sickness, physical handicaps and pain of all kinds would be dismissed as "merely" negative experiences, to be avoided as far as possible. However, viewed in their full context and for their long-term consequences, such experiences can turn out to be highly beneficial, humanly and spiritually. Not only the ancient Greeks but also Christians realized that we can learn much through the things we suffer (see Heb 5:8). So-called "bad" experiences may prove to be extremely enlightening and redemptive—a point that repeatedly emerges from many of the world's greatest dramas and novels.

There can be no such things as "purely negative" experiences or symbols. Some experiences may very well seem to be so: for example, a young mother dying of cancer, an unjust condemnation to a long-term prison sentence, or being victimized as an object of racial hatred. Some symbols may easily seem to be purely negative: for example, the mushroom cloud from an atomic bomb explosion, burning oil wells, extermination camps, or a man writhing to death on a cross. Yet the Jewish-Christian faith and classical metaphysics assure me that there neither is nor can be *pure* unadulterated evil or, in equivalent terms, the absolutely negative. Everything has come from the hands of the infinitely good God. Not even the ultimate in human or diabolic perversity can totally undo that fact. One can cling to the delusion that certain persons or events are the epitome of evil. But absolute evil would be pure absence, a total lack of the good which should be there—in other words, just nothing.

(9) In a way my next observation picks up on an aspect of the third point above: with varying degrees of intensity *the whole person* is involved in and revealed by his or her experiences. Every experience, even the most trivial one, enjoys at least a minimal "totality" by affecting the entire person. Any experience whatsoever is "my" experience and not simply that of my arm, my eye or my imagination alone. Of course, the more profound the experience, the greater its impact on the totality of my being, for good or evil.

On the objective side, even though as limited beings we experience only partial fragments of reality, our experiences somehow point to all reality. As we shall see in the next chapter, there is something total, absolute and unlimited about our relative and limited experiences of love. Objectively as well as subjectively, the whole of reality is involved in every experience. In and through experiencing parts of reality, nevertheless, as whole persons we stand in contact with the whole.

(10) Human beings come across not only as those who question, suffer, symbolize and *experience* but also as rational, *thinking* animals. How then does experience relate to and differ from thought?

Obviously thinking about joy differs from a joyful experience. There is a concrete particularity about experiences which differentiates them from universal concepts, discursive thought, general judgments and dictionary definitions. We use concepts and judgments to communicate our experiences. But they do not simply coincide with those experiences.

Here we might adapt and adjust Kant's dictum: "Thought without experience is empty; experience without thought is blind."[5] On the one hand, experiences make us think and lead us to understand. Consciously religious experiences lead us to think about God and understand at least a little of the divine-human relationship. Experiencing for the first time the symbolic drama of the Christian sacraments brings some people to a new and real knowledge of themselves, humanity and God. Without any personal contact with the Christian liturgy, at best they could enjoy only an abstract, "empty" appreciation of the sacraments—a notional knowledge through study rather than a real knowledge by acquaintance. On the other hand, thought may help to explain some experiences and to prepare us for new experiences. Thinking about what we witness in the sacramental life of the church can help us to participate more fully, intelligently and experientially in that life. Thought can clarify what we have experienced and prepare us to understand and interpret what we are going to experience.

The early development of Christian doctrine serves as well as any other phenomenon to illustrate the (distinguishable but inseparable) interplay between experience and thought. On the one hand, the apostolic and post-New Testament experience of Christ prompted his followers to think about him in certain ways. Clarifying their experiences led them to produce the christological teachings of the first general councils. On the other hand, that conciliar teaching about Christ as one divine person in two natures enriches our experience of him in prayer and daily life—or at least should do so.

This example suggests fashioning a further, related dictum: "Language without experience is empty; experience without language is mute." As well as plotting the basically inseparable relationship between thought and experience, we should do the same for language and experience. Without experience, language remains abstract and lifeless. Without language, experience remains confused and largely unintelligible. I can put this positively by citing my last example: Christian preaching about Christ which helped to prepare the way for the classic doctrines about Christ. From the very beginning, in the pre-Pauline formulations of faith (for instance, 1 Cor 15:3–5; Phil 2:6–11), Christians enjoyed a language that clarified their experience of the risen Lord in the Spirit. There was never a time when they lacked the language of faith not only to express but also to accompany and even constitute their experience: for instance, the experience of the Spirit prompting them to acclaim the risen Jesus as Lord (1 Cor 12:3).

In short, experience, thought and language form a distinguishable but inseparable unity.

(11) Thought and language remind us of yet a further observation that relates closely to our seventh and eighth points, as well as preparing for the twelfth point: experience is always *interpreted* experience. "Experience" without interpretation would be a mere sensation. We should denounce and banish the delusion that there could be non-interpreted

experiences. It is curious how much this fond delusion lingers on, as if, for example, the twelve first met Jesus and only later began to interpret him for themselves. In reality there never was a non-interpreted Jesus. Right from and in their earliest encounters the twelve and other disciples began to interpret him. It is impossible for us as thinking and speaking beings to have non-interpreted experiences. Right in every experience itself the process of interpretation begins, a process that may not run very long for trivial experiences, but that may last a lifetime for such profound and transformative experiences as Paul's encounter with the risen Christ. Anyone who continues to experience at depth the great biblical and liturgical symbols of Christianity knows how we never come to an end in our struggle to interpret and understand them.

Many of the victims of modern media saturation may simply glance at their experiences, without being willing or able to go very far toward understanding and interpreting them. Those, however, who bring a rich and informed judgment to their experiences can grasp them in a much more profound way. Paul's Damascus road experience was a one-off affair; he did not enjoy the great and ongoing grace of being closely associated with Jesus during his ministry. Yet the wealth of Paul's religious commitment, while radically turned around by his encounter with the risen Christ, helped to set him exploring and elucidating that experience for a lifetime.

This observation harkens back to my second point. Very experienced persons will often be led by their condition to discern and appreciate their new experiences in a more effective way than others do. However, one should also recognize how "experienced" persons may "bring so much" to fresh experiences that they are unable to open themselves to these experiences and be "found" by them. They fondly believe they already know it all. Being an expert has its own risks along with its advantages.

(12) Interpreting our experiences coincides largely with discovering their *meaning*. A meaningless experience—an experience that lacks all meaning and is literally "absurd"—seems as impossible to conceive as a totally negative experience. Every experience has some meaning. Nevertheless, the meaning or at least the full meaning of an experience may call for years of exploring before we find (and in a sense also create) its meaning. This is particularly true of some painful episodes; it can seem that some wounds will never be healed and some experiences will never make sense. However, time can not only heal all but also help to make sense of all.

The midlife journeys that I explored in *The Second Journey*[6] exemplify over and over again how it may take years of patient traveling before the painful experiences that initiated that midlife quest fall into place and yield their meaning. Grace is always stronger than evil. But the journey to discover meaning and truth may prove a long one. Paul acknowledged how experiencing Christianity's central symbol, the crucified Jesus, came across to many as scandalous nonsense (1 Cor 1:23) rather than meaningful and life-giving truth. In his own case it took a word from the risen Lord to make sense of some mysterious affliction he was enduring (2 Cor 12:7–10).

(13) My penultimate characteristic of experience concerns its *communicability*. If all experience is immediately personal (see point 4 above), how can we communicate it to others? When we "codify" our experiences in the attempt to express them to others, do we really get anywhere? People write autobiographies in the hope of expressing to others what they have been through. But in our desolation it can seem that we are nothing but solitaries living within our own skins and incapable of communicating with each other, or at least incapable of communicating the things which really matter. Yet we know also how the flesh of our experience can become a word for others. Despite the element, at times painful element, of incommunicability in our personal experiences, the miracle of dialogue can take place and we can communicate something of what we experience.

In communicating our experiences we enjoy the great benefits of many symbols. We can tell our story and use other symbolic language. Our style of life and body language (in the broadest sense of that term) can effectively symbolize what we experience. At the same time, as we saw in the last chapter, symbolic self-communication always involves something "kenotic." Even though our symbols make present what is symbolized (in this case, our experience), the symbols never perfectly coincide with what they symbolize. A gap opens up and a kenotic hiddenness remains to qualify whatever self-revelation we succeed in communicating.

(14) Lastly, a word about tradition, which may be understood as the transmission of a group's experiences. A wide range of symbols mediate socially the collective experience of a whole people, of a particular culture (which may not coincide with a given nation) and of the Church herself. The various monuments of tradition symbolize and express a group's identity.

As human beings and as believers we live through the tension between inherited traditions and contemporary experiences. On the one hand, tradition enables us to understand, evaluate and express our new experiences. On the other hand, new experiences challenge and modify past experiences, in that way altering the shape of the tradition we transmit to the coming generation. Ideally we are at ease with the tension, neither misusing tradition to protect ourselves against new experiences nor ignoring tradition as if our human and Christian experience began yesterday.

Talking about tradition (in the singular) should not be taken to imply that we inherit a monolithic block. The traditions we receive can vary in value and may be in tension with each other. There can likewise be a tension between contemporary experiences, which in any case also vary in value. Both our traditions and our experiences invite choice and discernment. It would be a delusion to imagine that either our inherited tradition or our contemporary experience constituted a clearly unified and self-justified whole.

Thus far this chapter has attempted to sketch some major characteristics of experience. The notion, language and reality of experience are notoriously polyvalent. Nevertheless, I needed to offer at least an interim report on experience to clarify what is meant by saying that we *experience* in faith God's symbolic self-communication.

This chapter would remain, however, patently incomplete if it lacked some reflection on consciously religious experience.

Religious Experience. Saintly persons who are truly contemplatives in action and find God in all things let their lives become a constant religious experience. They live in the presence of God. They see human and all created reality for what, with varying degrees of intensity, it all truly symbolizes—the divine reality. For those whose faith is magnificently alive, every moment is or can be a sign and sacrament of God's presence.

The synoptic gospels record for us the final years of one whose life shows itself to have been a constant religious experience, if ever there was one. From what we can glimpse of his "interior" existence, Jesus lived in the presence of the God whom he called "Abba (Father dear)," completely given over to the service of the divine kingdom that was breaking into the world.[7]

How frequent are religious experiences for rank and file believers? For those who are not (yet) believers but cling to the hope that one day they will suddenly understand "what it has all been for" (F.M. Dostoyevsky)? I am not claiming to know full and detailed answers to these questions. But what believers testify that they experience at common worship and personal prayer suggests some degree of frequency in their consciously explicit experience of God. Add too the kind of the data collected by Sir Alister Hardy and his subsequent collaborators at the Religious Experience Research Unit (Manchester College, Oxford)[8] about a wide range of "ordinary" people. Confronted with painful and sometimes downright tragic situations, many experience what must be described as the power of divine grace in their lives.

No one can enjoy contact with members of such organizations as Alcoholics Anonymous without becoming aware of how faith and religious experience flower in our mass age. The highly symbolic way people in such situations tell their life story as a quest to experience God's loving forgiveness must excite the interest of those interested in glimpsing how God's self-communication works in specific instances.

Explicitly religious experiences have often been named in a *spatial* way as occurring in "boundary-situations" (Karl Jaspers), as being "limit-experiences" (David Tracy) or peak experiences (Abraham Maslow), or as associated with "the ground of being and meaning" (Paul Tillich). To its advantage this spatial language allows us to glimpse two inseparable aspects of religious experience. (a) It puts us in conscious touch with the totality of things, that is to say, with God as the ground of everything and the all-determining reality. (b) In knowing God, we also know that it is we who know. We experience ourselves, in our radical dependence and contingency. We face God in our profound need but fundamental trust that, in its heart, the world holds together and our existence finally has worth.

Taking up in my own way the "spatial" language of Jaspers and others, I have invited readers to have an eye and an ear for the way explicitly religious experience means co-experiencing God and ourselves. I cannot imagine a religious experience in which we would encounter God without any sense whatsoever of ourselves. Here, as elsewhere, the principle enunciated in point 4 above holds good. All experience necessarily involves the subject as well as the object.

Besides reflecting on the frequency and nature of religious experiences, we need to add a word on their very possibility. Here I wish to align myself with those like Karl Rahner who expound the basic dynamism of the human spirit as creating the conditions for the possibility of religious experience. We can explicitly experience God because every human experience reveals its openness toward the infinite.[9] When we consciously experience God, what was hitherto dim and implicit becomes lit up and explicit. We are able to encounter God because all human experiences are already primordially religious. In any experience whatsoever we experience at least minimally ourselves and God.

In our century various authors have explored the dynamism of the human spirit, interpreting its openness to the infinite in terms of our intellect or our will.[10] One might put new heart into this approach by altering the terms and noting our primordial drive toward the fullness of life, meaning/truth and love. Spontaneously we seek to escape from death, absurdity and isolation. We long to live, to see the basic meaning and truth of things, and to love and be loved.

We may misinterpret our partial and provisional experiences of life, meaning and love (see point 7 above). We may mistakenly dismiss as merely "negative" experiences of death, absurdity and isolation what will ultimately turn out to be quite the opposite (see points 8 and 12 above). But our primordial drive toward life, meaning and love perdures. The next chapter will take shape around the story of the prodigal son (Lk 15:11–32) and the theme of love. We could also interpret that story in a threefold way. The young runaway faces death by starvation, experiences the absurdity of his situation and finds himself alone and abandoned by his good-time "friends." His follies have obscured his vision of where life, meaning and love are truly to be found. In deciding to return home, he is going back to where he will experience these realities.

The story of the two disciples on the road to Emmaus (Lk 24:15–35) suggests how religious experiences, especially any profound ones, yield life, meaning and love. The disciples know Jesus "in the breaking of the bread." His scripture lesson illuminates the sense of what they had just been through and had taken to be a meaningless tragedy. His words, actions and presence set their "hearts burning" within them. The quest to experience life, meaning and love constitutes the innate drive of all human beings. This quest has its center and climax in our primordial search to experience God as the fullness of life, the final meaning and the infinity of love. It is a process which hopefully will achieve its definitive condition in the world to come. Without ever intending to say all this, Luke in fact points toward our triple quest through that magnificent Emmaus story which sooner or later gives us the "I was there" feeling.

Having chosen to present divine revelation as God's symbolic self-communication which we experience, I needed in Chapters 9 and 10 to provide at least an interim account on symbols, self-communication and experience. They resist precise definition, but something must be and can be said. To complete this journey toward retrieving and developing a version of revelation rooted in the Second Vatican Council, several major tasks remain on the agenda. The first is to explain the central "content" of revelation, summed up by the Johannine "God is love." How should we interpret our experience of divine love (see point 11 above)?

10. THE REVELATION OF LOVE

God's "symbolic self-communication" describes the "how" or the route of divine revelation. "Love" catches up its essential content.

The Johannine epistles sum up what the divine self-disclosure has finally made clear by saying: "God [the Father] is love" (1 Jn 4:8, 16). Love is not only the way God acts in the world or the way human beings should relate to God and to one another. It is the very nature of God.

Without explicitly using the term "love," Luke's gospel nuances matters through the parable of the prodigal son, which would be more accurately named "the parable of the merciful father" (Lk 15:11–32). The divine love that has been revealed is a merciful, compassionate love.

In John's gospel five chapters of discourse and prayer (Jn 13–17) introduce the three chapters that tell the story of Jesus' passion, death, resurrection and imparting of the Holy Spirit (Jn 18–20). Love is the leitmotiv of those five chapters of discourse and prayer. They begin by emphasizing the revelation of Jesus' love (Jn 13:1) and end with his prayer that the love with which the Father has loved him may be communicated to his disciples (Jn 17:26). John's gospel expects that we read the story of the first Good Friday and Easter Sunday in the key of love. Years ago Rudolf Bultmann rightly identified John as *the* gospel of revelation.[1] The climax of this gospel of revelation comes with Christ's death and resurrection, and it is a climax to be understood primarily in terms of love. In the aftermath of Easter, Peter can become pastor to Christ's flock only after he has three times protested his love (Jn 21:15–19).

One needs, however, to bring alive the claim that love is *the* clue to the divine self-revelation. Some would do this by expounding the origin and meaning of the New Testament language of love.[2] But describing what we experience love to be could lead to a more vivacious version of God's loving self-disclosure. Either way, some account must be offered. It is simply not enough to repeat that "God is love."

Dimensions of Love. Ten inter-related themes wrap up most of what my human and Christian experience of love would encourage me to say.[3]

120

(1) Those who love "forget" themselves, "empty" themselves in their eagerness to help, and go beyond themselves in their orientation toward those whom they love. They find themselves in those others. Love has drawn them out of themselves. This loving reaching out and self-communication take place through a full range of words and deeds.

(2) The second reflection concerns love's motivation. By themselves rational motives are not enough to explain the choice and intensity of love. On the one hand, authentic love is never irrational and groundless. There are reasons to point to, and intelligible motives to offer. Certain characteristics of the other(s) help to motivate and "explain" our love. Nevertheless, on the other hand, you cannot plan love in a purely rational way. The motives *alone* can never clearly justify one's supremely free act of opening oneself up in love toward another. In the end love is a profoundly and mysteriously free gift of oneself.

(3) Love recognizes the *truth,* discovering the real worth, beauty and deepest values in those who are loved. Far from being blind, love predisposes the lover to understand and appreciate the truth about the beloved. At the same time, genuine love sees not only the positive merits but also the real self-destructiveness in those we know and love. Observing the faults and acknowledging their negative side, love acknowledges the potential of the sinners who can become saints.

Here as elsewhere, hatred alerts us to ways in which its contrary functions or rather misfunctions. Racial hatred, for example, is incapable of appreciating the humanity of those whom it despises and demonizes. Racism is notoriously and fatuously blind. It takes love to see that truth about others which justifies respect and high expectations.

(4) Truth links up with *growth.* Those who love others expect and make possible progress and new life in the objects of their love—at times a stunning transformation they never fully bargained for. Daily experience witnesses to this healing and transforming power of love. Here life merges with literature when we recall such figures as Raskolnikoff, the murderer in Dostoyevsky's *Crime and Punishment.* In a sequence that is presented as a resurrection from the dead, the depth and nobility of the love he persistently receives eventually arouse life and love in him. In the western world the classic example of the life-giving power of love is perhaps Dante Alighieri (1265–1321). According to what he says of himself, his life was rather reprobate until he met Beatrice Portinari. His immediate and deep love for her turned him to a much better way of living. In *Vita Nuova* he emphasizes the change love brought in him. Beatrice died young in 1290. The memory of Beatrice supported Dante right through life and inspired the writing of his greatest work, *The Divine Comedy.*

Love fed Dante's genial creativity. Sadly, those who lack or feel they lack the life-giving grace of love often remain psychologically handicapped. Physically as well, their failure to be nurtured by love can show through. They have not experienced, or at least not experienced adequately, the force of love that alone can properly feed their emotional, religious and whole human development.

(5) By its very nature love is *reciprocal* and dialogical. Unlike unilateral generosity, it is not a one-way street but looks for a response. Love, or at least authentic love, does not manipulate and force the beloved to respond. The one who loves hopes that his or her sentiments will be reciprocated.

Some bristle at this claim, arguing that agape or distinctive Christian love should be so utterly altruistic as to constitute unilateral self-sacrifice. Talk of mutuality means capitulating to merely human forms of love that are infected by egoism. Against those like Anders Nygren who wish to interpret Christian agape in such a unilaterally altruistic way, I join those for whom love, including distinctively Christian love, entails of its very nature the drive toward reciprocal, interpersonal communion. The desire for love to be reciprocated is intrinsic to the very nature of love.

In the case of the divine-human relationship, the mystery of God's loving self-communication aims at eliciting a response. The mystery of God's self-revelation completes itself in the mystery of human faith. Bilateral reciprocity essentially characterizes the relationship of divine revelation and human faith.

(6) *Union* results from the reciprocity of love. Those who love each other establish a "we," in a new joint identity. They no longer wish to live and decide unilaterally, but want to be together and decide together. A common home and the begetting of children form the most universal way of reflecting and expressing the union of a love relationship.

At the same time, genuine love does not entail a possessive or domineering union—on one side or the other. This union does not threaten the identity and liberty of the other. Far from destroying the distinction between lover and beloved or reducing the beloved's liberty, authentic love needs, respects and in fact enhances the other's independence. Love lets the other be the other and move away, if that is what the good and the growth of the other require. Love is not in the business of "smothering" the other and encouraging infantile dependence. The relationship of Jesus to his closest followers witnesses supremely to the way identity and freedom are enriched by the union of love.[4]

(7) If by its very nature love is reciprocal, it is also essentially *unconditioned.* To place conditions on love, in particular limits of time,

would be at the very least to blur the true dynamic of love. Diamonds are forever! The Song of Songs classically protests that unbounded love is stronger than the greatest forces of nature: fire, the sea and even death itself (Song 8:6–7). As such love aims to be eternal and refuses to tolerate even the "normal" limits of mortality. To cite Gabriel Marcel's now classical analysis, to say to someone "I love you" is tantamount to saying "You will not die." This is to say, "Our love will not die."

To be sure human frailty and death often terminate love, on one side or on both sides. Human beings want what no human beings can finally guarantee: infallible and eternal fidelity in love. Nevertheless, reflection not only on the human and Christian experience of love but also on literature (which even in its popular forms can fairly mirror life) supports the claim that love's desire is to prove unconditioned and even eternal.

(8) My eighth point concerns the cost of love. Authentic love never guarantees paradise at a discount price. To love is to leave our normal boundaries and references, making ourselves vulnerable by going out into open ground. Human and Christian experience, not to mention popular songs, repeatedly testifies to the way love places us at risk. Cordelia's honest love for Lear brings her great suffering and eventually leaves her dead in her father's arms. Our world is full of images emblematic of the fact that those who love "must" inevitably suffer: grieving parents, lonely widows and, above all, the persons on and around the cross.

(9) My last two points look at "happier" effects of love. First, of its very nature love tends to create a new and ever *wider community.* Love between a couple "realizes itself" in their children. But the new community does not limit itself to the family circle. Loving families open their doors to others, to friends and strangers alike. Paul lists love's characteristic actions in 1 Corinthians 13. We could well add to his list: "Love welcomes all people."

Where hatred isolates and pits people against each other, love works instead to bring about a new and ever widening solidarity. Far from being indifferent or even hostile, love reaches out to the hungry, the sick, the strangers and the imprisoned (Mt 25:35–36).

(10) Finally, love brings *joy,* at best deep and lasting joy. People who love each other rejoice in being with each other. They take great delight in the other and in giving delight to the other. Few human experiences match seeing those whom we love happy with us and made happy through us.

This last observation ties in closely with my fifth and sixth observations above. So often love's response takes the shape of shared joy and the sheer happiness of being together. That union of love which respects and enhances freedom gets expressed, in a special way, through parties that mark the passages of life: a birth, a baptism, a bar mitzvah, a marriage, an ordination, a wedding anniversary and all the other particular moments we celebrate with those whom we love. Even, or perhaps especially, the wake after a funeral can feature that playful joy which naturally characterizes people freely and deeply united through love for one another.

Applying the Analysis. As a human being and a Catholic Christian, I do not claim to know something special about love. Basing myself on my own experience, reflection and reading, I have chosen here to highlight significant aspects of what love means and invite readers to see whether this version is coherent and convincing.[5]

The account could be tested or at least further illuminated through the demonic counterpart of love. In its strange and sad fashion hatred sheds light on the nature of love. Under points 3 and 9 above I have already contrasted love with hatred. The blindness of hatred calls for a parody of Thomas Aquinas' lapidary phrase about love. When he said, "where there is love, there is sight/an eye" *(ubi amor, ibi oculus)*, we could say, "where there is hatred, there is blindness" *(ubi odium, ibi caecitas)*. Hatred, as I pointed out, differs from love through its disruptive, alienating impact.

Further reflection on hatred could lead us to match point for point the version I offered of love. Engrossed with itself, hatred remains utterly self-centered and blocks any self-forgetful reaching out to others (point 1). By themselves rational motives can never explain the choice and intensity of hatred (point 2). Far from seeking the growth and improvement of its objects, hatred wishes their destruction and extinction (point 4). Hatred is not completely "satisfying," unless and until it is reciprocated (point 5). Reflection on these and further dimensions of hatred might open our eyes to the full force of love. By and large we would have to carry this reflection through by ourselves. Unlike love, hatred has failed to inspire much writing. I have found no books and only a very few (dictionary) articles on the topic.

To complete this chapter in the way promised above, let me apply my account of love to the parable of the merciful father. I know no better way for unpacking the central Christian belief that God has been revealed as love.

Before doing so let me clear one difficulty away. Luke 15:11–32 is a parable, not an allegory which calls for a point-by-point interpretation that goes beyond what the narrative says on the surface to find deeper and further links with reality. In allegories every point carries an intended meaning. Parables convey one point only. Nevertheless, long parables like that of the merciful father can also yield meaning through their subordinate details. In such cases it would be a mistake in the name of a rigid and absolute distinction between parables and allegories to insist on recognizing only one point and refusing to entertain many richly nuanced elements in the story.[6]

(1) First, God's merciful love becomes transparent in the way the father of the prodigal "goes beyond himself" toward both his sons. With tender compassion (Lk 15:20) he is eager to help and forgive. He reaches out toward the prodigal through what he does: running to meet him, embracing him, seeing that he is once again clothed with dignity and holding a special feast to celebrate his return. With exquisite delicacy he speaks not directly to the boy himself but to the servants. The prodigal hears those words which dramatically express loving forgiveness and reconciliation (Lk 15:22–24). The father reaches out lovingly also toward the elder brother who sulks outside, refuses to call the prodigal "my brother" and insolently refers to him as "this son of yours." The father, who has come out to plead with his eldest son, brushes aside the insult and utters some of the loveliest words in the New Testament:

> Son, you are always with me, and all that is mine is yours. It was fitting to make merry and be glad, for this your brother was dead, and is alive. He was lost, and is found (Lk 15:31–32).

The father's meaning is clear: "You have missed the whole point. Why haven't you been happy? Why can't you love and joyfully welcome home someone who has suffered and who is after all your brother?" With his deeds (going out to plead with him) and words, the father reaches out in love toward the elder brother.

(2) How can one explain the merciful, forgiving love of the father toward his runaway son who began with prostitutes and ended by, in effect, denying his religion through his incessant contact with impure animals (Lk 15:13, 15–16, 30)? Undoubtedly one can point to some reasons. The prodigal is and remains the farmer's son. Nevertheless, how many fathers would receive back their disgraced son with such spontaneous joy and unaffected tenderness? The depth and intensity of this merciful love evade merely rational explanation. Here the parable leaves us with a mysterious question that goes to the heart of the divine attitude toward us: Why does God continue to love us no matter what we do (see Rom 5:6–8)? We are and remain made in the divine image

(Gen 1:27). But does our created dignity by itself rationally account for the depth of the divine love toward us that has been revealed in Christ?

(3) Unlike the prostitutes in the "far country" and the elder son at home, through his love the father sees the truth about the prodigal. He does not deny or fatuously overlook his sinful behavior. After all he twice speaks of the prodigal as having been "dead" and "lost" (Lk 15:24, 32). What the father sees and appreciates is the real worth of his prodigal son. By providing a robe, a ring and shoes, he lets the boy become what he should always have been—the honorable and free son of a free farmer (Lk 15:22). The father's gesture makes transparent God's vision of us. The divine love sees our real value and potential. We are God's free creatures who have sinned but who can become saints.

(4) In the parable the father's love makes it possible for the prodigal son who was "lost" and "dead" to be "found" and "come alive again." To be sure, when the lad makes his decision to return home, he is motivated by hunger (Lk 15:17). But he trusts that he will not be simply disowned by the man whom he still considers "my father" (Lk 15:18). Even if he is going to ask to be treated merely as a hired servant, he knows that he can still come home and speak to the one whom he continues to call "father" (Lk 15:18, 21). In the event his speech of repentance is cut short and he cannot end by saying to his father, "treat me as one of your hired servants" (Lk 15:21).

The father's love gives the prodigal new life and a fresh start. That love is there to feed the boy's further human and religious development.

(5) The prodigal's return home becomes a journey in which two people discover each other in love. The reciprocity of the relationship between the father and his younger son gets mirrored in the fact that even as the son is nearing home, his father runs out to meet and embrace him. Their new reciprocal relationship comes about through both of them moving physically toward the other.

Obviously the father's love has not died after the son left home. The boy himself cherishes at least enough affection to think of his father as "my" father (Lk 15:18). But their interpersonal communion of love is completed only when they meet and embrace each other on the road home.

(6) The common feast symbolizes the new union of love between father and son. But it is not a possessive, dominating union that the father's love has brought about. After all at the outset the father had not stopped the boy from having his share of the inheritance and leaving home (Lk 15:12–13). Nor does the father force his son to return home. All alone the prodigal must "come to himself" and take that decision. In

leaving and returning home his identity and liberty remain intact. There is no question of the father encouraging or engineering an infantile dependence in his younger son. The boy comes home to be received in a loving way that maintains his dignity and freedom without reducing him to the status of a semi-slave.

(7) Beyond question, the father's love exemplifies the seventh quality of love I noted above: its unconditioned character. His boundless love for both his boys imposes no conditions on either of them. His love is not withdrawn when one leaves home to fall into disgrace and the other sulks outside in a self-righteous and peevish mood.

In particular, the lapse of time does not threaten the father's love for the prodigal. The way the father catches sight of the boy when he was still a long way off (Lk 15:20) suggests someone whose unconditioned love remains firm in hoping to see his runaway come happily home again. When the boy does return, he forgives him unconditionally.

(8) Obviously, his love has made the father vulnerable to suffering. The pain that he has endured rings through his language about his son being "lost" and "dead." The moral and spiritual death of a son, a spouse or some other close relative can be much harder to bear than their physical death. His love sends the father out to face sulky insults from his older son who, unlike his younger brother, will not even address his father as "Father." The father's love makes him vulnerable to the hurt and suffering the two boys can cause him.

It is impossible to read the repeated refrain about a son who was "dead and is alive again" (Lk 15:24, 32) without hearing an echo of the cost of love in the case of Jesus himself. It takes no great leap of the imagination to attribute those words to God the Father and think of Jesus as sent into the "far country" of suffering and death, through love and not through trying to buy real happiness by spending money with dissolute friends.

(9) The return of the prodigal fills a gaping hole in the family circle. (It is frivolous to ask: Is the boy's mother still alive? Does he have sisters and other close relatives at home?) But the family community will be incomplete unless and until the elder brother puts away his self-righteousness and agrees to come in.

Jesus, of course, tells this and other parables to challenge those critics who were scandalized at his habit of receiving public sinners and eating with them (Lk 15:1–2). Jesus' merciful love realizes itself in a new and ever wider community.

(10) Lastly, love celebrates with joy. The father's love expresses itself by calling for a great feast to begin (Lk 15:23–24, 32). This and

other parables disclose God's delight at being with those willing to be raised from the death of sin (see Lk 15:7, 10). The playful fun of a family feast images forth the joy of God's redemptive love.

When presenting the paschal mystery as the effective revelation of God's love, John's gospel inevitably introduces the theme of joy (Jn 16:20–22). It comes as no surprise that the disciples rejoice when they see the risen Lord (Jn 20:20). The fourth gospel makes it quite clear how joy belongs essentially to the revelation of God's love in Christ.

In these pages I have tried to knit together ten inter-related aspects of love with Luke's parable of the merciful father. A few chapters later in that gospel we reach the story of the "prodigal" publican Zacchaeus and his repentance (Lk 19:1–10). Neither the parable nor the story of Zacchaeus introduces the word "love." But we would miss the point of both narratives if we refused to read them in the key of the effective revelation of God's compassionate love.

God's "symbolic self-communication" summarizes as well as any expression the "way" of divine revelation. The essential "content" of that revelation is summarized for all time by the Johannine "God is love." Without believing in that love, we are just voices echoing in the dark.

11. REVELATION AND THE BIBLE

The reality and definition of divine revelation have dominated this book. Admittedly the three opening chapters focused on theology. Yet theology, in any of its three major styles, necessarily draws its data from revelation. For these three styles theology is life, respectively seen, shaped and celebrated through *faith* and reason. Faith is nothing if not our human response to the experience of God's symbolic self-*revelation*.

My account of revelation would be more than patently incomplete if it failed to consider some aspects of the complex relationship between revelation and its inspired (and interpreted) record, the Bible.[1] Right from its first chapter, this book has been reflecting on and appealing to the biblical witness. It is time to examine attentively the relationship of revelation to the Bible. This task belongs, as we shall see in the next chapter, to the overall attempt to receive and retrieve adequately the teaching of *Dei Verbum*.

Right from the start it is worth insisting that, despite its high doctrine of biblical inspiration, Christianity is a religion of the word, not of the book. God's living word, above all in the form of the incarnate Word, takes precedence over the inspired book. The way revelation goes beyond the scriptures should become clear in the course of this chapter.

Convenience, no less than historical considerations, suggests looking at the formation of the Bible in the past and then its use today. The leitmotif will be the relationship between the scriptures and revelation.[2]

The Formation of the Bible. In considering the genesis of the Bible it seems advisable first to illustrate the differences between revelation and the scriptures and then reflect on the content of the scriptures.

(1) The Bible could not and cannot be simply identified with revelation. As a living interpersonal event, revelation takes place or happens. God initiates, at particular times and places and to particular persons, some form of symbolic self-communication. The divine initiative achieves

its goal and revelation happens when human beings respond in faith to the divine self-communication they experience.

As such the scriptures are not a living, interpersonal event in the sense just described. They are written records which through the inspiration of the Holy Spirit came into existence through the work of some believers at certain stages in the foundational history of God's people.

The scriptures differ from revelation in the way that written documents differ from an interpersonal event that happens. It makes perfectly good sense to say with exasperation, "I left my copy of the Bible behind in the New York subway." But you would have a good deal of explaining to do if you were to say to a friend, "I left revelation behind in the London underground." The bottom line in the difference between the Bible and revelation is the difference between a written text and an event, between a record and an actual happening.

In the history of the Bible's composition, the gift of revelation and the special inspiration to write the scriptures were not only distinguishable but also separable. This is another way of pointing up the difference we are concerned with. Either directly or through such mediators as the prophets and, above all, Jesus himself, revelation was offered to *all* the people. God's symbolic self-communication was there for everyone. The special impulse to write the scriptures was a charism given only to those who under the guidance of the Holy Spirit helped to compose the sacred texts. To be sure, the scriptures were written for everyone. But the charism of inspiration was given only to some persons.

Even in the case of the sacred writers themselves revelation and the charism of inspiration did not coincide. Opening themselves in faith to the divine self-manifestation was one thing, being guided by the Holy Spirit to set down certain things in writing was another. God's revelation impinged on their entire lives. In cases that we know of, the charism of inspiration functioned only in limited periods of their lives. The divine revelation was operative in Paul's life before and after his call/conversion (around 36 A.D.). Around 50 he wrote his first (inspired) letter that has been preserved for us, and composed his other letters during the 50s and into the early 60s. The divine self-communication affected the whole of Paul's life, the charism of inspiration only the last decade or so of his apostolic activity.

(2) Reflection on the *content* of the Bible offers another angle on the difference I an laboring to express. The Bible witnesses to and interprets various persons, events and words that mediated, more or less directly, the divine self-revelation. The letter to the Hebrews acknowledges the Son of God as the climax in a series of mediators of revelation (Heb 1:1–2). A wide variety of events manifested God and the divine

designs to the people: from an exodus, an exile, births of children through to a crucifixion and resurrection. Prophetic utterances, parables, creeds (for example, Deut 26:5–9; Rom 1:3–4), hymns (for example, Phil 2:6–11), kerygmatic summaries (for example, 1 Cor 15:3–5) and, supremely, the words of Jesus himself serve to disclose the truth about God and human beings. When we read the scriptures with an eye for the persons, events and words that are closely concerned with and witness to the divine self-revelation, we will certainly not lack material to report.

At the same time, the Bible also records matters that do not seem to be connected, or at least closely connected, with divine revelation. The language of human love and courtship fashions the Song of Songs, an inspired book which paradoxically has no explicitly religious content.

Alongside many lofty prescriptions to guide the worship and life of Israel as a holy people, Leviticus includes numerous regulations about wine and food, about the sick and diseased (in particular, lepers), about sexual relations and other matters which can hardly be derived from some special divine revelation. This book (which probably took its final shape in the sixth or fifth century) contains pages of rituals and laws, which usually look as if they come from old human customs rather than from some more or less dramatic divine disclosure. The book of Proverbs puts together the moral and religious instruction that professional teachers offered Jewish youth in the period after the Babylonian exile. This wisdom of the ages is based on the lessons of common human experience and is in part (Prov 22:17–24:22) modeled upon the Instruction of Amenemope, an Egyptian book of wisdom. Where religious faith supports Proverbs' view of an upright human life, Ecclesiastes seems to use reason alone to explore the meaning of human existence and the (limited) value of our life which ends in the oblivion of death.

Admittedly one might well argue that in human love, ancient religious traditions, the experience of the ages and the use of reason God is also at work to disclose the truth about our nature and destiny and the creator from whom we come and to whom we go. A theology that recognizes dramatic, special events, words and persons as the only appropriate means and mediators of the divine would be a diminished version of revelation. God can certainly use "ordinary" channels to communicate with human beings and shed new light on the divine and human mystery.

Nevertheless, it is clear that whole sections of the Bible (for example, much of the wisdom literature) speak much more of the human condition and less vividly of divine revelation. The mere fact that the inspiration of the Holy Spirit operated in the writing of these books is no necessary and immediate gauge of the "amount" of divine self-revelation to which they witness. On any showing, they report and proclaim matters of revelation less intensely and closely than other sections of the Bible. Simply from the presence of divine inspiration in the writing of a book one cannot draw any necessary conclusions about the degree to which divine revelation shows through that book.

Add too the way many chapters of the Bible focus on the human story of individuals and groups. To verify this assertion it would be enough to read some sections of the historical books from the Old Testament and Acts from the New Testament. Some of the material can seem a long way from God's saving self-communication. See, for instance, the story of a concubine's murder and the subsequent revenge on the Benjamites (Jgs 19:1–20:48), Saul's visit to the witch of Endor (1 Sam 3:25) and the death of Ananias and Sapphira (Acts 5:1–11). One might allege that such passages show how people failed to respond to the overtures of divine revelation. Stories of human failures, sins and atrocities got recorded under the impulse of divine inspiration. But that fact does not as such guarantee anything about their positive value for revelation. In brief, an inspired record is one thing, revelatory "content" is another.

The Use of the Bible. In distinguishing between revelation and inspiration this chapter has so far been directing attention to the formation of the scriptures in the past. If you like, it has been operating within the parameters of Chapter Three, Four and Five of *Dei Verbum*. What does the relationship of revelation and inspiration look like if we turn to Chapter Six of that document and the role of the scriptures in the life of the church today?

(1) First of all, Christian experience witnesses every day to the way biblical texts can convey to us the divine revelation. Passages from the prophets and the psalms, the words of Jesus from the gospel or reflections of Paul can let the truth about the divine and human mystery shine forth. These scriptural texts repeatedly bring us an inner light. We can hear God speaking to us through these words. What was long ago written down under the guidance of divine inspiration can become inspiring and illuminating for us today. To echo *Dei Verbum* and St. Ambrose, when we read the scriptures, we listen to God (DV 25).

It is also a fact of Christian experience that less "promising" parts of the Bible may also enjoy such a revealing impact. At first glance some scriptural texts can come across as "primitive" (like Saul's visit to the witch of Endor mentioned above), "boring" (like the genealogies in 1 Chronicles 1–9 or in the infancy narratives of Matthew and Luke) or so filled with hatred as to seem opposed to the revelation of the divine love (for example, Ps 137:7–9). Such passages can act as negative "foils" which bring out the true nature of divine revelation and our appropriate response to it. Saul's nocturnal visit to the witch of Endor is at the very least an inspired cautionary tale: we should not try to enter into contact that way with the other world. Some exiled Israelites did cry out for savage vengeance on their Babylonian and Edomite enemies (Ps 137:7–9). Their prayer for revenge works to illuminate God's loving concern for all (Jon 4:11) and Jesus' prayer that his executioners be forgiven (Lk 23:34). As regards the biblical genealogies, they may not always say much to the North Atlantic world. But for some non-western cultures to lack ancestors is to suffer diminishment in one's personal identity. Some years ago in England a friend with nerves of steel took one biblical genealogy as his text for the weekend retreat he led. He fed the prayer of his retreatants with the theme of God guiding human history and preparing for the birth of Jesus himself. Given the checkered career of some who are featured in our biblical genealogies, including those of Jesus himself (Mt 1:1–7; Lk 3:23–38), one can be helped to a deeper grasp of the truth that "God writes straight but with crooked lines."

In short, experience shows how any biblical text can lead people to know the truth about God and the human condition. Normally the "great" sections of the scriptures have this revelatory impact. But we need not be indignant that some thoroughly "unpromising" scriptural texts can trigger or renew people's knowledge of God. This point has more relevance nowadays, since the lectionary for reading at the Sunday and weekday eucharist contains a much broader selection from the Bible.

Before moving on from the revelatory power of the scriptures, let me add a few words on a theme already developed somewhat in Chapter 8 above. The heavily symbolic language of the scriptures greatly contributes to their power to evoke the truth and trigger moments of revelation. No book of the Bible surpasses John's gospel in its symbolic force. It would be enough to test that assertion by opening oneself in prayer to the way it uses the cure of a blind man to present Jesus as the light of the world (Jn 9:1–41). A sample from the book of Revelation easily exemplifies how well its imaginative, symbolic language communicates the divine promise:

And I saw the holy city, new Jerusalem, coming down out of heaven from God, prepared as a bride adorned for her husband. And I heard a loud voice from the throne saying, "Behold, the dwelling of God is with men. He will dwell with them, and they shall be his people, and God himself will be with them. He will wipe away every tear from their eyes, and death shall be no more, neither shall there be mourning nor crying nor pain any more, for the former things have passed away." And he who sat upon the throne said, "Behold, I make all things new" (Rev 21:2–5).

Two final examples of biblical symbolism. The opening words of Second Isaiah are unrivaled in their power to console and generate trust in God's tender concern for those homesick for "another" place where they shall truly be themselves (Is 40:1–11). From the beginning of Christianity the highly symbolic story of the passion told by all four gospels and culminating in Jesus' crucifixion at the place of the skull has invited all to "look upon him whom they have pierced" (Jn 19:37) and find in the events of Good Friday (and Easter Sunday) the climax of God's self-communication.

(2) Having sufficiently acknowledged the revealing power of the Bible, I should also call attention to certain limits and qualifications. It was not and is not the only means for receiving the divine revelation. Before the Hebrew scriptures came to be written, God had already initiated the special revealing and saving history for the chosen people. Christians saw in Christ the climax of that revelatory and salvific history, two decades before the first book of what came to be called the New Testament was written. Reading St. Paul proved decisive for Augustine's conversion. But it was a night of reading Teresa of Avila's autobiography that moved Edith Stein toward Christian faith and, eventually, martyrdom. Chapter 9 above should have done something to suggest the immense range of experiences that can communicate to Christians the divine self-communication, even to the point of radically changing their lives. Those experiences, at least initially, need not have anything to do directly with the scriptures. The data gathered by the Religious Experience Research Unit (at Manchester College, Oxford) amply supports that assertion.

We need also to recall what emerged in Chapter 6 above. God's revelation reaches non-Christians without their reading or hearing the Bible. To some extent at least their religious environment and personal experience can mediate to them the truth about God and our human condition. Only those out of touch with non-Christians and their world will deny the evidence for the divine saving and revealing activity on their behalf. God speaks to them through means other than the Bible.

The last limit to be noted in the Bible's revelatory impact is a sad one. It is more than possible to read or hear the scriptures without being open to the Spirit. A "merely scientific" knowledge of the Bible might yield little by way of knowing the God to whom the scriptures testify. The question of scientific and spiritual exegesis will turn up in the next chapter. Here I simply wish to observe the regrettable fact that an extensive knowledge of the Bible, whether "technical" or otherwise, does not automatically guarantee the scriptures being for me a vehicle of revelation.

Some Conclusions. (1) As an inspired text, the Bible illuminates constantly the divine and human mystery. It is indispensable for Christian existence, both collectively and individually. Nevertheless, revelation or the living word of God is a larger reality than the Bible and is not limited to the Bible. It is a gross error to identify revelation with the scriptures. God's living and authoritative word is not subordinated to a written text, even an inspired one. This fact explains and justifies the order in which *Dei Verbum* handles the matter. The greater reality of revelation is clarified (Chapter One) *before* the document turns to tradition (Chapter Two) and the inspired scriptures (Chapters Three–Six).

(2) At the same time, however, we are certainly justified in calling the scriptures "the word of God" (DV 9). First, unlike any other religious texts available for Christian (and, in the case of the Hebrew scriptures, Jewish) use, they were written under the special guidance of the Holy Spirit. In a unique way God was involved in the composition of these texts. Second, all the scriptures have some relationship to *foundational* revelation—to those persons, events and words that mediated God's salvific self-communication which reached its definitive climax with Christ and his apostles. Even in the case of those books and sections of the Bible that focus less vividly and immediately on the divine revelation, some link can be found. Thus the love poems that make up the Song of Songs relate themselves to the history of revelation and salvation by invoking key personages and places of that history (Solomon, David and Jerusalem). The bridegroom of these poems suggests Israel's God who like a loving husband wishes to woo again a faithless wife (Hos 2:14–23). Third, in the post-apostolic period of dependent revelation any section of the scriptures could become for us a living word of God. At the end John's gospel formulates its revelatory and salvific scope in terms that can be applied to the whole Bible: "These things are written that you may believe that Jesus is the Christ, the Son of God, and that believing you may have life in his name" (Jn 20:31; see 2 Tim 3:15–17). Our "believing" is the completion of, and "life" the salvific consequence of, divine revelation.

12. *DEI VERBUM* AND EXEGESIS

More than twenty-five years have passed since Pope Paul VI and the other bishops at the Second Vatican Council promulgated *Dei Verbum,* the Dogmatic Constitution on Divine Revelation (November 18, 1965). This document has much to teach about revelation, faith, tradition and the magisterium. But it can be reasonably argued that the Bible was the main object of the bishops' teaching in *Dei Verbum.* Four out of the six chapters which make up the document are explicitly dedicated to the scriptures. Moreover, the first two chapters have also important things to say about the scriptures. For Catholic biblical scholarship *Dei Verbum* is *the* document from the council.

I want to dedicate the first part of this chapter to that document and its teaching on exegesis. Then in the second part of the chapter I will take one example from the New Testament to indicate how the directives of *Dei Verbum* can be implemented.

In Chapters 8 and 11 of this book I invoked the symbolic quality of the scriptures. The Bible and its symbols are like a classical musical score to be experienced and interpreted ever anew. Using the instruments available today, conductors put a personal stamp on their performance, while remaining faithful to the text they have received.

I

The central thrust of the sixth and final chapter of *Dei Verbum* makes it quite clear that exegesis should serve the whole life of the church. The scriptures and biblical scholarship which helps to open up the scriptures must guide and nourish the church and the entire Christian life (DV 21). That is the headline for Chapter Six; let us see some of the small print.

That last chapter begins by endorsing a comparison between the eucharist and the scriptures which we find in the fathers of the church and which has its ultimate roots in the sixth chapter of John's gospel. Like the eucharistic body of Christ the scriptures are the bread of life; on our pilgrimage we are fed both by the word of God and by the eucharist (*ibid.*). The scriptures not only nourish but also guide Christian life. To cite *Dei Verbum,* "the scriptures, taken together with sacred tradition," are "the supreme rule" of the church's faith (*ibid.*). Hence by making their contribution to understanding, interpreting and actualizing the scriptures, biblical scholars are helping to nourish and guide the church.

Chapter Six of *Dei Verbum* indicates some specific areas in the life of the church which are nourished and guided by the scriptures: theology and the whole "ministry of the word" ("pastoral preaching, catechetics and all forms of Christian instruction, among which the liturgical homily should hold pride of place") (DV 24; see SC 24). The council's dream that, with help from biblical scholars, all those "officially engaged in the ministry of the word" should "immerse themselves in the scriptures by constant sacred reading and diligent study" (DV 25) has been far from fully realized. Some progress has been made, but biblical studies have still much to do toward providing that "profound understanding of the sacred scriptures" which can nourish the whole ministry of the word (DV 23) and the study of theology (DV 24).

The closing chapter of *Dei Verbum* offers us a wonderful dream about the way the scriptures in general (DV 21–26) and biblical scholarship in particular (DV 23) should guide and nourish the whole life of the church.[1] Those final pages of the document remain as topical and challenging as ever. They can serve as a timely examination of conscience for everyone: bishops, priests, biblical scholars, theologians, those engaged in the various forms of the ministry of the word, and all the faithful. I have no right to examine any conscience but my own. But one thing is clear: there is certainly no lack of material in that final chapter of *Dei Verbum* for an examination of our consciences and a deep pondering of that lapidary statement it quotes from St. Jerome: "Ignorance of the scriptures is ignorance of Christ" (DV 25).

So much for the great pastoral, theological and spiritual hopes the Second Vatican Council placed in a renewed study and use of the scriptures at every level of church life. The end, the closing vision of *Dei Verbum,* is where we started. Let us go back to earlier chapters of the document. They say and imply much about biblical scholarship and its role for Christian faith and life. There are, for example, the rich passages on the connection and interplay between the scriptures, tradition and the magisterium (DV 9–10). There is the teaching on the nature of biblical truth (DV 11), the indispensable importance of the Old Testament (DV 14–16) and our access through the gospels to the history of Jesus (DV 19). The opening five chapters of *Dei Verbum* offer a great deal of enduring and valuable teaching for biblical studies and scholarship. One could develop a year-long, in-depth course on all that.

In this chapter I would like to concentrate on one item for biblical scholarship which we find in the first five chapters of *Dei Verbum:* namely, the description of exegetical work offered by Chapter Three, article 12. According to *Dei Verbum* what principles should guide exegesis? What will help exegetes to understand for themselves and explain to others the meaning of scripture?

Article 12 of Chapter Three proposes at least four major points for the guidance of exegesis. In the first place, *Dei Verbum* firmly endorses the methods of historical-critical exegesis which aims to reach conclusions about three stages in the formation of our texts. At the third stage such exegesis tries to establish, as far as possible, the meaning and message of the final authors. Using this or that literary form, what did the biblical authors intend to say to the audiences they wrote for? In the contexts in which they wrote and using the resources of their culture, what did the sacred writers have in mind? In other words, at this third level historical-critical exegesis tries to understand and clarify the intention of the original author or the literal sense of the scriptures.[2]

As regards the second stage, the period of (oral or written) transmission in the community, such exegesis tries to identify the nature and extent of the traditions formed and handed on, for instance, during the early decades of Christianity, prior to the composition of the particular New Testament texts being studied. What traditions, for example, lie behind and were drawn on by John's gospel? What function did these traditions serve prior to the final composition of the gospel?

Finally, historical-critical exegesis also attempts to go back to stage one: the actual events that gave rise to the community's proclamation, teaching and traditions. In this way such exegesis studies three levels: for example, that of the evangelists themselves, that of the traditions in the early communities, and that of the events concerned with Jesus himself. Article 12 of *Dei Verbum* attends above all to level three, but implies things about the study of levels two and one (see also DV 19 on "the honest truth" about Jesus).

We call this exegesis *historical* (and diachronic) because it tries to overcome the temporal and cultural gap and go back to the historical contexts in which our biblical texts were formed and fashioned. It investigates and clarifies the historical genesis of these texts. We call this exegesis *critical,* because it requires professional knowledge and judgment to determine, even to some extent, what Mark, for example, wanted to communicate in his gospel and what were the sources he drew on. Thus far the first principle endorsed by *Dei Verbum.* The interpreter of the scriptures, following the methods of historical-critical exegesis, aims to establish what the biblical authors intended to witness to and express in their texts (= what they meant).

After some detail on the methods of scientific exegesis, the same article 12 of *Dei Verbum* adds, much more briefly, an ideal that will take exegetes beyond merely historical-critical procedures (with their orientation to the human authors in their particular contexts). Our document sees the exegetical task as more than simply elaborating an historical explanation of the origin and development of the biblical text. It enunciates an ideal which entails three considerations for exegetes in their work of understanding and explaining the meaning of scripture (= what it now means). The ideal is reading and interpreting the scriptures with the help of the same Spirit through whom they were written. Such "spiritual" interpretation attends to three points: 1) the unity of the entire Bible; 2) the living tradition of the whole church; and 3) the analogy of faith.

In parenthesis, let me warn those who use the Flannery translation of the council documents that this passage in *Dei Verbum* is not rendered all that well. For example, the original Latin text of *Dei Verbum* says: "since the sacred scripture is to be read and interpreted in the same Spirit through whom it was written" *(cum Sacra Scriptura eodem Spiritu quo scripta est etiam legenda et interpretanda sit)*. The Flannery version renders this: "since sacred scripture must be read and interpreted with its divine authorship in mind." "With its divine authorship in mind" weakens considerably the advice the Second Vatican Council drew from St. Jerome (*In Gal.* 5,19–21; PL 26, 417 A) about reading and interpreting the scriptures with the same Spirit through whom they were written. The earlier Abbott translation was more faithful to the Latin text of *Dei Verbum* when it rendered the clause as follows: "since holy scripture must be read and interpreted according to the same Spirit by whom it was written."

The general thrust of this principle from *Dei Verbum* is clear. One and the same Holy Spirit inspired the original writing of the scriptures and should inspire the reading and interpretation of them today. In this sense, exegesis is a spiritual experience. The interpreter of the scriptures should be a converted, prayerful and spiritual person. The Holy Spirit links the past formation of the sacred texts and their present interpretation. Light for understanding the scriptures now comes from the same Spirit who, back there and then, imparted the original charism of biblical interpretation.

To explain this "spiritual" dimension of biblical interpretation *Dei Verbum* mentions three points to be kept in mind: the first is "the content and unity of the whole of scripture." What is the focus of unity in the "whole of scripture"? Historical criticism can fragment (or at least seem to fragment) the biblical text. What unifies the content of the entire Bible? The scriptures find their dynamic unity through such elements as types and antitypes, patterns of promise-fulfillment-consummation, and the whole story providentially guided by "true divine pedagogy" (DV 15).[3] But the fullest Christian answer to the question of unity has always been: Jesus Christ himself (see DV 25). In his encyclical *Spiritus Paraclitus* (1920) Pope Benedict XV noted: "*In Christum enim velut centrum omnes utriusque Testamenti paginae vergunt* (All the pages of both testaments lead towards Christ as the center)."[4] Back in the sixteenth century William Tyndale wrote: "The scriptures spring out of Christ and were given to lead us to Christ. Thou must therefore go along by the scriptures as by a line, until thou come at Christ, which is the way's end and resting place."[5] The twelfth century Augustinian canon, Hugh of Saint Victor, shared a similar christological vision: "All divine scripture speaks of Christ and finds its fulfillment in Christ, because it forms only one book, the book of life which is Christ."[6]

Pope Benedict XV, William Tyndale and Hugh of Saint Victor are three among very many Christians who have witnessed to their faith that the divine authorship (or role of the Spirit in inspiring all the scriptures) gives a christological unity to the Bible and its content. Of course, the biblical authors show a great diversity in their environments, cultures and outlooks. But *Dei Verbum* recognizes unity as the first result of the Spirit's influence on the making of the scriptures, and that unity is found in Christ.

We can put matters in trinitarian terms. Through his life, death and resurrection (although not exclusively through those mysteries), Christ revealed and reveals his Father. Through the scriptures (although not exclusively through these inspired books) the Holy Spirit testifies to and reveals Christ, albeit with varying degrees of intensity and immediacy according to the nature of the biblical text in question (see Appendix One).

Dei Verbum article 12 then adds two further effects of the Spirit which help in understanding and explaining the scriptures: "the living tradition of the whole church" and the analogy of faith. "The living tradition of the whole church" obviously derives from the pneumatological principle. It is, after all, the living Spirit of God who, as the primary, if invisible, bearer of tradition, first inspired certain persons to write the scriptures and then helped the church to recognize these texts as canonical and normative. How has the church, guided by the Spirit, understood and actualized the scriptures through her preaching, worship, doctrines, theology, catechesis, art and whole life? "The living tradition of the whole church"—and, in particular, the liturgical tradition—invites us to interpret the scriptures in an ecclesial way.[7] The public worship of the church is a doxological hermeneutic of the scriptures. In a kind of *epiclesis* the liturgy implicitly calls on the Holy Spirit to turn the letter of the scriptures into a spiritual praise of God. Through the Holy Spirit the entire church, in her liturgy and beyond, has been living out and actualizing the scriptures. In fact, the post-New Testament tradition can be summed up as the way Christians have understood and lived the Bible. Thus the whole story of ecclesial interpretation, not only in teaching but also in life and worship, enlightens and guides the work of exegetes.

The third result of the Spirit's activity is located in "the analogy of faith" (Rom 12:6). Drawn from St. Paul, the phrase has been traditionally used to recall the unity in the whole of revelation. Particular biblical passages and specific Christian beliefs should be interpreted in the complete context of definitive revelation and integral faith. "The analogy of faith" moves us close to the First Vatican Council's vision of theology as exploring the coherent structure formed by the basic articles of faith and confessed in our Christian creeds (see Chapter 2 above).

The last part of *Dei Verbum* article 12 fills out the Second Vatican Council's judgment on biblical interpretation by encouraging a pneumatological exegesis, an exegesis which would attend to the unity of the scriptures in Christ, the church's living tradition and the analogy of faith that guides theology. In short, a pneumatological exegesis will be christological, ecclesial and theological.[8] By inspiring the scriptures and illuminating our understanding of them, the Holy Spirit leads us to Christ, his church and a theology based on the coherent structure of the divine revelation. A "spiritual" exegesis should bring us closer to Christ, the church and God. Conversely, a christological, ecclesial and theological outlook will guide us in understanding and interpreting the scriptures inspired by the Spirit.

To sum up the first part of this chapter: The sixth or last chapter of *Dei Verbum* offers a challenging vision of the role of the scriptures for the faith and life of the whole church. Earlier, in Chapter Three, the document spells out its advice for professional interpreters of the scriptures and the role they should play. On the one hand, their exegesis should follow the sane rules of the historical-critical method. On the other hand, their exegesis should also be pneumatological, which means being christological, ecclesial and theological in their approach. In brief, the integral version of biblical scholarship that we find in *Dei Verbum* article 12 includes both reason and faith, the right use of historical reason and the appropriate attention to the transformative guidance of the Holy Spirit. The first approach keeps some critical distance when in a scholarly way it reads the text. The second or pneumatological approach means being read by the text and transformed by it. It is the difference between grasping the meaning of the text and being grasped by its meaning, or between finding the truth and being found by it.

Like the proper Christian vision of the interaction between reason and faith, the two "readings" of scripture, while distinguishable, may not be separated. Scholars who study the scriptures historically should (a) read these texts in the believing community because they have been received into the normative canon by that community, (b) recognize the scriptures as inspired by the Holy Spirit and (c) accept some kind of biblical unity in Christ. Historical exegesis, while rationally critical, does not and should not entail reading the scriptures without faith. Rightly understood, scholarly interpretation of the Bible is also an exercise of a shared and personal faith.

The pneumatological reading of the Bible, precisely as pneumatological, cannot ignore the historical issues. The scriptures witness to Christ who lived, died and rose from the dead; they reach us because the church historically acknowledged them as canonical, and for nearly two thousand years they have been understood to mirror our common faith. Thus the christological, ecclesial and theological nature of "spiritual" exegesis necessarily involves historical considerations. In short, the pneumatological meaning of the Bible (what it means) cannot be separated from the historically established meaning of the original author (what it meant) and the subsequent history of the text.

II

The first part of this chapter has been theoretical—idealistic and Platonic, if you like. It is high time to turn practical and Aristotelian and offer at least one detailed example. What would the directives of *Dei Verbum* do for our exegesis when we apply them to one such case?

The example I have selected comes from a field in which I have been teaching and writing since 1967, the resurrection of Jesus Christ. The issue concerns the Easter appearances and one specific question: Are these encounters to be interpreted as experiences of the Holy Spirit? This is a question prompted by John's gospel, where during an appearance the risen Christ breathes on the disciples and imparts to them the Holy Spirit. That scene led Rudolf Bultmann to speak of Easter and Pentecost "falling together."[9] In his commentary on John, C.K. Barrett suggests that originally the first Christians had one experience, a christological and pneumatological experience which included the resurrection of Jesus, his appearances, his exaltation and the gift of the Holy Spirit. Later on, Christians described all this in terms of separate incidents. Originally, however, according to Barrett the resurrection and appearances of Jesus coincided with the gift of the Holy Spirit.[10]

Let me put the issue quite clearly. Were the appearances of the risen Christ (= the christophanies) really the same event as the gift of the Holy Spirit? Was the theme of Jesus' appearances simply an alternate way of speaking about the disciples' first experiences of the Holy Spirit after Jesus' death and burial? An affirmative answer would deny any special, distinct reality to the christophanies. The appearances of the risen Christ would be nothing more than the first experiences of the Spirit in which we later Christians can all share.

To begin with, what does historical-critical exegesis have to say about the issue? Clearly John 20:22 links at least one christophany with the receiving of the Holy Spirit. In an act of new creation the risen Christ, after commissioning the disciples, breathes into them the Spirit. In the power of the Spirit they will be enabled to fulfill their mission. However, on the one hand, the same gospel reports appearances of the risen Jesus without speaking of the gift of the Spirit (Jn 20:11–18, 26–29; 21:1–23). On the other hand, John represents Jesus in death as imparting the Spirit without there being an appearance of him as risen from the dead (Jn 19:30, 34–37). In dying Jesus gives up "his Spirit" and then his side is pierced. The reader of the gospel has been prepared to associate the gift of the Spirit with the blood and water coming from the open side of Christ (Jn 7:37–39). To interpret that scene on Calvary, John cites the scriptures: "They shall look on him whom they have pierced" (Jn 19:37). The contemplation of the crucified Jesus, *not* the appearance of the risen Christ, is here linked with the Spirit. Even in John's gospel the gift of the Spirit and the christophanies are by no means always associated.

Beyond question, this gospel wants to link Jesus' death, resurrection and exaltation with the imparting of the Holy Spirit. It sees the paschal mystery in this unifying way. Nevertheless, even John's gospel observes some limits in its unifying vision. Only once does it add the imparting of the Spirit to a christophany (Jn 20:19–23). What C.K. Barrett suggests is theoretically possible: that in one original experience the first Christians saw the risen Christ and received the Spirit and that, even if it is the last gospel to be written, John 20:22 preserves a memory of that original experience. It seems much more likely, however, that John 20:22 represents the end-point of a theological development toward a more unified vision of the paschal mystery. Even in John's gospel that process is not complete. As we have seen, John can present separately christophanies and the gift of the Spirit. Even the very Johannine scene that links a christophany with the gift of the Spirit *also* distinguishes them to some extent. Christ appears and commissions his disciples before communicating to them the Holy Spirit.[11]

What of the earlier New Testament witnesses? Mark, Matthew and Luke do not identify the christophanies with the gift of the Spirit. In Mark's brief Easter narratives, there is a promise of one or more appearances in Galilee (Mk 16:7) but not a word about the Holy Spirit.[12] Matthew's final chapter reports two appearances but no gift of the Spirit. That chapter includes a liturgical formula about baptism "in the name of the Father and of the Son and of *the Holy Spirit,*" but that is all.[13] Luke's Easter narrative includes Jesus' appearance to "the eleven and those who were with them" (Lk 24:33) and his assurance that they would be "clothed with power from on high" (Lk 24:49)—a promise fulfilled at Pentecost (Acts 2:1–4).[14] However we interpret the content and sources of the Easter stories in the synoptic gospels, they hardly support the thesis that the appearances of the risen Christ were really nothing other than experiences of the Holy Spirit.

Our earliest New Testament writer is St. Paul. His summary of the Easter appearances in 1 Corinthians 15:5–8 says nothing about the gift of the Spirit, nor does he make that link earlier in the same letter when he asks: "Am I not an apostle? Have I not seen the Lord?" (1 Cor 9:1).[15] Likewise in Galatians, where Paul speaks about his vocation coming through the revelation of Jesus Christ (Gal 1:12, 16) there is no mention of the Holy Spirit. It was the manifestation of the risen Christ which founded Paul's call to be apostle to the Gentiles.[16] In short, the data from Paul does not support the case of the christophanies coinciding with the gift of the Holy Spirit.

We can reinforce this conclusion by noting a converse feature in Paul's letters. For the apostle, the Spirit brings a profound change in believers, making them move from being and living as "old" persons to become and live as "new" persons (Rom 8:2, 4, 11; 1 Cor 2:12–15; 2 Cor 3:8, 17–18; Gal 3:2; 5:16–25; Col 3:9–10; Eph 2:15; 3:16; 4:22–24). Paul often refers to our participating in the life of the risen Christ (Rom 6:4; 7:6; 1 Cor 15:45) through the indwelling Spirit (Rom 8:9, 14–16; Gal 4:6). The power of the Spirit makes us grow in the new life initiated through faith, baptism and incorporation into Christ. But Paul never identifies the believers' common experience of the Spirit with the once-and-for-all encounter with the risen Christ that gave him and others their special, apostolic mission.[17]

To sum up the data from Paul: When the apostle cites the appearances of the risen Christ to himself or others, he never mentions the Holy Spirit. When he refers to the experience and effects of the Spirit

(for example, 1 Cor 12:1–13; 14:1–40), he never does so in the context
of the risen Lord's appearances and the apostolic mission. Admittedly
Paul names the Holy Spirit as "the Spirit of him who raised Jesus from
the dead" (Rom 8:11). But that is to refer to the Spirit's "source," God
(the Father) to whom a recurrent formula attributes the event of Jesus'
resurrection (for example, 1 Cor 6:14; Gal 1:1; 1 Thess 1:10). Paul does
not "speak of the Holy Spirit of him who rose and appeared to me/us."
The Holy Spirit is linked to the resurrection but not to the appearances.

Thus far I have briefly examined our issue by applying the rules for
(historical-critical) exegesis endorsed by article 12 of *Dei Verbum*. An
examination of the New Testament evidence does not support the conclusion that either the authors themselves (third stage) or their sources
(second stage) point to the Easter appearances as being identical with
the gift of the Holy Spirit (first stage). The only exception to this conclusion is found in John 20:22 which looks more like a later (theological)
development than a guide to what originally happened at the first stage.

What might the other three, "spiritual" considerations for exegesis say
about our issue? The unity of the whole Bible in Christ suggests the
importance of distinguishing between the appearances and the gift of the
Spirit. It is the risen Christ and not the Holy Spirit who commissions his
disciples. Paul is an apostle, because he has seen the Lord (1 Cor 9:1),
not because he has received the Spirit. Mark's Easter narrative promises
a rendezvous in Galilee (Mk 16:7), a promise explicitly fulfilled in Matthew's Easter narrative when the risen Jesus sends the eleven to "make
disciples of all nations" (Mt 28:19). Luke-Acts understands the apostles
to be sent as witnesses "to the ends of the earth" (Acts 1:8), empowered
by the Holy Spirit but commissioned to do so by the risen Christ (Lk
24:49; Acts 1:8). The Johannine Easter narratives center on the commission: "As the Father has sent me, even so I send you" (Jn 20:21). The
Spirit is imparted in function of this sending (Jn 20:22). The apostles are
foundational witnesses (Eph 2:20; Rev 21:14), through their association
with and mandate from Christ. The christological unity of the Bible
illuminates the significance of the distinction between the appearances
of the risen Jesus (who sends his apostles) and the gift of the Spirit (who
dwells within and empowers all Christians).

The second consideration for reading and interpreting the scriptures in the same Spirit through whom they were written is the living
tradition of the whole church—a lovely phrase which corresponds to the
dynamic and wholistic view of tradition expressed by the second chapter
of *Dei Verbum*.[18] Eastern Christians remind us that the church's liturgy
is the pre-eminent witness to her living tradition.[19] The liturgical separa-

tion of Easter and Pentecost is not simply the triumph of Luke's scheme found at the end of his gospel and the beginning of Acts. The voice of the liturgy testifies to the fact that, while closely related, Christ's resurrection made known through the appearances does not simply coincide with the gift of the Holy Spirit. The living tradition that celebrates first Easter and then Pentecost does not encourage us to collapse into one the christophanies and the gift of the Holy Spirit.

Third, the analogy of faith also has something to say about the issue we have chosen. In particular it is the mediation of the definitive revelation through Christ at specific times and in specific places that is illuminating here. Their association with Christ and, above all, their special Easter encounters with him made the apostles the foundational witnesses to the fullness of revelation manifested in Christ. All subsequent Christians depend on the foundational testimony of the apostles. It was their association with Christ, not just their experience of the Spirit, that made the apostles foundational and normative witnesses to God's definitive self-communication in Christ.

The nature of revelation is an utterly basic and all-pervading element in our understanding of Christian faith. Our Christian interpretation of revelation is integrally bound up with its apostolic character and the normative role of the apostles as witnesses to revelation. To understand the Easter appearances as really nothing else than the first experiences of the Holy Spirit risks undercutting the function of the apostles as foundational witnesses to revelation. Experiences of the Spirit are common to all Christians. Encounters with the risen Christ were limited to a small group of witnesses at the start of Christianity.

In short, by encouraging us to see all the elements together and in depth, the analogy of faith encourages us to distinguish between the Easter appearances to a limited number of foundational witnesses and the gift of the Spirit to all.

One of the most valuable documents from the Second Vatican Council is its Constitution on Divine Revelation. Among the treasures of *Dei Verbum* is its teaching on exegesis—a vision of exegesis that embraces both the historical-critical method and an approach which is led by the Spirit to be properly christological, traditional (or ecclesial) and theological. It is a vision of exegesis that respects both reason and faith, that is both rational and pneumatological.

I have taken up one specific issue to illustrate how this integral vision of exegesis might work. The historical and "spiritual" guidelines outlined by *Dei Verbum* converge in distinguishing between the appearances of the risen Christ and the coming of the Holy Spirit. In the light of the farewell discourse of John's gospel, this conclusion is not surprising.

In that discourse Jesus promises the gift of the Spirit. So far from being a substitute, let alone a rival, the Spirit will bear witness to Christ and glorify Christ (Jn 15:26; 16:14). A coming of the Spirit, distinct from the Easter appearances, allows for a witnessing to Christ which does not replace him. The Spirit does not glorify a Christ whom no one ever saw alive after his resurrection. To remove the distinct Easter appearances of the risen Christ or reduce them to the first experiences of the Spirit would be a step toward collapsing christology into pneumatology. Here, as elsewhere, christology and pneumatology are related but properly distinct, just as Christ and the Holy Spirit are related but personally distinct.

CODA: THE "OPEN" BIBLE AND EXEGETICAL CONTROL

In commenting above on DV 12, I recalled the need to attend to a) the original authors, b) their texts and c) their hearers, readers and interpreters (see also note 2 of this chapter). In privileging the role of a), historical-genetic exegesis of the Bible aims to reconstruct and understand "from within" the world, the lived experience and the mind of the authors—as it were reliving their consciousness and "thinking their thoughts after them." Such exegesis seeks to recapture, as far as possible, the original authorial intention and its message for the original readers or hearers of the text.

When it operates in isolation, such biblical exegesis can ignore the fact that meaning is not confined to the intention which was originally embedded in the text by the author and is to be excavated scientifically from the text by later interpreters. A one-sided historical exegesis slips over the role now played in interpretation by the cultural-social-religious world of the individual exegetes and the community to which they belong. They bring to the work of understanding and interpretation their assumptions, questions, expectations and all their experiences of faith, action and prayer. Their act of interpretation is conditioned, religiously and culturally. Nevertheless, so far from merely creating problems, the present situation of the exegetes themselves, their cultural and temporal distance from the original authors and the whole intervening history of interpretation offer productive opportunities to those who ask: What do the scriptural texts mean?

As we saw, DV 12 champions approach a), but it does not make authorial intention the sole norm of meaning. It recognizes other elements involved in biblical interpretation. In particular, its encouragement of "spiritual" exegesis includes an appeal to c), the role which past and present readers, hearers and interpreters of the scriptural texts have played in actively co-producing, with the help of the Holy Spirit, the meaning of the Bible. What is not so clear in *Dei Verbum* is a sense of b), the function of the *text itself* in producing meaning. That is to say, we need to hear more of synchronic or final-form study.

As regards c), the reader response to the scriptures has been one major element in that wider process of living tradition in which the church hands on "all that she herself is, all that she believes" (DV 8). Within that broader process, reader response and engagement have actively received and creatively realized the biblical texts. The Bible has proved itself to be an "open" book, with its readers constantly discovering and creating fresh meaning. This history of the reception of the Bible within the living tradition of the community is a history of its inexhaustible potential for meaning being continually unfolded, brought alive and actualized. Here, if anywhere, there can be no such thing as the *final* meaning of a work.

This active, living reception of the scriptures includes but goes far beyond the work of professional scholars in understanding and interpreting these texts. Led by the Holy Spirit (Jn 16:13), Christian communities, their leaders and individual members have been creatively interpreting, responding to and actualizing the scriptures in an endless variety of ways. This very wide reader response to the biblical texts belongs to that "living tradition of the whole Church" which *Dei Verbum* recognizes as a key element in integral exegesis.

As we have seen, what does not emerge clearly from DV 12 is the role of b), the text itself, which has its afterlife independently of its author. It forms the bridge between the authors in the past a) and the readers in the present c). The type and paper now used to print the Hebrew and Greek books of the Bible set our scriptures apart from the handwritten parchments and papyri of the past. But the text itself, thanks to the unique witnesses of so many scrolls, papyri and manuscripts, is substantially the same text, an extraordinary, physical bridge between the readers now and the writers then. Thanks to textual criticism, we can retrieve more or less the original text.

Insights into different aspects of the final text itself permit a wide variety of complementary interpretations. This final-form exegesis can prove very enriching, but leaves us with a challenging question.

We have seen how in the exegetical vision of *Dei Verbum* living tradition has provided the reader response to the "open" Bible. But were there and are there limits to and controls over this response? What stands in the way of arbitrary interpretations in the name of final-form exegesis? *Dei Verbum* invokes the magisterium (DV 9–10, 23) and the intentions of the original authors (DV 12). What one misses is a sense of the way the very text itself b) also functions to control exegesis, whether it styles itself "reader response" or "final-form" exegesis.

In its "otherness" the biblical text remains what it is, an alien, inspired text from the past which, in strange and new ways, can question, challenge, and transform the expectations and interpretations of the reader. This is simply a lesson drawn from Christian experience of the Bible. All classical texts, and in a peculiar way the scriptural texts, can interact in this way so as to oppose, as well as fulfill, our expectations and lead us to fresh understanding.

To sum up the point of this coda: Critical theories of interpretation should, in one way or another, take into account a) the authors of texts, b) the texts themselves and c) the readers of these texts. Some theories focus on the relationship between b) text and c) reader even to the point of discounting completely the role of the original authors and their intentions. Or else meaning becomes virtually identified with b) the text itself, leaving both authorial intention a) and active reader response c) disregarded as irrelevant. *Dei Verbum*, however, rightly attends to a) and c) reminding us in particular of the creativity and community of interpretation constituted by the "living tradition" as it reads and responds to the "open" Bible. The intention of the original authors and the guidance of the magisterium function to set some limits to the reader response today. To this schema of biblical interpretation we need to add the role of the very text itself, which in its inspired otherness can become for us the living and guiding word of God.

CONCLUSION

In the seventh of his *Duino Elegies* Rainer Maria Rilke wrote: "One earthly thing, truly experienced even once, is enough for a lifetime." Specifically in terms of the Second Vatican Council, we might adapt and appropriate these words to say: "One ecumenical council, truly experienced and interpreted, is enough for a lifetime of theology."

This book has set itself above all to experience and interpret more satisfactorily the Second Vatican Council's teaching that is significant for fundamental theology. In particular, this has meant tuning in to texts that bear on the central theme of FT, God's self-revelation. Chapter 4 has aimed to throw further light on the genesis and content of *Dei Verbum*. At the same time, other conciliar documents not only reiterate the teaching of this Constitution on Divine Revelation but also develop further what *Dei Verbum* teaches and even add new points (for example, the correlation between the human condition and the salvific self-disclosure of God in Christ). Hence an adequate reception of the conciliar doctrine on revelation has involved examining what the "other" documents indicate about divine revelation (Chapter 5) and the saving knowledge of God mediated through non-Christian religions (Chapter 6).

The retrieval of the integral conciliar teaching on revelation prepared the way for drawing some systematic conclusions about revelation as past and foundational and revelation as present and dependent (Chapter 7), the nature of revelation as God's symbolic self-communication (Chapter 8), our experience of this self-communication (Chapter 9), and the identification of revelation's essential "content" as love (Chapter 10).

Among the basic questions which will not go away are those which concern the revelationship between revelation and the Bible and a related issue, the nature of integral exegesis. The final two chapters tackled those issues.

The key aim of this book has been to see and retrieve what *Dei Verbum* and related texts are all about—in particular, as regards the divine self-revelation. To achieve this aim it was necessary to clarify and

150

take a stand about postconciliar theological orientations (Chapter 1), the nature of theology (Chapter 2) and the specific role of FT (Chapter 3). The (largely) theoretical considerations of those three chapters weave in and out of practically all that follows. In particular, the opening chapter and its three styles of theology can guide the reader right through to the appendix.

Those three styles are ideal types, theoretically distinct approximations that classify and clarify much that is happening in modern theology and certainly a very great deal that this book has reported and argued for. Take, for example, "the anthropological turn" *(die anthropologische Wende)* that drew our attention in Chapters 2, 3, 5 and elsewhere. The human condition can be interpreted in a triple fashion: as a questioning and thinking condition *(homo interrogans et ratiocinans),* a suffering condition *(homo dolens)* and a praying condition *(homo orans).* These three versions of the human condition match, respectively, the academic, the practical and the contemplative styles of theology. Chapter 9, when considering religious experience, was obviously developing the second version of the human condition (and second style of theology) when it noted how we suffer from death, absurdity and isolation (in all their various forms) and enjoy a primordial drive toward the fullness of life, meaning/truth, and love.

Let me add three further examples to illustrate further the importance of the opening chapter for the whole of this book. The chapter on God's *symbolic* self-communication might have quoted Paul Ricoeur's classic dictum about a symbol inviting thought. Yet the logic of this present work would demand two additions. If symbols invite thought (style one of theology), they also invite action (style two) and prayer/ adoration (style three). What Chapter 8 presented about symbols could be usefully reread in terms of symbols "inviting" thought, action and prayer.

The concern for the language of revelation (Chapter 7), experience (Chapter 9) and love (Chapter 10) represents what some have called "the linguistic turn" in modern theology. Undoubtedly twentieth century philosophy and other influences have encouraged such a "linguistic turn" in theology, which is closely interwoven with the "anthropological turn" and gets reflected in such fine works as Janet Martin Soskice's *Metaphor and Religious Language* (Oxford, 1985). Both within this book and beyond, the linguistic turn expresses itself hermeneutically, praxiologically and liturgically. It is concerned with understanding and interpreting texts (style one of theology), language as an agent of change (the speech acts of style two) and the language of public worship and private prayer (style three). Those with a taste for the linguistic turn in theology have doubtless observed where this book and its language betrayed the hermeneutical interests of style one, the performative interest of style two or the liturgical interest of style three.

My third example refers to something the reader has not yet come to, the criticism of *Dei Verbum* found in the first appendix. That plea to emphasize the liturgical character of biblical interpretation becomes even more enlightening when interpreted as expressing the third style of theology (and church teaching).

Much of the shape of this book has come from the schema proposed in Chapter 1. But the "matter" has largely come from the Second Vatican Council and its teaching on God's saving self-revelation. As indicated right from the outset, the book embodies an attempt to receive and retrieve creatively some conciliar teaching that is vitally significant for fundamental theology. Nearly three decades have gone by since the council promulgated *Dei Verbum* and closed in 1965. Very many of the authors of the conciliar texts have died and the readers have kept changing. But I hope to have shown how those texts still have much to say for Christian life and theology.

NOTES

INTRODUCTION

1. On the reception of conciliar teaching see Y. Congar, "Reception as an Ecclesiological Reality," *Concilium* 77 (1972) pp. 43–68, A. Grillmeier, "The Reception of Chalcedon in the Roman Catholic Church," *The Ecumenical Review* 22 (1970) pp. 382–411; E.J. Kilmartin, "Reception in History: An Ecclesiological Phenomenon and Its Significance," *Journal of Ecumenical Studies* 21 (1984) pp. 334–54; W.G. Rusch, *Reception: An Ecumenical Opportunity* (Philadelphia, 1988). On the reception of teaching of the Second Vatican Council see A. Acerbi, "Receiving Vatican II in a Changed Historical Context," *Concilium* 146 (1981) pp. 77–84; G. Alberigo et al. (eds.), *The Reception of Vatican II* (Washington, 1987); K. Rahner, "Towards a Fundamental Interpretation of Vatican II," TS 40 (1979) pp. 716–27; this essay also appeared as "Basic Theological Interpretation of the Second Vatican Council," ThInv 20, pp. 77–89.

2. A. Franzini's *Tradizione e Scrittura* (Brescia, 1978) is, for example, an excellent study of the background to and teaching of *Dei Verbum* on tradition and scripture. However, apart from a little material on *Lumen Gentium,* this book does not explore what the conciliar documents other than *Dei Verbum* might contribute to our renewed understanding of tradition and scripture.

CHAPTER 1.

1. This chapter addresses the question of Catholic (and Christian) *theology,* not as such wider questions of church life as a whole.

2. See R. Tucci, in *Commentary on the Documents of Vatican II,* ed. H. Vorgrimler, vol. 5 (New York, 1969) p. 285. Tucci is commenting on GS 62 and quoting remarks made at Vatican II by (Cardinal) G. Lercaro and C. Moeller about opening theological faculties to lay people. GS 62 expressed the hope that "more lay persons will receive an appropriate formation in the sacred sciences and that some of them will take up these

studies professionally and contribute to their advancement." See also R. Latourelle, "Lay Theologians," *Theology. Science of Salvation* (New York, 1969) pp. 219–31.

3. It would be false to contrast the Catholic manualist theology that dominated between the two Vatican Councils with postconciliar theology as if the former were deductive and the latter inductive. In its own rather positivistic way, manualist theology was inductive. It made current church teaching its point of departure and then, using a "regressive" rather than a "genetic" method, went back to scripture and tradition to find data that proved the "pre-established" conclusion (see J. Wicks, "Teologia manualistica," *Dizionario di Teologia Fondamentale*, eds. R. Latourelle and R. Fisichella [Assisi, 1990] pp. 1265–69). As we shall see in the next chapter, the Second Vatican Council encouraged not only a "genetic" approach (that traces doctrines *from* their origins to the present) but also a more accurate study and use of scriptural and historical sources.

4. The 1990 document of the International Theological Commission, "On the Interpretation of Dogma," calls the liturgy "the living and comprehensive *locus theologicus* of faith," constituting with prayer "an important hermeneutical locus for the knowledge and transmission of the truth" (*Origins* 20 [1990] pp. 1–14, at pp. 6, 11; there is a translation offered by the *Irish Theological Quarterly* 56 [1990] pp. 251–77 but it is not as satisfactory. For the original German text see *Internationale katholische Zeitschrift* 19 [1990] pp. 246–66). See also J. Leclercq, "Theology and Prayer," NCE, vol. 14, pp. 64–65.

5. The particular "time focus" of each style can be clarified through the theme of experience. The first style seeks to understand and explain someone else's experience, above all the apostolic experience of God's definitive self-relevation in Christ. The second style takes as its point of departure our present experience of physical suffering and other evil. The point of departure for the third style is our experience (both liturgical and extra-liturgical) of the beautiful and our yearning for complete fulfillment.

6. After identifying three styles of theology, I should add that all theology operates through thought, words and writing. Differences emerge, inasmuch as the thought, words and writing are primarily in the service of knowledge and understanding (style one), in the service of action (style two), or in the service of prayer (style three).

7. If we were to pursue the question "What is truth?" we might associate the first style of theology with the classical correspondence theory of truth (for which truth is found in the intellect when its judg-

ments correspond to the facts), the second style with the pragmatic theory of truth (for which truth is proved in action or verified by its consequences) and the third style with the coherence theory of truth (which fits everything into a "beautiful," comprehensive account of the universe). For an initial bibliography see A.N. Prior, "Correspondence Theory of Truth," *The Encyclopedia of Philosophy,* ed. P. Edwards (New York, 1967), vol. 2, pp. 223–32; G. Ezorsky, "Pragmatic Theory of Truth," *ibid.,* vol. 2, pp. 130–33; idem, *Truth* (London, 1971); C.J.F. Williams, *What Is Truth?* (Cambridge, 1976).

8. The axiom "legem credendi lex statuat supplicandi" ("let the law of prayer establish the law of belief") goes back to St. Prosper of Aquitaine (ca. 390–ca. 463). He included the axiom in the *Indiculus,* a dossier on grace which he drew from St. Augustine and composed for Pope Celestine I (DS 238–49, at 246).

9. Different images of Christ match the three styles. Titian's painting of the boy Jesus (now in Dresden) shows him in the temple long ago, engaged in dialogue with contemporary theologians (style one). The tortured Christ of Latin American iconography presents the second style through the one who presently identifies with the wretched of this earth and is "in agony until the end of the world" (Blaise Pascal). The Pantocrator of eastern Christian churches (and of such western churches as San Clemente, in Rome) pictures Christ now reigning in radiant glory and to come at the end of time (third style).

10. See E. Dhanis (ed.), *Resurrexit* (Rome, 1974) pp. xii–xiii; AAS 62 (1970) pp. 220–24. Paul VI was citing St. Augustine, *De Doctrina Christiana* III, 56; PL 34, 89.

CHAPTER 2.

1. For Vatican I's teaching on faith and reason see H.J. Pottmeyer, *Der Glaube vor dem Anspruch der Wissenschaft* (Freiburg, 1968) especially pp. 349–459.

2. See D.L. Lane, "Eschatology," *The New Dictionary of Theology,* ed. J.A. Komonchak et al. (Wilmington, 1987) pp. 329–42; G. O'Collins, "Prolepsis," *A New Dictionary of Christian Theology,* ed. A. Richardson and J. Bowden (London, 1983) p. 472.

3. See G.A. Maloney. "Apophatic Theology," NCE, vol. 18, pp. 23–24.

4. For commentaries on *Optatum Totius* see R. Latourelle, "Absence and Presence of Fundamental Theology at Vatican II," *Vatican II. Assessment and Perspectives,* ed. R. Latourelle (Mahwah, 1989) vol. 3,

pp. 378–415, at p. 412. To that bibliography one should add J. Neuner, *Commentary on the Documents of Vatican II,* ed. H. Vorgrimler, vol. 2 (New York, 1968) pp. 371–404.

5. On this image of the Bible as the soul of theology see E. Rasco, "Biblical Theology. Its Revival and Influence on Theological Formation," *Vatican II. Assessment and Perspectives,* vol. 3, pp. 337–60, at pp. 341–42.

6. On these images of "supporting," "strengthening" and "rejuvenating," see *ibid.,* pp. 340–41.

7. The council encourages here the "genetic" method in theology or, in other words, a return to the sources by studying first the biblical themes and then the subsequent story of tradition and dogmatic development.

8. On the meaning of "authentic" magisterium see F.A. Sullivan, *Magisterium* (Mahwah, 1983) pp. 26–28. On the magisterium and the role of theologians see *ibid.,* pp. 174–218.

9. On the place of philosophy in programs of priestly formation see later in this chapter reference to two documents from the Sacred Congregation for Catholic Education (of 20 January 1972 and 22 February 1976). On the relationship between philosophy and theology see my *Fundamental Theology* (Mahwah, new ed., 1986) pp. 24–31 and what will come at the end of this chapter.

10. The beginning and the end of GS 62 make this one of the richest articles from the council on the role of theologians. The article leaves us with a challenge to which we will return later in this chapter: the fruitful tension between a) the theologians' scientific research and their struggle to understand more deeply God's revelation, and b) their service within the church in presenting the truth of faith to our contemporaries. In its teaching on faith and reason the First Vatican Council spoke of sciences (*disciplinae*) using their own proper principles and method (*propriis utantur principiis et propria methodo*) and of the church as "acknowledging this just freedom (*iustam hanc libertatem agnoscens*)" (DS 3019). GS 62 applies this language to the "sacred sciences," when it refers to theologians "adhering to the methods and requirements proper to theological science (*servatis propriis scientiae theologicae methodis et exigentiis*) and to the "just freedom of inquiry" (*iusta libertas inquirendi*) which all the faithful, both clerical and lay, should be accorded. CIC 218 reproduces this language of *iusta libertas.*

11. On the council's "silence" about fundamental theology see note 4 above.

12. W. Bousset, *Apophthegmata* (Tübingen, 1923) pp. 309–10.

13. PG 79, 1180.

14. It is significant, however, that even when it talks about "the mys-

teries of salvation" in the plural, *Optatam Totius* states that "students should learn how these mysteries are *interconnected*" (UR 16; italics mine; see DS 3016).

15. See K. Rahner, "The Concept of Mystery in Catholic Theology," ThInv 4, pp. 36–73 (especially pp. 60–73); idem, "Reflections on Methodology in Theology," ThInv 11, pp. 68–114 (especially pp. 101–14).

16. See A.T. Henelly (ed.), *Liberation Theology. A Documentary History* (New York, 1990).

17. *Normae Quaedam* were not published in AAS.

18. In its section on theological studies (76–81) the "Basic Plan for Priestly Formation" issued by the Sacred Congregation for Catholic Education on 6 January 1970 parallels the vision of theological study and teaching expressed by *Normae Quaedam* and the council itself. This 1970 document is found in *Norms for Priestly Formation. A Compendium of Official Documents on Training Candidates for the Priesthood,* issued by the National Conference of Catholic Bishops (Washington, 1982) pp. 15–60.

19. *Gravissimum Educationis* was using here a terminology taken from Pope Pius XI's *Deus Scientiarum Dominus* of 24 May 1931 (AAS 23 [1931] pp. 241–61). "Faculties of sacred sciences" are university faculties which teach and study the theological disciplines, whereas "ecclesiastical faculties" are various independent faculties which may teach and study theology but may also teach and study such related disciplines as exegesis and philosophy.

20. *Norms for Priestly Formation,* pp. 61–95. It should be noted that the "Theological Formation of Future Priests" did not appear in Latin nor was it published in AAS.

21. *Ibid.,* pp. 97–107.

22. The 1980 papal encyclical *Dives in Misericordia* exhibits the same *reductio in mysterium,* referring thirty-nine times to the "mystery" (of God, of Christ, etc.) and only twice to "mysteries." The text likewise speaks of "truth" (in the singular) twenty-six times and never of "truths" (in the plural). Chapter 7 of this book will discuss the encyclical in some detail.

23. *Ibid.,* pp. 225–61.

24. See CIC 218.

25. For the use of "scientific" in connection with theology see the Code of Canon Law for the Latin Church (CIC 810, 815). At the same time, the Code requires a "mandate" from the competent ecclesiastical authority for those who teach theology in Catholic universities and in other Catholic institutes of higher learning (CIC 812).

26. See I.G. Barbour, "Ways of Relating Science and Theology," *Physics, Philosophy and Theology,* ed. R.J. Russell et al. (Vatican City,

1988) pp. 21–48; G. O'Collins, *Fundamental Theology,* pp. 140–41; idem, *Jesus Risen* (Mahwah, 1987) pp. 47–49, 52, 134–35.

27. In his *Idea of a University* (the first section originally published as "Discourses on University Education" in 1853 and the second as "Lectures and Essays on University Subjects" in 1858) Newman devoted two chapters in the first section to theology. See the critical edition by Ian Ker (Oxford, 1976).

28. W. Pannenberg, *Theology and the Philosophy of Science* (Philadelphia, 1976) pp. 3–20, 228–345. See also K. Rahner, ThInv 13, Part One, "Theology as Science," pp. 3–102.

29. See F.A. Sullivan, "The Theologian's Ecclesial Vocation and the 1990 CDF Instruction," *TS* 52 (1991) pp. 51–68.

30. See International Theological Commission, *Texts and Documents 1969–85,* ed. M. Sharkey (San Francisco, 1989).

31. *Ibid.,* pp. 129–43. See also the translation and commentary provided by F.A. Sullivan in *Magisterium,* pp. 174–218.

32. On the service of theologians in their relationship both to the bishops and to the community of Christian believers see F.G. Brambilla, "La figura del teologo nei pronunciamenti ecclesiali dal Concilio a oggi," *Teologia* 12 (1987) pp. 201–31.

33. Y. Congar, *A History of Theology* (Garden City, 1968); G. Ebeling, *The Study of Theology* (London, 1979); C. Geffré, *A New Age in Theology* (New York, 1974); W.J. Hill, "Theology," *The New Dictionary of Theology,* ed. J.A. Komonchak et al., pp. 1011–27; B. Lonergan, *Method in Theology* (London, 1972); J. Macquarrie, *Principles of Christian Theology* (London, 1977); J. Moltmann, *Theology Today* (London, 1988); W. Pannenberg, *Theology and the Philosophy of Science;* K. Rahner, *Foundations of Christian Faith* (New York, 1978); J.L. Segundo, *The Liberation of Theology* (Maryknoll, 1976); P. Tillich, *Systematic Theology* (London, 1978) vol. 1, pp. 3–68; D. Tracy, *Blessed Rage for Order* (New York, 1975); idem, *The Analogical Imagination* (New York, 1981).

34. See my *Foundations of Theology* (Chicago, 1971) pp. 1–20; idem, *Fundamental Theology,* pp. 5–21, 24–31.

35. See note 9 above and K. Rahner, "The Current Relationship between Philosophy and Theology," ThInv 13, pp. 61–79.

CHAPTER 3.

1. See F. Schüssler Fiorenza, *Foundational Theology* (New York, 1984); R. Fisichella, *La Rivelazione: evento e credibilità* (Bologna, 1985); W. Kern et al., *Handbuch der Fundamentaltheologie,* 4 vols. (Freiburg, 1985–88); R. Latourelle and R. Fisichella (eds.), *Dizionario*

di Teologia fondamentale (Assisi, 1990); R. Latourelle and G. O'Collins (eds.), *Problems and Perspectives of Fundamental Theology* (Ramsey, 1982); J.B. Metz, *Faith in History and Society* (New York, 1979); G. O'Collins, *Fundamental Theology;* H. Verweyen, *Gottes letztes Wort* (Düsseldorf, 1991); H. Waldenfels, *Kontextuelle Fundamental-theologie* (2 ed., Paderborn, 1988).

2. See my *Fundamental Theology,* pp. 140–45; idem, *Jesus Risen,* pp. 130–47.

3. On the issue of credibility see R. Fischella, "Credibilità," *Dizionario di Teologia Fondamentale,* pp. 212–30.

4. On P. Tillich and the method of correlation see J.H. Thomas, "Correlation," *A New Dictionary of Christian Theology,* ed. A. Richardson and J. Bowden, p. 124.

5. On faith see my *Fundamental Theology,* pp. 130–60.

6. See Y. Congar, *Tradition and Traditions* (London, 1966); F. Lambiasi, "Spirito Santo," *Dizionario di Teologia Fondamentale,* pp. 1168–77; H.J. Pottmeyer, "Tradizione," *ibid.,* pp. 1341–49.

7. See my *Fundamental Theology,* pp. 225–49; J. Wicks, "Canone Biblico," *Dizionario di Teologia Fondamentale,* pp. 130–40; R. Fisichella, "Ispirazione," *ibid.,* pp. 620–25; I. de la Potterie, "Verità," *ibid.,* pp. 1449–55.

8. See my *Fundamental Theology,* pp. 249–59; Chapter 12 of this book; M. Gilbert, "Esegesi Integrale," *Dizionario di Teologia Fondamentale,* pp. 395–403; P. Grech, "Ermeneutica," *ibid.,* pp. 382–92; J. Wicks, "Chiesa: Interprete della Scrittura," *ibid.,* pp. 186–89.

9. See I.U. Dalferth, *Religiöse Rede von Gott* (Munich, 1981); J. Macquarrie, *God-Talk* (London, 1967).

CHAPTER 4.

1. With Joseph Cassar, S.J., I prepared a bibliography on *Dei Verbum* which appears in this book as Appendix Two.

2. G. Caprile, "Tre emendamenti allo schema sulla Rivelazione," *Civiltà Cattolica* 117 (1966/I) pp. 214–31.

3. J. Ratzinger, in K. Rahner and J. Ratzinger, *Revelation and Tradition* (London, 1966) pp. 50–68.

4. See Chapter 3, nn. 7 and 8 above, and Chapter 12 below.

5. J. Gnilka, *Jesus von Nazareth. Botschaft und Geschichte* (Freiburg, 1990).

6. His 1980 encyclical *Dives in Misericodia* uses "mystery" thirty-nine times, but "mysteries" only twice.

7. J.M. Lera, " 'Sacrae paginae studium sit veluti anima Sacrae

Theologiae' (Notas sobre el origen y procedencia de esta frase)," *Palabra y Vida. Homenaje a J. Alonso Diaz,* ed. A. Vargas Machuca and G. Ruiz (Madrid, 1984) pp. 409–22.

8. On the use of the notion of "self-communication" by R. Bultmann and R. Guardini, as well as by K. Rahner, see E. Biser, "Dialogischer Glaube," *Lebendige Seelsorge* 34 (1983) pp. 265–72, at p. 267, n. 7. Earlier than any of the three writers listed by Biser (who also overlooks Karl Barth), back in 1900 Hermann Schell spoke of revelation as follows: *Die übernaturliche Offenbarung Gottes bedeutet die freie Selbstmitteilung Gottes durch Wort und Tat zu persönlicher und sachlicher Lebensgemeischaft mit dem geschöpflichen Geist* ("The supernatural revelation of God means the free self-communication of God through word and deed to a personal and real community of life with the created spirit") (*Katholische Dogmatik,* ed. J. Hasenfuss and P.-W. Scheele, vol. 1 (Munich, 1968) p. 28, n. 1.

9. In a modified form this draft (= Chapter One of a revised version of *De Divina Revelatione,* see n. 22 below) and its accompanying report (also in a modified form) appear in *Acta Synodalia S. Concilii Oecumenici Vaticani II,* vol. III, pars III, (Vatican, 1974) pp. 69–78. The original draft and report by Smulders are found in his archives in Amsterdam.

10. *Ibid.,* p. 72; see p. 78.

11. *Ibid.,* p. 813.

12. The texts of July and November 1964, which both modified Smulders' draft of April 1964, are found in *ibid.,* vol. IV, pars 1 (Vatican, 1976) pp. 336–74. As we have seen, it is in the November 1964 revision that we read: "God wished to communicate himself" (*Deus seipsum . . . communicare voluit*). In his comments on Chapter One of *Dei Verbum* Max Seckler recognizes the document's endorsement of the notion of revelation as God's *"Selbst-mitteilung* (self-communication)." But he fails to notice the explicit use of the theme of God's wishing "to communicate himself" in DV 6. See Seckler, "Der Begriff der Offenbarung. Das dritte Modell: Offenbarung als Selbstmitteilung Gottes," *Handbuch der Fundamentaltheologie,* vol. 2 (Freiburg, 1985) pp. 66–67.

13. Postconciliar documents receive and develop the theme of revelation being essentially salvific: see, for example, nn. 3, 6 and 7 of the 1980 encyclical *Dives in Misericordia;* Chapter 7 will discuss this papal text in some detail. The radically salvific nature of revelation is a commonplace in biblical and fundamental theology: see, for example, H. Hübner, *Biblische Theologie des Neuen Testaments,* vol. 1 (Göttingen, 1990) pp. 101–239, where the author's treatment of revelation repeatedly emphasizes that God is revealed as Savior.

14. See my *Foundations of Theology* (Chicago, 1971) pp. 47–52; *Fun-*

damental Theology, passim; and *Theology and Revelation* (Cork, 1968) *passim.*

15. That next meeting took place three days later. On all this see J. Feiner, "La contribution du Secrétariat pour l'unité des chrétiens à la Constitution dogmatique sur la Révélation divine," *La Révélation divine, Unam Sanctam,* 70a, ed. B.-D. Dupuy (Paris, 1968) p. 137.

16. I wish to thank Fr. Smulders very warmly for making available to me a copy of this text from his archives in Amsterdam. The Latin original and my English translation appear at the end of the notes to this chapter. The text is dated 29 November [1962], a date which puts it after the next full meeting of the "mixed commission" (November 27, 1962) but before a group (Barnabas Ahern, Gregory Baum, Alexander Kerrigan and Smulders) delegated by a sub-commission of the "mixed commission" met on December 2, 1962. It does not seem that the text delivered by Smulders to Scherer on November 25 had undergone any substantial changes by November 29. The eleven members of the "mixed commission's" sub-commission are listed by Kerrigan in "Il Vecchio Testamento," *Commento alla Costituzione dogmatica sulla Divina Rivelazione,* ed. U. Betti et al. (Milan, 1966) p. 176.

17. J. Feiner (n. 15 above) p. 138.

18. See *DV* 2, 4, 14, 15.

19. *Acta Synodalia S. Concilii Oecumenici Vaticani II,* vol. I, III (Vatican, 1971) p. 260. See n. 8 above for Hermann Schell's remarkable anticipation of this language.

20. See DV 2, 4, 14, 17.

21. "Vatican II's Constitution on Divine Revelation: History and Interpretation," *TS* 28 (1967) pp. 51–75.

22. To call *either* Chapter Three of *De Divina Revelatione* or, for that matter, its earlier form in SD a "corrected" version of Chapter Three of *De Fontibus Revelationis* could be misleading. Between Chapter Three of *De Fontibus Revelationis* and SD there are hardly any verbal links whatsoever. As regards content, in some form or another the following points were already there in that chapter of *De Fontibus Revelationis:* Romans 15:4 as supporting the permanent authority of the Old Testament (15); God's covenantal relationship with the people (15) but without any reference to Abraham or Moses; the Old Testament prophets (15, 16, 17); God's salvific plans (15, 17); the Old testament pointing to and being clarified by the New (16, 17) but not vice versa (as in SD); and God as author and inspirer of both Testaments (17). As we shall see immediately, Chapter Three of *De Divina Revelatione* was substantially the same as SD. Neither text in any proper sense of the word "corrects" Chapter Three of *De Fontibus Revelationis;* they replace it. *De Fontibus*

Revelationis is found in *Schemata Constitutionum et Decretorum,* Series prima (Vatican, 1962) pp. 8–22. In its original (April 1963) and then its revised (July 1964) form, as debated in the third session of the council, *De Divina Revelatione* is found in *Acta Synodalia S. Concilii Oecumenici Vaticani II,* vol. III, pars III, (Vatican, 1974) pp. 69–123.

23. G. Baum (n. 21 above) p. 57.

24. A. Kerrigan (n. 16 above) p. 156.

25. On a number of points contained in this excursus see P. Smulders, "Zum Werdegang des Konzilskapitels 'Die Offenbarung Selbst'," *Glaube im Prozess,* ed. E. Klinger and K. Wittstadt (Freiburg, 1984) pp. 99–120.

DE LIBRIS VETERIS TESTAMENTI
(Draft by Smulders)

Eventus revelationis

1. Deus hominem numquam sine testimonio reliquit (Act 14,17). Foedere tamen cum Abraham inito et cum Moyse renovato seipsum populo sibi acquisito intimius revelavit, ut vias Dei cum hominibus experientia discerent, ac verbo Dei per prophetas facto profundius clariusque intelligerent. Ita autem populus in Abraham electus praeparabatur adventui Filii Dei in carne venientis, et persona, gestis, verbis suis revelationem consummantis.

fit Scriptura

Quae historia, Deo inspirante narrata et a prophetis interpraetata ac praedicta, nobis adhuc exhibetur in libris Veteris Testamenti, qui ipsi etiam Ecclesiae Christi sunt verbum Dei sensu pleno, quisquis sit auctor uniuscuiusque libri humanus (Rom 15,4).

2. De relatione inter Vetus et Novum Testamentum.

valor apologeticus
dogmaticus

moralis

Libri itaque Veteris Testamenti non solum Ecclesiae Christi praebent argumenta, quibus missio ac veracitas Christi valide confirmatur, sed insuper in Christo credentibus cognitionem Dei et hominis praebent, eosque docent quibus mirabilibus modis Deus cum hominibus agat, et quo modo se homo ad Deum ac proximos gerere debeat.

In ordine ad Xtum

Post adventum Christi hi libri Veteris Testamenti Ecclesiae commissi sunt tamquam pars unius revelationis totalis. Ideo plura in illis quae tempori praeparationis exclusive conveniebant, Nova Lege abrogata sunt. Pleraque autem revelationi christianae incorporata per hanc revelationis plenitudinem profundiorem sensum, acquirunt et ostendunt. "Quando enim Salvator evangelium in carne praestituit, per evangelium, omnia quasi evangelium fecit" (Origenes, *in Joann.* I 6,8 PG 14,53s). Sicut ergo Vetus Testamentum ex Novo plene aperitur (Lc 24,32), ita ex altera parte ad sapidam ac ditiorem Novi Testamenti intellectum summopere confert. Nam "in Veteri Testamento est occultatio Novi, in Novo Testamento est manifestatio Veteris" (August., *De Catechizandis Rudibus* 4,8 PL 40,315).

CONCERNING THE BOOKS OF THE OLD TESTAMENT
(Translation by O'Collins)

The Event of Revelation

1. God had never left man without witness (Acts 14:17). Nevertheless, through the covenant which was entered into with Abraham and renewed with Moses, he more intimately revealed himself to the people he had acquired for himself, so that by experience they might learn the ways of God with men, and more profoundly and clearly understand [these ways] by the word of God delivered through the prophets. Thus the people who had been chosen in Abraham were being prepared for the coming of God's Son, who came in the flesh and completed revelation by his person, deeds [and] words.

becomes Scripture

This history, recounted through God's inspiration and interpreted and predicted by the prophets, is still presented to us in the books of the Old Testament. These books, no matter who is the human author of each book, are also for Christ's church the word of God in the full sense (Rom 15:4).

2. Concerning the relation between the Old and the New Testament.

Apologetic value

Dogmatic value
Moral value

With a view
to Christ

Hence the books of the Old Testament not only provide Christ's church with arguments which validly confirm the mission and truth of Christ, but also provide those who believe in Christ with a knowledge of God and man, and teach them about the wonderful ways God acts with men, and how man should behave toward God and neighbors.

After Christ's coming these books of the Old Testament were entrusted to the church as part of one whole revelation. A number of things in these books which belonged exclusively to the time of preparation were abrogated by the new law. More things, however, when incorporated into the Christian revelation, acquire and show forth through this fullness of revelation a more profound meaning. "For when in the flesh the Savior presented the good news, through the good news he made all things as it were good news" (Origen, *In Joann.* I, 6, 8; PG 14, 53f). Therefore, just as the Old Testament is fully opened up from the New (Lk 24:32), so on the other hand it has greatly contributed to our richer understanding and relish of the New Testament. For "in the Old Testament the New is hidden, in the New Testament the Old is revealed" (Augustine, *De Catechizandis Rudibus* 4, 8; PL 40, 315).

CHAPTER 5.

1. See J. van Laarhoven, "The Ecumenical Councils in the Balance: A Quantitative Review," *Concilium* 167 (1983) pp. 50–60.

2. H. Waldenfels, "Das Offenbarungsverständnis auf dem 2. Vatikanischen Konzil," *Handbuch der Dogmengeschichte,* ed. M. Schmaus et al., vol. I, 1b (Freiburg, 1977) pp. 193–208.

3. H. Pfeiffer, *Gott offenbart sich* (Frankfurt, 1982).

4. In the Old Testament many psalms speak of the kingly God present in the sanctuary and in cult (see, for example, Pss 24, 48, 68, 84, 96, 132, 150). For Ezekiel revelation is characteristically the event of God becoming present and remaining present in worship (see Ez 43; see also Ez 8–11 where the glory of the Lord leaves the temple).

5. The council text here follows the Vulgate in reading *adventus* (advent), whereas the Greek text of Titus 2:13 has *epiphaneia* (appearing).

6. This passage exemplifies the experiential approach of GS to revelation and other themes. As regards statistics, GS uses the noun "experience" eleven times and the verb "experience" also eleven times. The other fifteen documents from the council use the noun twenty times and the verb only six times, for a total of twenty-six occurrences over against the total in GS alone of twenty-two occurrences.

7. Once again the council here associates the disclosure of "the mystery of God" with the disclosure of "the innermost truth" of the human condition. Knowing the divine mystery means knowing the human mystery (see GS 22). Men and women are understood here as beings in search of meaning and truth (first style of theology), rather than as beings in search of justice/goodness (second style) or beauty (third style).

8. This paragraph thinks in terms of the church directly revealing God. It could have spoken of manifesting "the mystery of *Christ's* love for us," thus maintaining the scheme of the church being the sign/symbol revealing Christ and Christ being the sign/symbol revealing God.

9. In his *Enarr. in Ps.* 138,14, Augustine says of God: *Quaesivit vos antequam quaereretis eum; et invenit vos ut inveniretis eum* (He has searched for you before you search for him; and he has found you so that you will find him) (*Corpus Christianorum,* Series Latina 40, p. 2000). Augustine echoes here Isaiah 65:1 (cited by Paul in Romans 10:20).

10. As it does elsewhere, GS here holds together the order of creation and redemption (God who "created" and "redeemed" us). The "perfect" answer to our radical questioning (as opposed to imperfect, partial or inadequate answers) is found in Christ, the final mediator of revelation and redemption.

CHAPTER 6.

1. E. Stakemeier, *Die Konzilskonstitution über die göttliche Offenbarung* (Paderborn, 1966) p. 112.

2. On the "general" and "special" history of revelation and salvation, see my *Fundamental Theology,* pp. 122–29.

3. *Ecclesiam Suam,* AAS 56 (1964) pp. 654–55.

4. See my *Fundamental Theology,* pp. 114–29.

5. As with its translation of LG 17, the Flannery version here wrongly translates *sanare* as "purified."

6. Like *Dei Verbum,* both *Lumen Gentium* and *Ad Gentes,* by referring to the customs, rites and cultures of peoples, suggest that the community, rather than the individual, is the primary addressee of God's revelatory and salvific self-communication.

7. *Ad Gentes* here remedies an omission on the part of *Sacrosanctum Concilium* which curiously failed to recall the presence of Christ in "the word of preaching" (see SC 7).

8. See Frank Sullivan, *Salvation Outside the Church?* (Mahwah, 1992).

9. See Jacques Dupuis, *Jesus Christ at the Encounter of World Religions* (Maryknoll, 1991). On many questions connected with God's revealing and saving self-communication in and according to Christianity and other religions, see such numbers of *Studia Missionalia* as *Revelation* 20 (1971), *Salvation* 29 (1980) and *Voies de Salut* 30 (1981).

CHAPTER 7.

1. So far as I know, no one has ever written on the rich teaching for a theology of revelation to be found in *Dives in Misericordia.* This neglect reflects, I presume, a general (partial) neglect of such central themes of FT as revelation.

2. Apropos of this growth in understanding, *Gaudium et Spes* talks rather of a task: the church (aided by the Holy Spirit) should reflect on and interpret "the many voices of our times . . . in the light of the divine word, so that the revealed truth may be more deeply penetrated, better understood and more suitably presented" (GS 44).

3. See G. O'Collins, *Theology and Revelation,* pp. 45–57, 49–50, and *Fundamental Theology,* pp. 101–02. P. Tillich speaks of "original and dependent revelation" (rather than "foundational and dependent revelation") and uses that language with the nuances of his own system (*Systematic Theology,* vol. 1 [London, 1978], pp. 126–28). In *Der apostolische Abschluss der Offenbarung Gottes* (Freiburg, 1979) pp. 144 and 146–47, J. Schumacher contrasts revelation "in actu primo" (the revelation which reached its complete fullness with Christ and his apostles) and revelation "in actu secondo" (revelation as it happens in the post-apostolic church).

4. On this dependence from the apostolic witnesses see K. Rahner, *Foundations of Christian Faith,* pp. 274–76. On the normative, founda-

tional role coming to the apostles through their encounters with the risen Jesus see G. O'Collins and D. Kendall, "The Uniqueness of the Easter Appearances," *Catholic Biblical Quarterly* 54 (1992) pp. 287–307.

5. See J. Schumacher, *Der apostolische Abschluss,* pp. 121–36.

6. "The Death of Jesus and the Closure of Revelation" ThInv 18, pp. 132–42, at pp. 140–41. In *Der apostolische Abschluss* Schumacher reports a number of others who propose similar views and then marshalls the arguments of those who hold that the apostolic age also belonged to what Schumacher calls the constitutive period of revelation or "revelatio in actu primo" (pp. 153–69).

CHAPTER 8.

1. Calling *Dei Verbum* a point of departure for a theology of God's symbolic self-communication does not mean ignoring either the way the theme of the divine self-communication stretches back through Rahner and others to Kierkegaard (see Chapter 4, n. 8 above) or the way Rahner developed theologically the theme of symbol in an article (on devotion to the Sacred Heart) originally published in 1959, six years before the appearance of *Dei Verbum* in 1965: "The Theology of the Symbol," ThInv 4, pp. 221–52. Rather *Dei Verbum* is a point of departure, in that postconciliar theology has begun developing an approach to revelation as God's symbolic self-communication: see, for example, A. Dulles, *Models of Revelation* (New York, 1983), H. Fries, Fundamental-theologie (Graz, 1985) pp. 158–61, 167–69, and A. Shorter, *Revelation and Its Interpretation.*

2. See G. Aulén, *The Drama and the Symbols* (London, 1970); E.R. Bevan, *Symbolism and Belief* (London, 1962); E. Cassirer, *The Philosophy of Symbolic Forms* (New Haven, 1970); idem, *Symbol, Myth and Culture* (New Haven, 1979); B.J. Cooke, *The Distancing of God* (Minneapolis, 1990); F.W. Dillistone, *The Power of Symbols* (London, 1986); idem, *Traditional Symbols and the Contemporary World* (London, 1973); M. Eliade, *Images and Symbols* (London, 1961); idem, *Symbolism* (New York, 1986); C.G. Jung (ed.), *Man and His Symbols* (London, 1964); W.W. Müller, *Das Symbol in der dogmatischen Theologie* (Frankfurt, 1990); P. Ricoeur, *Interpretation Theory* (Fort Worth, 1976) pp. 45–69; W.A. Van Roo, *Man the Symbolizer* (Rome, 1981); A.N. Whitehead, *Symbolism: Its Meanings and Effect* (Cambridge, 1928).

3. See W. Kasper, *The God of Jesus Christ* (New York, 1989) pp. 275–76.

4. The fact that symbols, in some way or another, always make present what is symbolized should outlaw such expressions as "a *mere* symbol"

or "*only* symbolically present." Reporting debates at the Second Vatican Council, Enzo Bianchi accepts without demur this misleading language which wrongly understands talk of "a symbolic presence" to be necessarily a reductive view of things; see his "The Centrality of the Word of God," *The Reception of Vatican II*, ed. G. Alberigo et al., p. 118.

5. The expression "symbolic stories" should not be misconstrued to mean that there are or could be non-symbolic stories.

CHAPTER 9.

1. See Kasper, *The God of Jesus Christ*, pp. 116–17.

2. See F.W. Dillistone, "Experience, Religious," *A New Dictionary of Christian Theology*, ed. A. Richardson and J. Bowden, pp. 204–07; W.J. Hill, "Experience, Religious," NCE, vol. 5, pp. 751–53; K. Lehmann, "Experience," *Sacramentum Mundi*, vol. 2, pp. 307–09; J.A. Martin, "Religious Experience," *The Encyclopedia of Religion*, ed. M. Eliade, (New York, 1987) vol. 12, pp. 323–30; J. Mouroux, "Religious Experience," *Sacramentum Mundi*, vol. 5, pp. 292–93; H. Pinard de la Boullaye, "Experience Religieuse," *Dictionnaire de Théologie Catholique*, vol. 4, col. 1786–1867; H. Wissmann et al., "Erfahrung," TRE, vol. 10, pp. 83–141. Right from his first encyclical, *Redemptor Hominis* of 1979, Pope John Paul has repeatedly reflected on human experience and explicitly used the terminology of experience. His 1980 encyclical *Dives in Misericordia* began by appealing to collective and individual experience (4) and went on to use "experience" as a noun thirteen times and as a verb six times. His studies of phenomenology help to explain this interest in human experience. What is curious, however, is the way no Catholic theologian that I know has ever noticed and reflected on the theme of experience that runs through the present pope's teaching. I have already remarked how he has developed two items to be found in *Dei Verbum:* the *reductio in mysterium* (Chapter Two) and the divine self-communication (Chapter Four). He does the same for the theme of experience—something the theological world has failed to notice (see Chapter 5, n. 6 above and Chapter 9 below).

3. Kasper, *The God of Jesus Christ*, p. 79.

4. See C.S. Lewis, *Surprised by Joy* (London, 1955).

5. Immanuel Kant wrote: "Thoughts without content are empty, intuitions without concepts are blind" (*Critique of Pure Reason*, tr. Norman Kemp Smith [London, 1933] p. 93).

6. Mahwah, rev. ed. 1987.

7. See G. O'Collins and D. Kendall, "The Faith of Jesus," TS 53 (1992) pp. 403–23.

8. See A. Hardy, *The Spiritual Nature of Man* (Oxford, 1984).

9. See K. Rahner, *Foundations of Christian Faith,* pp. 19–23, 31–35, 51–71.

10. See Kasper, *The God of Jesus Christ,* pp. 104–06.

CHAPTER 10.

1. R. Bultmann, *The Gospel of John* (Philadelphia, 1971).

2. See C. Spicq, *Agape in the New Testament,* 3 vols. (St. Louis, 1963–66).

3. On love and further related matters see S.J. Pope, "The Order of Love and Recent Catholic Ethics: A Constructive Proposal," TS 52 (1991) pp. 255–87. To Pope's extensive bibliography on love one could add works by Augustine, Abelard, Bernard, Dante, Eric Fromm, Goethe, Gabriel Marcel, Rollo May, Maurice Nedoncelle and Josef Pieper. See also E. McDonagh, "Love," *The New Dictionary of Theology,* ed. J.A. Komonchak et al., pp. 602–16.

In my analysis of love I will concentrate on its personal and interpersonal characteristics. Love can also be understood as a cosmic force that creates, sustains, informs and moves every being to its proper end. This is the "Love which moves the sun and the other stars," celebrated by Dante at the close of the *Divine Comedy* and expounded by Teilhard de Chardin.

4. W. Kasper expresses this point as follows: "In the unity established by Jesus Christ unity and independence increase in direct and not in inverse proportion. Ever greater unity means ever greater independence, and conversely true independence is to be achieved only through and in unity in love" (*The God of Jesus Christ,* p. 284).

5. One could highlight further aspects of love: for example, the approval, activity, adoration and astonishment of love. One could explore the link between love and beauty. The version I have offered here of love suits better the context of this book; it is in no way intended to take back what I wrote on love in *Jesus Risen,* pp. 188–200.

6. On the parables of Jesus see R. Brown, C. Osiek and P. Perkins, NJBC, pp. 1364–69.

CHAPTER 11.

1. On biblical inspiration see J. Barton, "Verbal Inspiration," *A Dictionary of Biblical Interpretation,* ed. R.J. Coggins and J.L. Houlden (London and Philadelphia, 1990) pp. 719–22; R.F. Collins, "Inspiration," NJBC, pp. 1023–33; J. Goldingay, "Inspiration," *A Dictionary of*

Biblical Interpretation, pp. 314–16; G. O'Collins, *Fundamental Theology,* pp. 225–41.

2. This chapter faces the question left open by the section in Chapter 4 above about the biblical orientation of *Dei Verbum,* a document which presented itself as a constitution on the divine self-revelation. What is the relationship between revelation and the inspired scriptures?

CHAPTER 12.

1. For a Lutheran version of the way the Bible should become again the source of Christian consensus and community see George Lindbeck, "Scripture, Consensus and Community," *Biblical Interpretation in Crisis,* ed. R.J. Neuhaus (Grand Rapids, 1989) pp. 74–101. On this book and the two-day meeting that produced it see Jared Wicks, "Biblical Criticism Criticised," *Gregorianum* 72 (1991) pp. 117–28.

2. a) Some scholars deny that the recovery of the original authorial intention is possible. b) Others doubt the relevance of such a quest, not only because we now live in cultures very different from those of the biblical authors, but also because neither biblical nor any other authors determine or fix the meaning of their texts. c) Others again emphasize the degree to which "critical" conclusions about the historical origins and meaning of our biblical texts are deeply affected by the presuppositions of exegetes. As regards a) and b), provided our interpretation makes room also for the intention of the reader or interpreter and of the text itself, the recovery (or at least the partial recovery) of the original author's intention is a necessary, possible and relevant quest. Our temporal and cultural distance from the setting in which the biblical texts were finally fashioned creates difficulties but it also serves as a critical advantage. As regards c), it is true that every act of interpretation, including biblical exegesis, is affected by the personal understanding, cultural formation and faith (or lack of faith) that scholars bring to their work. But the fact that we cannot expect from exegetes utterly "objective," "scientifically" assured results does not mean that we cannot expect any results at all. Some, at times many, exegetical conclusions can be well established, to the point of high probability and even historical certainty. See further Robert Alter, *The Art of Biblical Narrative* (London, 1981); idem, *The Pleasures of Reading* (New York, 1989); idem, with Frank Kermode (eds.), *The Literary Guide to the Bible* (Cambridge, 1987); Raymond Brown and Sandra Schneiders, "Hermeneutics," NJBC, pp. 1146–65; C. Conroy, "Reflections on the Exegetical Task; *Pentateuchal and Deuteronomistic Studies,* eds. C. Brekelmans and J. Lust (Louvain, 1990) pp. 255–68; T. Eagleton, *Literary Theory: An Introduction* (Min-

neapolis, 1983); N. Frye, *The Great Code: The Bible and Literature* (New York, 1982); H.-G. Gadamer, *Truth and Method* (rev. ed., London, 1989); W. Iser, *The Art of Reading: A Theory of Aesthetic Response* (Baltimore, 1978); G. O'Collins, *Fundamental Theology*, pp. 249–59; R. Selden, *A Reader's Guide to Contemporary Literary Theory* (2nd ed., Lexington, 1989).

3. Once again the Flannery translation falters over this phrase, translating *veram paedogogiam divinam* as "authentic divine teaching." This is to weaken the reference *Dei Verbum* makes at this point to Pope Pius XI's 1937 encyclical *Mit brennender Sorge* which speaks of God's "pedagogy of salvation" (*Heilspädagogik*) revealed at work in the Old Testament (AAS 29 [1937] 1951).

4. *Enchiridion Biblicum*, p. 172.

5. *The Work of William Tyndale*, ed. G.E. Duffield (Philadelphia, 1965) p. 353.

6. *De Arca Noe Morali* II, 8–9. Nearly a thousand years before Hugh of Saint Victor, St. Irenaeus called "the Son of God" a "seed scattered everywhere in his scriptures" (*Adv. Haer.* IV, 10, 1). In its 1989 document "On the Interpretation of Dogmas" (*Origins* 20 [1990] 1–14, at p. 11) the International Theological Commission emphasized the way in which, for both scripture and tradition, Christ should be seen as the center of unity and *the* criterion of interpretation.

7. In its 1989 document the International Theological Commission recalled the way in which, along with tradition, the scriptures are "realized and actualized in the liturgy" (*ibid.,* p. 12).

8. The council's attention to the "spiritual" side of exegesis reminds biblical scholars that they should not (and really cannot) ignore theological considerations. In its closing chapter *Dei Verbum* associates exegesis with theology when it speaks of "Catholic exegetes *and other* workers in the field of sacred theology" (*aliique Sacrae Theologiae cultores*) (DV 23).

9. *The Gospel of John* (Oxford, 1971) p. 692.

10. C.K. Barrett, *The Gospel According to St. John* (London, 1962) p. 475. In *The Holy Spirit and the Gospel Tradition* (London, 1954) Barrett, however, is somewhat more reserved about identifying the gift of the Spirit with the appearances (pp. 159–60). In his *A Commentary on the First Epistle to the Corinthians* (London, 1968) Barrett is cautious about identifying the resurrection appearance to more than five hundred with the gift of the Holy Spirit to the disciples in Acts 2. But he at once adds: "The early tradition (including Paul—and John) knows nothing of a corporate bestowal of the Holy Spirit distinct from appearances of the risen Christ" (p. 342). But, apart from John 20:22 and Acts 2:1–4, what corporate bestowals of the Spirit does Barrett have in mind? John 19:30–

34? Acts 8:17? As we shall see, the whole tradition (from Paul to John) tells of appearances to groups and individuals without any mention of the Holy Spirit being bestowed.

11. On John 20:19–23 see further R.E. Brown, *The Gospel According to John* (xiii–xxi) (New York, 1970) pp. 1033–45; R. Schnackenburg, *The Gospel According to John,* vol. 3 (New York, 1987) pp. 300–07, 321–28. Surprisingly R.H. Fuller maintains that John 20:22 "is likely to be *more original* in holding together the two events of christophany to the apostles and the giving of the Spirit." But Fuller weakens the claim that "the gift of the Spirit and the appearances *must* coincide" by four times introducing "if" into his argument (*The Formation of the Resurrection Narratives* [London, 1972] pp. 140, 214; italics mine).

12. Mark 1:8 announces a general gift of the Spirit, a promise the evangelist presumably saw fulfilled in the community's reception of the Spirit (see Acts 1:5; 2:16). The late appendix to Mark's gospel speaks of signs which will accompany Christians (Mk 16:7–8). The passage does not name the Holy Spirit, but the signs "are those which are commonly ascribed to the activity of the Spirit" (C.K. Barrett, *The Holy Spirit and the Gospel Tradition,* p. 133; see p. 116). Nevertheless, the fact remains that neither Mark's gospel nor its appendix identifies the appearances of the risen Christ with the gift of the Holy Spirit.

13. See R.E. Brown, "The Resurrection in Matthew (27:62–28:20)," *Worship* 64 (1990) pp. 157–70; reprinted in *A Risen Christ in Eastertime* (Collegeville, 1991) pp. 23–38; C.K. Barrett interprets the reference of the Father, the Son and the Holy Spirit as being rather "a theological formula, a defense of the doctrine of the Trinity." But he is quite clear in holding that this trinitarian formula "is not specifically related to the gift of the Spirit" (*The Holy Spirit and the Gospel Tradition,* pp. 132–33); it does not have "any relationship to the eschatological outpouring of the Spirit" (*ibid.,* p. 103), for example, during an appearance of the risen Christ.

14. From the last part of the travel narrative (from Luke 13:1 on) and right through the accounts of Jesus' ministry in Jerusalem and his passion, there is no word about the Holy Spirit. Even the resurrection stories contain only the reference to "the promise of my Father" (Lk 24:49), an enigmatic phrase which will be clarified in Acts 1:4–5; 2:33. See J.A. Fitzmyer, *The Gospel According to Luke, I–IX* (New York, 1981) pp. 227–28, 230.

15. Since C.H. Weisse in 1838, a number of authors have identified the appearance to "more than five hundred" followers of Christ (1 Cor 15:6) with the Pentecost story of Acts 2:1–4; see S. MacLean Gilmour, "The Christophany to More Than Five Hundred Brethren," *Journal of*

Biblical Literature 80 (1961) 248–52. In a subsequent article, "Easter and Pentecost," *ibid.*, 81 (1962) 62–66, Gilmour presented and endorsed again the thesis that holds the resurrection, the appearance of the risen Christ and the gift of Spirit to be merely different versions of the same experience. In his *Theology of the New Testament,* vol. 1, *The Proclamation of Jesus* (London, 1971) J. Jeremias similarly maintained that the appearance to more than five hundred and the coming of the Spirit to the one hundred and twenty followers of Jesus at Pentecost (Acts 2:1–3) are simply two traditions of one and the same event (pp. 307–08). In his 1961 article Gilmour mentioned a number of authors who did not agree with the Weisse hypothesis. C. Freeman Sleeper, in his "Pentecost and Resurrection," *Journal of Biblical Literature* 84 (1965), examined and rejected again the hypothesis as based on insufficient evidence (pp. 389–99). Since then others have also questioned the linking of 1 Corinthians 15:6 with Acts 2:1–4; see F.F. Bruce, *1 and 2 Corinthians* (London, 1971) p. 141; W.L. Craig, *Assessing the New Testament Evidence for the Historicity of the Resurrection of Jesus* (Lewiston, 1989) pp. 58–59; X. Léon-Dufour, *Resurrection and the Message of Easter* (London, 1974) p. 204; W.F. Orr and J.A. Walter, *1 Corinthians* (New York, 1976) pp. 321–22. As Bruce remarks, "there is no good reason for regarding" the appearance reported by 1 Corinthians 15:6 "as a variant account of the Pentecostal event of Ac 2.1–41" (*1 and 2 Corinthians,* p. 141).

16. J.P. Lemonon observes that, whereas the third and fourth chapters of Galatians refer eighteen times to the Spirit, the first two chapters (where Paul writes of his original vocation and subsequent relations with the other apostles) never mention the Spirit. Lemonon explains this silence as due to Paul's desire to show that his vocation did not come through some action of the Spirit but through an appearance of the risen Jesus ("L'Esprit Saint dans le corps paulinien," *Dictionnaire de la Bible Supplément,* vol. 11 [Paris, 1986] col. 241).

17. See H. Kessler, *Sucht den Lebenden nicht bei den Toten: Die Auferstehung Jesu Christi* (Düsseldorf, 1985) pp. 155–56.

18. In translating, "*vivae totius Ecclesiae Traditionis* (DV 12) the Flannery version weakens the reference to Chapter Two of *Dei Verbum* by omitting "living" and giving us simply "the tradition of the entire church."

19. See Appendix One.

APPENDIX ONE: A NEGLECTED CONCILIAR INTERVENTION

On October 5, 1964, the Melkite archbishop Neophytos Edelby delivered a speech on the interpretation of the scriptures during a four day (October 1–2, 5–6, 1964) discussion of *De Divina Revelatione,* a draft which in its final form was promulgated by the council as *Dei Verbum.* The text of his speech is found in *Acta Synodalia Sacrosancti Concilii Oecumenici Vaticani Secundi,* vol. 3, part 3 (Vatican, 1974), pp. 306–08. In their *Third Session. Council Speeches of Vatican II* (Glen Rock: Paulist Press, 1966) pp. 79–97, W.K. Leahy and A.T. Massimini published an English translation of six speeches from that October 1964 debate on *De Divina Revelatione.* Those six speeches were all worth having in English. The Leahy/Massimini volume would have been considerably enriched at that point if it had also included a seventh speech, that of Archbishop Edelby. This appendix intends to remedy that long-standing omission.

From the many valuable points briefly mentioned by Archbishop Edelby, let me emphasize these. We should interpret the scriptures in the light of the temporal "missions" of the incarnate Word and the Holy Spirit. Second, being a liturgical and prophetic reality, the scriptures belong in a special way to the church's proclamation and worship. There the Holy Spirit witnesses through the scriptures to the risen Christ, who in turn reveals his Father within the whole context of salvation history. Third, tradition relates to salvation history as a kind of epiclesis or theophany of the Holy Spirit. Hence, fourth, the scriptures should be interpreted within the entire plan of salvation history. Finally, the "apophatic" nature of revelation means that the divine mystery goes beyond not only any theological reflections but even the text of the Bible itself.

Here follows my translation of the archbishop's speech, which focused on paragraph 12 of *De Divina Revelatione* (= DV 12).

"Venerable fathers, as regards the properly theological principles for interpreting sacred scripture, let me put forward for your consideration the witness of the eastern churches. I am certain that our Orthodox brethren will recognize in my presentation authentic teaching which is common to them and to us.

"Undoubtedly the timidity found in paragraph 12 of this draft comes from the difficulty which the church experiences of emerging from the post-tridentine problematic. Yet the period of controversy with the reformers should now be over. For the eastern churches, as for the new churches of Africa and Asia, a preoccupation of this kind does not exist.

"The reformers set over against each other scripture and the church. The main remedy for this, as we think, pseudo-problem consists in returning to the intimate mystery of the church, while rejecting an excessively juridical, almost nominalistic, mentality in which the theology both of the reformers and of our theologians has been shut up. One cannot separate the mission of the Holy Spirit from the mission of the incarnate Word. This is the first theological principle for any interpretation of sacred scripture.

"It should not be forgotten that beyond the auxiliary disciplines of any kind, the final goal of Christian exegesis is the spiritual understanding of sacred scripture in the light of the risen Christ, just as our Lord himself taught the apostles according to Luke 24.

"A second principle: Sacred scripture is a *liturgical* and *prophetic* reality. It is proclamation rather than a written book. It is the witness of the Holy Spirit to Christ. The principal and privileged time for this witness is the celebration of the eucharistic liturgy. Through this witness of the Holy Spirit, the saving plan ("economy") of the Word reveals the Father. The post-tridentine controversy, however, sees in sacred scripture first and foremost a written norm. But the eastern church sees rather in sacred scripture under the appearances of a human word a certain consecration of salvation history which cannot be separated from the eucharistic consecration in which the whole body of Christ is summed up ("recapitulated").

"A third principle: This consecration requires some kind of *epiclesis*—that is to say, the invocation and the action of the Holy Spirit. But epiclesis is precisely sacred tradition. *Thus tradition is the epiclesis of salvation history,* namely, the Holy Spirit's theophany without which the world's history is incomprehensible and sacred scripture remains a dead letter. This idea could be developed at greater length when dealing in line twenty-three with "the living tradition of the church." Thus our proposal is inserted into the intimate mystery of the church—that is to say, into the mystery of the people of God gathered through the Holy Spirit to become the body of Christ in its maturity.

"This gives rise also to the fourth principle, according to which sacred scripture should be interpreted within *the totality of salvation history.* At the first stage, namely, the Holy Spirit brings about salvific events and some kind of human community which is to be simultaneously the witness and the protagonist of such events. The Old Testament books are the first epiphany of God among his people. At a second stage, the saving events [literally, "event"] and the community are brought to an issue, in a definitive way, in Christ Jesus: this is the saving plan ("economy") of the incarnate Word, of whom the New Testament books are as it were a unique epiphany. Finally, at a third stage— namely, in the last times in which we live—the Holy Spirit is personally poured out so as to make present in the whole of history the saving plan ("economy") of the incarnate Word and the power of his resurrection: this is the saving plan ("economy") of the Spirit—that is to say, sacred tradition in the age of the church.

"Hence, it appears that tradition, or the church, in handing on the outpouring of the saving plan ("economy") of the Word, is essentially *liturgy.* The law of praying is the law of believing (*lex orandi, lex credendi*). We began the work of this most holy council with the mystery of the sacred liturgy, from which we passed to the sacramentality of the collegial episcopate, so as to reach at the end the whole mystery of tradition which is the mystery of the church.

"From all the ways of thinking which we may apply to the interpretation of sacred scripture, one touches the living criterion of this interpretation. The Spirit is the Spirit of the body of Christ. Tradition, therefore, should be regarded and lived above all in *the light of the sacrament of apostolicity—that is to say, the episcopate.* This liturgical and prophetic sign is also a kind of epiclesis of the unity in unfailing faith of the people of God. In this sense it would be desirable, let me say in parenthesis, that the infallibility of the successor of Peter should be better set forth according to this mystery of epiclesis. For authority in the church, as a juridical reality, comes from a liturgical and prophetic reality, and not vice versa, just as a canonical mission is not the source of episcopal orders [literally, "order"].

"Finally, a last but not least principle is this: *the meaning of mystery.* The God who reveals himself is a "hidden God." Revelation should not make us forget the depths of the triune God's life, which the faithful people live but can in no way exhaust. The eastern church says that revelation is above all "apophatic"—that is to say, it is lived in mystery before it can be expressed in words. Within the church this apophatic characteristic of revelation is the foundation for those riches of tradition, which are always alive. One of the causes of the difficulties which theology has experienced in these last [few] centuries consists precisely in this fact that theologians wanted to imprison the mystery in formulas. But the fullness of the mystery transcends not only theological formulation but even the limits of the letter of sacred scriptures."

APPENDIX TWO: *DEI VERBUM:* A BIBLIOGRAPHY

[VATICAN II'S DOGMATIC CONSTITUTION ON DIVINE REVE-LATION (*DEI VERBUM*): A Bibliography prepared by Joseph Cassar, S.J. and Gerald O'Collins, S.J.]

The absence of any adequate bibliography on *Dei Verbum* prompted the preparation of this one. The bibliographies prepared by Franzini (1978), Pfeiffer (1982), Waldenfels (1977), and Kubis (1968) were very useful but incomplete even when they appeared (see below under 2.2). Moreover, other publications on *Dei Verbum* have come out since they were published in the 1970s or early 1980s. In our bibliography we have tried to be as complete as possible: from 1965 to mid-1991. Our work was made considerably easier by the listings on *Dei Verbum* which have apepared in the *Elenchus Bibliographicus* of the *Ephemerides Theologicae Lovanienses* and the *Elenchus Bibliographicus Biblicus* (compiled by Peter Nober [till 1978] and Robert North [from 1979 onward, and known as the *Elenchus Bibliographicus of Biblica*).

It may seem puzzling that it has taken nearly three decades before anyone provided anything like a complete bibliography. One reason for this lack comes from the fact that there have been very few doctoral theses on *Dei Verbum*. A strong doctoral candidate is just the kind of person likely to gather and publish such a bibliography. Apart from A. Franzini, M.A. Molina Palma and R.H. Miller, we have not traced any other theses on *Dei Verbum* that have been published, either completely or in part. Three doctoral dissertations involving *Dei Verbum* are currently being written at the Gregorian University but have not yet been presented and defended.

As the reader will see, our bibliography includes not only items that have appeared in English, French, German, Italian, Portuguese and Spanish but also in other languages, in particular those of central and eastern Europe. There are a fair number of listings from Poland, including a 1968 book edited by the future Pope John Paul II.

178

We begin with the translations of *Dei Verbum* that have been published in the languages officially used at the Gregorian. Some of these translations have an enhanced value because they appear together with the original Latin text.

Some comments on *Dei Verbum* have the advantage that they come from bishops who actively contributed to the documents of Vatican II (see Butler and Wojtyla below). Other comments and commentaries have been offered by *periti* who were not only officially appointed to assist the bishops at the council but who also in various ways worked on the preparation of *Dei Verbum* (see Baum, Betti, Congar, de Lubac, Grillmeier, Kerrigan, Ratzinger, Rigaux and Smulders below). Further valuable material has been published by such scholars as Alonso Schökel, de la Potterie, Dulles, Dupuy, Feiner and Latourelle who, although not official *periti,* followed the council's proceedings closely and intelligently.

Several non-Catholic observers at the council (see Cullmann, Schutz and Thurian below) recorded their helpful reflections on *Dei Verbum.* While unable to be such an observer, Karl Barth offered some valuable reflections on the text (see 2.3 below).

As an attentive reading of our bibliography will show, the great wave of work on *Dei Verbum* goes back to the late 1960s and the early 1970s. The twentieth anniversary of the document in 1985 encouraged a minor burst of writing, especially from Spanish scholars. As will be argued in this book, there is still much to be done in retrieving and receiving *Dei Verbum* and, in general, the range of Vatican II's teaching that is significant for fundamental theology. Nevertheless, it is satisfying to note how the reception of *Dei Verbum* has often expressed itself through the fact that works in biblical studies and fundamental theology often contain specific chapters or sections on *Dei Verbum* (see, for example, Brown, Martini and Pfeiffer below).

We are both strongly convinced of the enduring value of *Dei Verbum.* A recent (Lutheran) introduction to the theology of the New Testament repeatedly stressed the need to recognize the deep link between revelation and salvation, a theme which emerges clearly from *Dei Verbum* (see H. Hübner, *Biblische Theologie des Neuen Testaments,* vol. 1, [Göttingen, 1990]). The present book has hoped to illustrate how two further themes from *Dei Verbum* (God's self-communication in art. 6 and human experience in art. 8 and 14) have been taken up and developed in subsequent magisterial teaching. The question of the need not only to practice but also to go beyond merely historical exegesis (see *Dei Verbum,* art. 12) has gained rather than lost importance (see the 1991 official Vatican response to *The Final Report* produced by ARCIC, the Anglican-Roman

Catholic International Commission). These are just some of the questions from *Dei Verbum* which have maintained their lasting relevance.

1. THE TEXT OF "DEI VERBUM"

"Constitutio Dogmatica de Divina Revelatione." In *Acta Apostolicae Sedis* 58 (1966) 817–35.

"Constitutio Dogmatica de Divina Revelatione." In *Sacrosanctum Oecumenicum Concilium Vaticanum II—Constitutiones, Decreta, Declarationes* (Vatican, 1966) 421–47.

"Dogmatic Constitution on Divine Revelation." In *The Documents of Vatican II,* eds. W.M. Abbott and J. Gallagher (New York, 1966) 111–28.

"Dogmatic Constitution on Divine Revelation." In *Vatican Council II. The Conciliar and Post Conciliar Documents,* ed. A. Flannery. Revised ed. (Boston, 1988) 750–65.

"Dogmatic Constitution on Divine Revelation." In *Decrees of the Ecumenical Councils* [Latin and English text], ed. N.P. Tanner, vol. 2 (London–Georgetown, 1990) 971–81.

"Constitution dogmatique sur la Révélation divine." In *Vatican II. Enseignements, éducation, culture. Receuil de textes conciliaires latin/français.* Collection Orientations (Paris, 1966).

"Constitution dogmatique sur la Révélation divine. Texte latin et traduction française." *Nouvelle Revue Théologique* 88 (1966) 170–88.

"Constitution dogmatique 'Dei Verbum'." In *Vatican II. Les seize documents conciliaires. Texte intégral,* ed. P.-A. Martin. Collection La Pensée Chrétienne (Montréal–Paris, ²1967) 101–20.

"La Révélation divine 'Dei Verbum'. Constitution dogmatique." In *Concile Oecuménique Vatican II. Constitutions–Décrets–Déclarations.* Trans. G. Martelet (Paris, 1967) 123–46.

"La Révélation divine. Constitution dogmatique 'Dei Verbum'. Texte et traduction française." Trans. J.-P Torrell. In *La Révélation divine,* ed. B.-D. Dupuy. Collection Unam Sanctam 70a (Paris, 1968) 19–57.

"Dogmatische Konstitution über die göttliche Offenbarung." In *Vatikanum II. Vollständige Ausgabe der Konzilsbeschlüsse,* ed. K.W. Kraemer (Osnabrück, ²1966) 215–35.

Dogmatische Konstitution über die göttliche Offenbarung." In *Kleines Konzilskompendium. Sämtliche Texte des Zweiten Vatikanums mit Einführungen und ausführlichem Sachregister,* eds. K. Rahner and H. Vorgrimler. Herderbücherei, 270 (Freiburg–Basel–Wein, ²²1990) 367–82.

Costituzione dogmatica sulla divina Rivelazione." In *Enchiridion Vaticanum. Documenti del Concilio Vaticano II. Testo ufficiale e traduzione italiana.* Revised and enlarged (Bologna, ⁹1971) 488–517.

"Costituzione dogmatica 'Dei Verbum' sulla divina rivelazione." In *I Documenti del Concilio Vaticano II* (Milano, ⁷1989) 151–69.

"Costituzione dogmatica sulla divina rivelazione." In *Conciliorum Oecumenicorum Decreta* [Latin and Italian text], eds. G. Alberigo et al. (Bologna, 1991) 971–81.

"Costituzione dogmatica su 'La divina rivelazione'." In *Tutti i Documenti del Concilio* (Milano–Roma, ¹⁷1991) 81–96.

"Constitución dogmática sobre la divina Revelación." In *Vaticano II. Documentos* (Madrid, ³⁴1979) 118–33.

For the drafts, reports, debates, written comments and voting, as well as the final text, see *Acta Synodalia Sacrosancti Concilii Oecumenici Vaticani Secundi,* 29 vols. (Vatican, 1970–86) I/3, 14–110, 121–370; III/3, 69–151, 181–276, 283–324, 330–66, 425–511, 782–941; IV/1, 49–50, 336–83, 418, 423–24, 574–75, 597; IV/2, 54–55, 301, 947–99; IV/5, 681–753; IV/6, 597–609, 687.

2. COMMENTARIES ON *DEI VERBUM*

Note: *In the opening section we have listed some translations of* "Dei Verbum" *in English, French, German, Italian and Spanish (in that order). Some other texts listed below have also appeared in various languages. In such cases, after giving the details for the English version, we have noted the existence of other versions. We have not done this for items from* "Concilium." *Where we refer to* "chap." *or* "art." *the reference is always to* "Dei Verbum."

2.1 ENTIRE BOOKS:

Alonso Schökel, L. *Comentarios a la Constitución 'Dei Verbum' sobre la divina Revelación.* BAC, 284 (Madrid, 1969).

———— and A.M. Artola eds. *La Palabra de Dios en la História de los Hombres. Comentario Temático a la Constitución 'Dei Verbum' del Vaticano II sobre la Divina Revelación* (Bilbao, 1991); a revised edition of the book just listed.

Arenhoevel, D. *Was sagt das Konzil über die Offenbarung?* (Mainz, 1967).

Associazione Biblica Italiana. *Costituzione Conciliare 'Dei Verbum'.* Atti della XX Settimana Biblica (Brescia, 1970).

Bea, A. *The Word of God and Mankind* (London, 1968); also in French, German, and Italian.

Betti, U., E. Florit, A. Grillmeier, A. Kerrigan, R. Latourelle, L. Randellini, and O. Semmelroth. *Commento alla Costituzione dogmatica sulla Divina Rivelazione* (Milano, 1966).

————, P. Dacquino, E. Galbiati, A.M. Javierre, C.M. Martini, and A. Penna. *La Costituzione Dogmatica sulla Divina Rivelazione.* With a Preface by A. Favale. Magistero Conciliare, 3. Revised and enlarged ed. (Torino, ³1967).

————. *La Dottrina del Concilio Vaticano II sulla Trasmissione della Rivelazione. Il Capitolo II della Costituzione dommatica 'Dei Verbum.'* Spicilegium Pontificii Athenei Antoniani, 26 (Roma, ²1985).

Blum, G.G. *Offenbarung und Überlieferung. Die dogmatische Konstitution 'Dei Verbum' des II. Vaticanums im Lichte altkirchlicher und moderner Theologie.* Forschungen zur systematischen und ökumenischen Theologie, 28 (Göttingen, 1971).

Buit, F.M. du, *La Parole de Dieu. Le Concile parle de la Bible.* Évangile, 69 (Paris, 1968).

De Lubac, H. *La Révélation divine. Commentaire du Préambule et du Chapitre I de la Constitution 'Dei Verbum' du Concile Vatican II* (Paris, ³1983).

Dupuy, B.-D. ed., H. De Lubac, C. Moeller, P. Grelot, L. Alonso-Schökel, X. Léon-Dufour, and A. Grillmeier. *La Révélation divine.* 2 vols. (Paris, 1968).

Franzini, A. *Tradizione e Scrittura. Il Contributo del Concilio Vaticano II.* Pubblicazioni del Pontificio Seminario Lombardo in Roma. Richerche di Scienze Teologiche, 15 (Brescia, 1978).

Granados, A. *La 'Palabra de Dios' en el Concilio Vaticano II.* Patmos, 127 (Madrid, 1966).

Harrington, W. and L. Walsh. *Vatican II on Revelation* (Dublin, 1967).

Höslinger, N. *Zeit der Bibel. Die Bibel im Leben der Christen nach dem 2. Vatikanischen Konzil* (Klosterneuburg, 1967).

Indices verborum et locutionum decretorum Concilii Vaticani II. Constitutio dogmatica de Divina Revelatione 'Dei Verbum'. Testi e ricerche di scienze religiose, 11 (Firenze, 1969).

Lyonnet, S., K. Hruby, I. de la Potterie, L. Alonso Schökel, M. Zerwick and C.M. Martini. *La Bibbia nella Chiesa dopo la 'Dei Verbum', studi sulla costituzione conciliare.* Collana Punti scottanti di teologia, eds. V. Schurr and B. Häring (Roma, 1969).

Magrassi, M., B. Pastorino and M. Turicani, eds. *La Parola di Dio e il Concilio.* Temi conciliari, 4 (Milano, 1968).

Molina Palma, M.A. *La interpretación de la Escritura en el Espíritu. Estudio histórico y teológico de un principio hermeneútico de la Constitución 'Dei Verbum' 12* (Burgos, 1987).

Nicolau, M. *Escritura y Revelación según el Concilio Vaticano II. Texto y comentario de la Constitución dogmática 'Dei Verbum'* (Madrid, 1967).

Pacomio, L., ed. *Dei Verbum: Genesi della Costituzione sulla Divina Rivelazione. Schemi annotati in sinossi* (Torino, 1971).

Perarnau, J. *Constitución dogmática sobre la Revelación divina* (Castellón de la Plana, 1966).

Persson, P.E. *Skriften och Kyrkan. Studiepan till Andra Vatikankonciliets dogmatiska kontitution Om den gudomliga uppenberelsen* (Stockholm, 1967).

Sandfuchs, W., ed. *Die Kirche und das Wort Gottes. Eine Einführung in die dogmatische Konstitution 'Dei Verbum'* (Würzburg, 1967).

Schutz, R. and M. Thurian. *Revelation. A Protestant View. The Dogmatic Constitution on Divine Revelation. A Commentary* (Westminster–Amsterdam, 1968); also in French and Italian.

Semmelroth, O. and M. Zerwick. *Vaticanum II über das Wort Gottes.* Stuttgarter Bibelstudien, 16 (Stuttgart, 1966).

Silanes, N., A. Gonzáles Nuñez, J.R. Scheifler, A. Ortega, I. Saade, and J. Solano. *Dios al encuentro del hombre en la Constitución 'Dei Verbum'*. Semana de Estudios Trinitarios, 3 (Salamanca, 1970).

Stakemeier, E. *Die Konzilskonstitution über die göttliche Offenbarung. Werden, Inhalt und theologische Bedeutung* (Paderborn, [2]1967).

Stramare, T. *La Parola di Dio vivente nella Chiesa* (Napoli, 1968).

Tavard, G.H. *The Dogmatic Constitution on Divine Revelation of Vatican Council II* (London, 1966); also in French.

Toiviainen, K. *Kirkko ja Raamattu. Raamatun asema konstituution Dei Verbum valossa* [Church and Scripture. The place of Scripture in the light of the Constitution 'Dei Verbum']. Suomalaisen Teologinen Kirjallisuusseuran julkasuja, 83 (Helsinki, 1970).

Waldenfels, H. *Offenbarung: Das Zweite Vatikanische Konzil auf dem Hintergrund der neuren Theologie. Beiträge zur Ökumenischen Disput,* ed. H. Fries, no. 3 (München, 1969).

Welte, P. *T'ienchu ch'ishih te chiaoi hsienchang shihi* [Commentary on the Constitution on Divine Revelation] (Taichung, Taiwan, 1968).

Wojtyla, K., ed. *Idee przewodnie soborowej Konstytucji o Bozym Objawieniu* [The Main Ideas of the Conciliar Constitution on Divine Revelation] (Krakow, 1968).

2.2 SECTIONS OF BOOKS:

(*Note: the books in question are listed under either 2.1 or 2.2*)

Ahern, B. "Scriptural Aspects [of 'Dei Verbum']." In *Vatican II, An Interfaith Appraisal,* ed. J.H. Miller, 54–67.

Aland, K. "De duplici fonte revelationis. Ein Bericht zum Problem von Schrift und Tradition auf dem II. Vaticanum." In *Erneuerung der einen Kirche. Arbeiten zur Kirchengeschichte und Konfessionskunde.* Heinrich Bornkamm zum 65. Geburtstag gewidmet. Ed. J. Lell (Göttingen, 1966) 168–78.

Alonso Schökel, L. "Sur l'Ancien Testament." [On chap. IV] In *La Révélation divine,* ed. B.-D. Dupuy, vol. 2, 383–400.

————. "E' attuale il linguaggio del Vecchio Testamento?" In *Bibbia nella Chiesa,* by S. Lyonnet et al., 109–33.

————. "Carattere Storico della Rivelazione." In *Costituzione Conciliare,* by Associazione Biblica Italiana, 31–56.

————. "Unidad y Composición de la Constitución 'Dei Verbum.' In *La Palabra de Dios,* eds. L. Alonso Schökel and A.M. Artola, 167–76.

————. "Unidad y Composición." [On art. 2] In *ibid.,* 179–82.

————. "Carácter histórico de la Revelación." [On art. 3] In *ibid.,* 183–205.

————. "Revelación y doctrina." [On arts. 5–6] In *ibid.,* 229–35.

————. "Unidad y Composición." [On art. 7] In *ibid.,* 239–41.

————. "El dinamismo de la tradición." [On art. 8] In *ibid.,* 243–83.

————. "Unidad y Composición." [On chap. III] In *ibid.,* 335–36.

———. "Utilidad de la Escritura." In *ibid.*, 383–84.

———. "Interpretación de la Sagrada Escritura." [On art. 12] In *ibid.*, 385–417.

———. "La Condescendencia de Dios." [On art. 13] In *ibid.*, 427–29.

———. "La Interpretación de la Escritura. Comentario Literal." [On arts. 14–16] In *ibid.*, 433–54.

———. "Comentario temático. [On arts. 14–16] El Antiguo Testamento, incorporado al Nuevo." In *ibid.*, 455–89.

———. "Excelencia del Nuevo Testamento." [On art. 17] In *ibid.*, 493–95.

———. "Unidad y Composición." [On chap. IV] In *ibid.*, 583–85.

———. "Pan de Vida." [On art. 21] In *ibid.*, 587–606.

———. "Perspectivas." In *ibid.*, 669–75.

Alszeghy, Z. " 'Sensus Fidei' and Development of Dogma." In *Vatican II. Assessment and Perspectives*, ed. R. Latourelle, vol. 1, 138–56; also in French, Italian and Spanish.

Antón A. "Tradizione." *Dizionario del Concilio Ecumenico*, ed. S. Garofalo, cols. 1923–35.

———. "La comunidad creyente, portadora de la revelación." [On art. 10] In *La Palabra de Dios*, eds. L. Alonso Schökel and A.M. Artola, 285–330.

———. "El Ministerio de la Palabra." In *ibid.*, 631–41.

Artola, A.M. "La inspiración y la inerrancia según la Constitución 'Dei Verbum'." In *XXVI Semana Española de Teología 2 (1969)* 471–96.

———. "La inspiración de la sagrada Escritura." [On art. 11a] In *La Palabra de Dios*, eds. L. Alonso Schökel and A.M. Artola, 337–57.

Ashton, J. "Cristo, mediador y plenitud de la revelación." [On art. 4] In *ibid.*, 207–28.

Asveld, P. "Theologia Anglicana de doctrinis fundamentalibus." In *Acta Congressus,* ed. A. Schönmetzer, 506–12.

Barsotti, D. "Sacra Scriptura Eodem Spiritu Quo scripta est etiam legenda et interpretanda ('Dei Verbum' 12)." In *Costituzione Conciliare,* by Associazione Biblica Italiana, 301–20.

Barth, K. "Conciliorum tridentini et vaticani I inhaerens vestigiis?" In *La Révélation divine,* ed. B.-D. Dupuy, vol. 2, 513–22.

Bea, A. "Die göttliche Inspiration der Heiligen Schrift und ihre Auslegung." In *Die Kirche und das Wort Gottes,* ed. W. Sandfuchs, 63–76.

Benoît, P. "De indole veritatis in Sacra Scriptura." In *Acta Congressus,* ed. A. Schönmetzer, 513–23.

Betti, U. "Cronistoria della Costituzione Dogmatica sulla Divina Rivelazione." In *Commento,* by U. Betti et al., 33–67.

———. "La Trasmissione della Divina Rivelazione." [On chap. II] In *ibid.*, 91–117.

———. "Storia della Costituzione dogmatica 'Dei Verbum'." In *Costituzione Dogmatica,* by U. Betti et al., 13–67.

———. "La trasmissione della divina Rivelazione." [On chap. II] In *ibid.*, 219–62.

———. "De sacra Traditione iuxta Constitutionem dogmaticam 'Dei Verbum'." In *Acta Congressus,* ed. A. Schönmetzer, 524–34.

———. "Le magistère de l'Église au service de la Parole de Dieu: à propos du nr. 10 de la Constitution dogmatique 'Dei Verbum'." In *Au service de la Parole du Dieu,* ed. C. Troisfontaines, 245–61.

Beumer, J. *La tradition orale* (Paris, 1967) 225–34.

Bianchi, E. "The Centrality of the Word of God." In *The Reception of Vatican II*, ed. G. Alberigo et al. (Washington, 1987) 115–36; also in French, German and Italian.

Boschi, B. "Impostazione del problema ermeneutico dalla 'Providentissimus' alla 'Dei Verbum'." In *Costituzione Conciliare*, by Associazione Biblica Italiana, 283–99.

Bouillard, H. "Le concept de révélation de Vatican I à Vatican II." In *Révélation de Dieu et langage des hommes*, ed. J. Audinet (Paris, 1972) 35–49.

Boyer, C. "De propositione Concilii: 'Quo fit ut Ecclesia certitudinem suam de omnibus revelatis non per solam Sacram Scripturam hauriat' (Constitutio dogmatica de divina Revelatione, c. 2, n. 9)." In *Acta Congressus*, ed. A. Schönmetzer, 535–39.

Brown, R.E. and T.A. Collins. "Church Pronouncements." In *New Jerome Biblical Commentary*, eds. R.E. Brown et al. (Englewood Cliffs, 1990) 1166–74 (esp. 1169).

Butler, C. "The Constitution on Divine Revelation." In *Vatican II, An Interfaith Appraisal*, ed. J.H. Miller, 43–53.

———. "Revelation and Inspiration." In *The Theology of Vatican II*. Rev. ed. (London, 1981) 25–51.

Caba, J. "El problema de la historicidad de los evangelios en el concilio Vaticano II: Constitución dogmática 'Dei Verbum'." Chap. in *De los evangelios al Jesús histórico. Introducción a la Cristología* (Madrid, ²1980) 50–73; also in Italian.

———. "En torno a los autores de los evangelios: Constitución dogmática 'Dei Verbum'." Chap. in *ibid.*, 107–17.

———. "Historicity of the Gospels ('Dei Verbum,' 19). Genesis and Fruits of the Conciliar Text." In *Vatican II*, ed. R. Latourelle, vol. 1, 299–320; also in French, Italian and Spanish.

Casanova, A. "Aspects du Concile: la Révélation au XXe siècle." Chap. in *La Nouvelle Critique* (Paris, 1966) 28–48.

Congar, Y.M.J. "Une deuxième condition: La question de la Révélation." In *La nouvelle image de l'Église. Bilan du Concile Vatican II,* ed. B. Lambert (Tours, 1967) 217–38.

Coppens, J. "Aspectus luminosi necnon umbrosi Constitutionis 'Dei Verbum'." In *Acta Congressus,* ed. A. Schönmetzer, 540–49.

Cullmann, O. "Die kritische Rolle der Heiligen Schrift." In *Die Autorität,* ed. J.C. Hampe, vol. 1, 189–97.

Dacquino, P. "L'ispirazione dei libri sacri e la loro interpretazione." [On chap. III] in *Costituzione Dogmatica,* by U. Betti et al., 263–322.

de la Potterie, I. "La verità della Sacra Scrittura secondo la dottrina del Concilio." [On chap. III] In *Bibbia nella Chiesa,* by S. Lyonnet et al., 77–107.

———. "Interpretation of Holy Scripture in the Spirit in Which It Was Written (Dei Verbum 12,3)." In *Vatican II,* ed. R. Latourelle, vol. 1, 220–66; also in French, Italian and Spanish.

Delhaye, P. "Quelques souvenirs du Concile." In *Au service de la Parole de Dieu,* ed. C. Troisfontaines, 149–77 (esp. 164–71).

de Lubac, H. "Commentaire du chapitre I sur la Révélation." In *La Révélation divine,* ed. B.-D. Dupuy, vol. 1, 159–302.

———. "Constitution 'Dei Verbum'." In *Essor et permanence de la Révélation,* by M. Philipon et al. (Paris, 1970) 265–78.

Dulles, A. "The Constitution on Divine Revelation in Ecumenical Perspective." Chap. in *Revelation and the Quest for Unity* (Washington, 1968) 82–99.

———. "Das I. Vatikan und die Wiedergewinnung der Tradition." In *Glaube im Prozeß,* eds. E. Klinger and K. Wittstadt, 546–62.

Duncker, P.G. "Transmission of Divine Revelation." In *Biblical Studies in Contemporary Thought,* ed. M. Ward (Burlington, 1976) 14–26.

Dupont, J. "Storicità dei Vangeli e metodo storico nella 'Dei Verbum'." In *A vent'anni dal Concilio*, eds. S. Consoli et al. (Palermo, 1983), 51–73.

Dupuy, B.-D. "Historique de la Constitution." In *La Révélation divine*, ed. B.-D. Dupuy, vol. 1, 61–117.

———. "La portée de la Constitution 'Dei Verbum' pour le dialogue oecuménique." In *ibid.*, vol. 2, 557–66.

Eicher, P. *Offenbarung. Prinzip neuzeitlicher Theologie* (München, 1977) 502–43.

Feiner, J. "La Contribution du Secrétariat pour l'unité des chrétiens à la Constitution dogmatique sur la Révélation divine." In *La Révélation divine*, ed. B.-D. Dupuy, vol. 1, 119–53.

Ferrier-Welti, M. "La Constitution sur la Révélation divine et la controverse entre catholiques et protestants." In *Points de vue de théologiens protestants. Études sur les décrets du Concile Vatican II*, by J. Bosc et al. Unam Sanctam, 64 (Paris, 1967) 47–73.

Filthaut, T., ed. *Umkehr und Erneuerung. Kirche nach dem Konzil* (Mainz, 1966). See entries under Kasper and Lengeling below.

Fisichella, R. *La rivelazione: evento e credibilità*. Corso di Teologia Sistematica, 2 (Bologna, 1985) 79–84, 122–31, 157–62, 171–77.

——— and R. Latourelle. "Dei Verbum." In *Dizionario di Teologia Fondamentale*, eds. R. Latourelle and R. Fisichella (Assisi, 1990) 279–91.

Floristan, C. "La Renovación Bíblica (Constitución dogmatica 'Dei Verbum' sobre la revelación divina)." In *Vaticano II, Un Concilio Pastoral*. Pedal, 208 (Salamanca, 1990) 61–79.

Florit, E. Introduction to *Commento*, by U. Betti et al., v–xxi.

Florkowski, E. "Objawienie Boze wedlug [Divine Revelation according to] Konstytucji 'Dei Verbum'." In *Idee przewodnie*, ed. K. Wojtyla, 31–43.

Fries, H. "Die theologische Situation vor dem Konzil." In *Die Kirche und das Wort Gottes,* ed. W. Sandfuchs, 17–26.

———. "Kirche und Offenbarung Gottes." In *Die Autorität,* ed. J.C. Hampe, vol. 1, 155–69.

Galbiati, E. "Il Nuovo Testamento." [On chap. V] In *Costituzione Dogmatica,* by U. Betti et al., 367–415.

Garofalo, S., ed. *Dizionario del Concilio Ecumenico Vaticano Secondo.* Roma, 1969.

———. "Scrittura Sacra." In *ibid.,* cols. 1783–825.

———. "Testamento, Antico e Nuovo." In *ibid.,* cols. 1903–16.

———. "Vangeli." In *ibid.,* cols. 1964–68.

Geenen, G. *Magistère de l'Église, dépôt de la foi et progrès du dogme dans la constitution 'Dei Verbum' du concile Vatican II.* Miscellanea Lateranense (Roma, 1975), 46–84.

Gesteira, M. "Comentario a la Constitución dogmática sobre la divina Revelación." In *La Divina Revelación* (Madrid, 1965) 5–48.

Gnutek, W. "Drugi Sobor Watykanski o Tradycji swietej. [The Second Vatican Council on Tradition]." In *Idee przewodnie,* ed. K. Wojtyla, 45–65.

González, Nuñez, A. "História y Revelación." In *Dios al encuentro,* by N. Silanes et al., 21–55.

Gonzáles Ruiz, J.-M. "Der Gebrauch der Bibel in der Kirche des Konzils." In *Die Autorität,* ed. J.C. Hampe, vol. 1, 232–39.

Grant, F.C. "A Response [to 'Dei Verbum]." In *The Documents of Vatican II,* eds. W.M. Abbott and J. Gallagher, 129–32.

———. "Divine Revelation." In *The Second Vatican Council, Studies by Eight Anglican Observers,* ed. B.C. Pawley (London–New York, 1967) 28–53.

Grelot, P. "L'inspiration de l'Écriture et son interprétation." [On chap. III] In *La Révélation divine,* ed. B.-D. Dupuy, vol. 2, 347–80.

Grillmeier, A. "L'Ispirazione Divina e l'interpretazione della Sacra Scrittura." [On chap. III] In *Commento,* by U. Betti et al., 118–50.

———. "Chapter III. The Divine Inspiration and the Interpretation of Sacred Scripture." In *Commentary,* ed. H. Vorgrimler, Vol. 3, 199–246.

———. "La sainte Écriture dans la vie de l'Église." [On Chap. VI] In *La Révélation divine,* ed. B.-D. Dupuy, vol. 2, 435–60.

Grzybek, S. "Rys historyczny [The historical development of] Konstytucji 'Dei Verbum'." In *Idee przewodnie,* ed. K. Wojtyla, 12–30.

———. "Pismo swiete historia zbawienia [Sacred Scripture Is the History of Salvation]." In *ibid.,* 89–120.

Hampe, J.C. ed. *Die Autorität der Freiheit. Gegenwart des Konzils und Zukunft der Kirche im ökumenischen Disput.* Vol. 1 (München, ²1967). See entries under Cullmann, Fries, Gonzáles Ruiz, Ott, Reid, Schmithals, Stakemeier, Zerwick.

Holstein, H. "De testimonio Traditionis in fide populi christiani." In *Acta Congressus,* ed. A. Schönmetzer, 550–54.

Homerski, J. "O natchnieniu i interpretacji Pisma Swietego [On the inspiration and interpretation of sacred Scripture]." In *Idee przewodnie,* ed. K. Wojtyla, 67–88.

Ibáñez Arana, A. "La Constitución 'Dei Verbum' y los estudios bíblicos." In *Balance del Concilio Vaticano II a los veinte años* (Vitoria, 1985) 58–82.

Jacob, R. "La verdad de la Sagrada Escritura." [On art. 11b] In *La Palabra de Dios,* eds. L. Alonso Schökel and A.M. Artola, 359–83.

Javierre, A.M. " 'Prooemium' (n. 1)." In *Costituzione Dogmatica,* by U. Betti et al., 155–74.

———. "La Divina Rivelazione." [On chap. I] In *ibid.,* 175–218.

Kasper, W. "Schrift-Tradition-Verkündigung." In *Umkehr und Erneuerung. Kirche nach dem Konzil,* ed. T. Filthaut, 13–41.

Kerrigan, A. "Il Vecchio Testamento." [On chap. IV] In *Commento,* by U. Betti et al., 151–81.

Klinger, E. and K. Wittstadt, eds. *Glaube im Prozeß. Christsein nach dem II. Vatikanum.* Festschrift für Karl Rahner (Freiburg–Basel–Wien, 1984) 66–120, 514–62. See entries in 2.2 under Dulles, Sauer, Schauf and Smulders.

Kniazeff, A. "Réflexions sur les chapitres III à VI de la Constitution sur la Révélation divine." In *La Révélation divine,* ed. B.-D. Dupuy, vol. 2, 541–56.

Kubis, A. "Bibliografia Konstytucji soborowej o Bozym Objawieniu [A Bibliography on the conciliar Constitution on Divine Revelation]." In *Idee przewodnie,* ed. K. Wojtyla, 192–208.

Kudasiewicz, J. "Powstanie i historycznosc Ewangelii [The origins and historicity of the Gospels]." In *ibid.,* 121–52.

Latourelle, R. "Revelation and its transmission according to the Constitution 'Dei Verbum'." Chap. in *Theology of Revelation* (New York, 1966) 453–88; also in French, Italian, Portuguese and Spanish.

———. "La Rivelazione." [Commentary on chap. I] In *Commento,* ed. U. Betti, 68–90.

———. "Rivelazione." *Dizionario del Concilio,* ed. S. Garofalo, cols. 1729–45.

———. "Il Vaticano II e il tema della Rivelazione." In *Mysterium Salutis,* ed. J. Feiner and M. Löhrer. Vol. 1, part 1 (Brescia, ³1972) 238–55.

———. "La Costituzione Dogmatica sulla Divina Rivelazione." In *I Libri di Dio,* eds. C.M. Martini and L. Pacomio, 242–69.

———, ed. *Vatican II. Assessment and Perspectives.* Vol. 1 (New York–Mahwah, 1988); also in French, Italian and Spanish. See entries in

2.2 under Alszeghy, Caba, de la Potterie, Lyonnet, O'Collins and Vanni.

Laurentin, R. *Bilan du Concile. Histoire, Textes, Commentaires* (Paris, 1966) 153–57, 275–88.

Lengeling, E.J. "Liturgie: Dialog zwischen Gott und Mensch." In *Umkehr und Erneuerung. Kirche nach dem Konzil,* ed. T.I. Filthaut, 92–135.

Lengsfeld, P. "De mutua interpretatione S. Scripturae et dogmatum Traditionis." In *Acta Congressus,* ed. A. Schönmetzer, 555–59.

Léon-Dufour, X. "Sur le Nouveau Testament." [On chap. V] In *La Révélation divine,* ed. B.-D. Dupuy, vol. 2, 403–31.

Lera, J.M. " 'Sacrae paginae studium sit veluti anima Sacrae Theologiae' (Notas sobre el origen y procedencia de esta frase." In *Palabra y vida. Homenaje a J. Alonzo Diaz,* ed. A. Vargas Machuca and G. Ruiz. Miscellanea Comillas, 41 (Madrid, 1983) 411–22.

Leuba, J.L. "La Tradition à Montréal et à Vatican II: Convergences et differences." In *La Révélation divine,* ed. B.-D. Dupuy, vol. 2, 475–97.

Lohfink, N. "Bibel und Bibelwissenschaft nach dem Konzil." In *Bibelauslegung im Wandel* (Frankfurt, 1967) 13–28.

———. "Das heutige Verständnis der Schriftinspiration in der katholischen Theologie." In *Abhandlung zum christlich-jüdischen Dialog,* 2 (München, 1967) 15–26; cf. 195–98.

———. "Das Alte Testament." In *Die Kirche und das Wort Gottes,* ed. W. Sandfuchs, 77–94.

Lyonnet, S. "La nozione di rivelazione." [On chap. I] In *Bibbia nella Chiesa,* by S. Lyonnet et al., 9–37.

———. "L'unità dei due Testamenti ('Dei Verbum' 16)." Chap. in *Il Nuovo Testamento alla luce dell'Antico.* Studi Biblici Pastorali dell'Associazione Biblica Italiana, 3 (Brescia, 1972) 9–27.

————. "A Word on Chapters IV and VI of 'Dei Verbum'. The Amazing Journey Involved in the Process of Drafting of the Conciliar Text." In *Vatican II*, ed. R. Latourelle, vol. 1, 157–207; also in French, Italian and Spanish.

MacKenzie, R.A.F. "Introduction [to 'Dei Verbum']." In *The Documents of Vatican II*, eds. W.M. Abbott and J. Gallagher, 107–10.

Marangon, A. "Il Senso Cristiano dell'Antico Testamento." In *Costituzione Conciliare*, by Associazione Biblica Italiana, 343–65.

Martini, C.M. "La Sacra Scrittura nella vita della Chiesa." [On Chap. VI] In *Costituzione Dogmatica*, by U. Betti et al., 417–65.

————. "La Sacra Scrittura nutrimento e regola della predicazione e della religione." [On chap. VI] In *Bibbia nella Chiesa*, by S. Lyonnet and others, 157–72.

———— and L. Pacomio, eds. *I Libri di Dio* (Torino, 1975). See entry in 2.2 under Latourelle.

Mattioli, A. "Realtà e Senso della Pienezza della Rivelazione in Cristo." In *Costituzione Conciliare*, by Associazione Biblica Italiana, 57–110.

Miller, J.H. *Vatican II, An Interfaith Appraisal.* International Theological Conference, University of Notre Dame, March 20–26, 1966 (Notre Dame, 1966). See entries in 2.2 under Ahern, Butler and Minear.

Miller, R.H. *Revelation in Franz Rosenzweig's "The Star of Redemption" and in Vatican Council II's 'Dei Verbum'.* Dissertation, Northwestern University, 1978. Dissertation Abstracts (Ann Arbor) 39, 8 (1978–79) 4987.

Minear, P.S. "A Protestant Point of View [on 'Dei Verbum']." In *Vatican II, An Interfaith Appraisal*, ed. J.H. Miller, 68–88.

Moeller, C. "Le texte du chapitre II dans la seconde période du Concile (Sessions II, II, IV)." In *La Révélation divine*, ed. B.-D. Dupuy, vol 1, 305–44.

Neyrey, J.H. "Interpretation of Scripture in the Life of the Church." In *Vatican II: The Unfinished Agenda*, ed. L. Richard et al. (Mahwah, 1987) 33–46.

O'Collins. "Revelation Past and Present." In *Vatican II*, ed. R. Latourelle, vol. 1, 125–37; also in French, Italian and Spanish.

Ortega, A. "Jesucristo, plenitud de la Revelación." In *Dios al encuentro*, by N. Silanes et al., 79–137.

Ott, H. "Die Offenbarung Gottes nach dem Konzil." In *Die Autorität*, ed. J.C. Hampe, vol. 1, 169–74.

Padberg, R. "Neue Akzente der Glaubensverkündigung." In *Umkehr und Erneuerung. Kirche nach dem Konzil*, ed. T. Filthaut, 136–55.

Penna, A. "Il Vecchio Testamento." [On chap. IV] In *Costituzione Dogmatica*, by U. Betti et al., 323–66.

Petuchowski, J.J. and W. Strolz, eds. *Offenbarung im jüdischen und christlichen Glaubensverständnis*. Quaestiones disputatae, 92 (Freiburg–Basel–Wien, 1981). See entry in 2.2 under Seckler.

Pfeiffer, H. "Das Verständnis von Offenbarung im zweiten vatikanischen Konzil." In *Gott offenbart sich* (Frankfurt am Main–Bern, 1982) 55–240.

Plate, M. "Wort Gottes. Die Konstitution über die göttliche Offenbarung." Chap. in *Weltereignis Konzil*. (Freiburg–Basel–Wien, 1966) 229–50.

Quacquarelli, A. "Riscontro patristico della Dei Verbum." In Costituzione Conciliare, by Associazione Biblica Italiana, 19–29.

Rahner, K. "Kritische Anmerkungen zu Nr. 3 des dogmatischen Dekrets 'Dei Verbum' des II. Vatikanums." In *Neues Testament und Kirche*. In honour of R. Schnackenburg, ed. J. Gnilka (Freiburg, 1974) 543–49.

———. "On the 'History of Revelation' according to the Second Vatican Council." In *Theological Investigations*, vol. 16, trans. David Morland (London, 1979) 191–98.

Ramazzotti, B. "Studio sulla Costituzione 'Dei Verbum'." In *Presentazione dei sedici documenti del Concilio Ecumenico Vaticano II* (Verona, 1966) 91–145.

Randellini, L. "Il Nuovo Testamento." [On chap. V] In *Commento*, ed. U. Betti, 182–230.

Ratzinger, J. "Dogmatic Constitution on Divine Revelation. Origin and Background." In *Commentary*, ed. H. Vorgrimler, vol. 3, 155–66.

―――. "Preface." [On art. 1] In *ibid.*, vol. 3, 167–69.

―――. "Chapter I. Revelation Itself." In *ibid.*, vol. 3, 170–80.

―――. "Chapter II. The Transmission of Divine Revelation." In *ibid.*, vol. 3, 181–98.

―――. "Chapter VI. Sacred Scripture in the Life of the Church." In *ibid.*, vol. 3, 262–72.

Reid, J.K.S. "Die Heilige Schrift und das Vaticanum II." In *Die Autorität*, ed. J.C. Hampe, vol. 1, 223–31.

Rigaux, B. "Chapter IV. The Old Testament." In *Commentary*, ed. H. Vorgrimler, vol. 3, 247–51.

―――. "Chapter V. The New Testament." In *ibid.*, vol. 3, 252–61.

―――. "L'interprétation de l'Écriture selon la Constitution 'Dei Verbum'." In *Au Service de la Parole de Dieu*, ed. C. Troisfontaines, 262–89.

Ruiz, G. "Historia de la constitución 'Dei Verbum'." In *La Palabra de Dios*, eds. L. Alonso Schökel and A.M. Artola, 45–151.

Saade, I. "Espíritu, Iglesia y Revelación." In *Dios al encuentro*, by N. Silanes et al., 141–51.

Salvador, J. "A Verdade da Sagrada Escritura na 'Dei Verbum'." In *Atualidades Bíblicas*, ed. S. Voigt et al. (Petrópolis, 1971) 154–71.

Sánchez Caro, J.M. "Escritura y Teología." [On art. 24] In *La Palabra de Dios,* eds. L. Alonso Schökel and A.M. Artola, 607–29.

————. "La lectura eclesial de la Biblia." In *ibid.,* 643–67.

Sandfuchs, W. "Ein entscheidendes Dokument." In *Die Kirche und das Wort Gottes,* ed. W. Sandfuchs, 7–10.

Sauer, H. "Von den 'Quellen der Offenbarung' zur 'Offenbarung Selbst'. Zum theologischen Hintergrund der Auseinandersetzung um das Schema 'Über die göttliche Offenbarung' beim II. Vatikanischen Konzil." In *Glaube im Prozeß,* eds. E. Klinger and K. Wittstadt, 514–45.

Schauf, H. "Auf dem Wege zu der Aussage der dogmatischen Konstitution über die göttliche Offenbarung 'Dei Verbum' Art. 9 'quo fit ut Ecclesia certitudinem suam de omnibus revelatis non per solam Sacram Scripturam hauriat'." In *ibid.,* 66–98.

Scheffczyk, L. "Die Weitergabe der göttlichen Offenbarung." In *Die Kirche und das Wort Gottes,* ed. W. Sandfuchs, 45–61.

Scheifler, J. "El Dios de la Revelación." In *Dios al encuentro,* by N. Silanes et al., 59–76.

————. "Los Evangelios." [On arts. 18–19] In *La Palabra de Dios,* eds. L. Alonso Schökel and A.M. Artola, 497–557.

Schlink, E. "Écriture, Tradition et magistère selon la Constitution 'Dei Verbum'." In *La Révélation divine,* ed. B.-D. Dupuy, vol. 2, 499–511.

Schmitz, J. *Offenbarung in Wort und Tat* (Aschaffenburg, 1973) 47–56.

————. *Offenbarung* (Düsseldorf, 1988) 67–78.

————. "Das Christentum als Offenbarungsreligion im kirchlichen Bekenntnis." In *Handbuch der Fundamentaltheologie,* eds. W. Kern, H.J. Pottmeyer and M. Seckler. Vol. 2 Traktat Offenbarung (Freiburg–Basel–Wien, 1985) 15–28 (esp. 23–28); also in Italian.

Schmitz van Vorst, J. "Die Bibel im Brennpunkt." In *Kirche gestern–Kirche morgen* (Stuttgart, 1966) 187–97.

Schmithals, W. "Die Wahrheit der Heiligen Schrift und das Konzil." In *Die Autorität,* ed. J.C. Hampe, vol. 1, 197–208.

Schnackenburg, R. "Das Neue Testament." In *Die Kirche und das Wort Gottes,* ed. W. Sandfuchs, 95–128.

Schönmetzer, A. ed. *Acta Congressus Internationalis de Theologia Concilii Vaticani II* (Vatican City, 1968). See entries in 2.2 under Benoît, Betti, Boyer, Coppens, Holstein and Lengsfeld.

Schröffer, J. "Die Heilige Schrift im Leben der Kirche." In *ibid.,* ed. W. Sandfuchs, 109–24.

Schutz, R. and M. Thurian. "La Révélation selon le chapitre Ier de la Constitution." In *La Révélation divine,* ed. B.-D. Dupuy, vol. 2, 463–74.

Scrima, A. "Révélation et Tradition dans la Constitution dogmatique 'Dei Verbum' selon le point de vue orthodox." In *ibid.,* 523–39.

Seckler, M. "Dei Verbum religiose audiens: Wandlungen im christlichen Offenbarungsverständnis." In *Offenbarung im jüdischen und christlichen Offenbarungsverständnis,* eds. J.J. Petuchowski and W. Strolz, 214–36.

Seifert, P. "Die Bibel–das Buch der ganzen Christenheit." In *Erneuerung oder Restauration,* ed. C. Klinkhammer (Essen, 1967) 101–15.

Semmelroth, O. "La Sacra Scrittura nella Vita della Chiesa." [On chap. VI] In *Commento,* ed. U. Betti, 231–41.

Senior, D. "Dogmatic Constitution on Divine Revelation 'Dei Verbum'." In *Vatican II and Its Documents. An American Reappraisal.* Theology and Life Series, 15, ed. T.E. O'Connell (Wilmington, 1986), 122–40.

Skydsgaard, K.E. "Schrift und Tradition. Eine vorläufige Untersuchung zur Entstehung und Aussage des Dokumentes Constitutio dogmatica de Divina Revelatione 'Dei Verbum'." In *Wir sind gefragt. Antworten evangelischer Konzilsbeobachter,* eds. F.W. Kantzenbach and V. Vajta (Göttingen, 1966) 13–61.

Smereka, W. "Pismo swiete w zyciu Kosciola [Sacred Scripture in the life of the Church]." In *Idee przewodnie,* ed. K. Wojtyla, 153–90.

Smith, J.J. "An Introduction to the Constitution on Divine Revelation." In *Ecumenism and Vatican II. Select Perspectives.* Cardinal Bea Studies, 1. Ed. P.S. De Achutegui (Manila, 1973) 15–63.

Smulders, P. "Zum Werdegang des Konzilkapitels 'Die Offenbarung selbst' [Chap. I]." In *Glaube im Prozeß,* eds. E. Klinger and K. Wittstadt, 99–120.

Solano, J. "Respuesta y acceso del hombre a Dios." In *Dios al encuentro,* by N. Silanes et al., 155–67.

Stakemeier, E. "Die Weitergabe der Offenbarung Gottes." In *Die Autorität,* ed. J.C. Hampe, vol. 1, 174–89.

Subilia, V. "La divina rivelazione." Chap. in *La nuova cattolicità del Cattolicesimo. Una valutazione protestante del Concilio Vaticano II.* Nuovi Studi Teologici, 1 (Torino, 1967) 179–218.

Thurian M. "Renewal and the Scripture-Tradition Problem in the Light of Vatican II." In *Renewal of Religious Thought,* ed. L.K. Shook (Montréal, 1968) vol. 1, 66–82.

Troisfontaines, C. ed. *Au Service de la Parole de Dieu.* Mélanges offerts à Mgr. André Marie Charue (Gembloux, 1969). See entries in 2.2 under Betti, Delhaye and Rigaux.

Ubieta, J.A. "Los Escritos Apostólicos del Nuevo Testamento." [On art. 20] In *La Palabra de Dios,* eds. L. Alonso Schökel and A.M. Artola, 559–80.

Vanni, U. "Exegesis and Actualization in the Light of Dei Verbum." In *Vatican II,* ed. R. Latourelle, 344–363; also in French, Italian and Spanish.

Vögtle, A. "Die Offenbarung in sich." In *Die Kirche und das Wort Gottes,* ed. W. Sandfuchs, 27–44.

Volta, G. "La Nozione di Rivelazione al Vaticano I e al Vaticano II." In *La Teologia Italiana Oggi.* In honour of C. Colombo. Ed. Facoltà Teologica dell'Italia Settentrionale (Brescia, 1979) 195–244 (esp. 211–23).

Vorgrimler, H. ed. *Commentary on the Documents of Vatican II,* vol. 3 (New York–London, 1969); also in German. See entries in 2.2 under Grillmeier, Ratzinger and Rigaux.

Waldenfels, H. "Das Offenbarungsverständnis im zwanzigsten Jahrhundert." In *Handbuch der Dogmengeschichte,* eds. M. Schmaus, A. Grillmeier and L. Scheffczyk. Vol. I/1b, *Die Offenbarung. Von der Reformation bis zur Gegenwart,* by H. Waldenfels and L. Scheffczyk (Freiburg–Basel–Wien, 1977) 108–208 (esp. 193–208).

Weber, J.-J. "La Révélation. Introduction [à 'Dei Verbum']." *Documents Conciliaires,* vol. 4 (Paris, 1966) 15–37.

———. "L'Écriture Sainte d'après la constitution 'De divina Revelatione' du IIᵉ Concile du Vatican." In *Où en sont les études bibliques?* eds. J.-J. Weber and J. Schmitt (Paris, 1968) 9–25.

Wojtyla, K. "Znaczenie Konstytucja 'Dei Verbum' w teologii." In *Idee przewodnie,* ed. K. Wojtyla, 7–11.

Zerwick, M. "Konzil und Bibelauslegung." In *Die Autorität,* ed. J.C. Hampe, vol. 1, 209–23.

———. "Il divino attraverso l'umano nei Vangeli." [On Chaps. III and V] In *Bibbia nella Chiesa,* by S. Lyonnet and others, 135–156.

2.3 ENTIRE ARTICLES:

Adinolfi, M. "La rivelazione divina nell'insegnamento della Chiesa ieri e oggi." *Antonianum* 43 (1968) 3–20.

Ahern, B.M. "On Divine Revelation." *Homiletic and Pastoral Review* 56 (1965) 557–65.

Aleu, J. "La constitución 'Dei Verbum' del Concilio Vaticano II. Tonalidad ecuménica de la Constitución dogmática sobre la divina Revelación." *Unitas* 5 (1966) 278–388.

———. "La Constitución dogmática sobre la Divina Revelación." *Estudios Eclesiásticos* 43 (1968) 23–59.

Alonso Schökel, L. "La Palabra de Dios según la Constitución conciliar." *Sal Terrae* 54 (1966) 1–7.

———. "La Constitución 'Dei Verbum' en el momento actual." *Razon y Fe* 178 (1968) 237–44.

Antón, A. "Revelación y Tradición en la Iglesia: 'Gesta et Verba' sus elementos constitutivos." *Estudios Eclesiásticos* 43 (1968) 225–58.

———. "La tradición viva en la comunidad viviente." *Studia Missionalia* 20 (1971) 75–99.

Aranda, Perez, G. "Acerca de la verdad contenida en la Sagrada Escritura. (Una quaestio de Santo Tomás citada por la Constitución 'Dei Verbum')." *Scripta Theologica* 9 (1977) 393–422.

Arenhoevel, D. "Das Verhältnis zwischen Altem und Neuem Testament nach der Dogmatischen Konstitution über die göttliche Offenbarung." *Freiburger Rundbrief* 18 (1966) 10–12.

Arróniz, J.M. "Notas a la Constitución dogmática sobre la Revelación." *Lumen* 15 (1966) 386–94.

Artola, A.M. "La inspiración según la Constitución 'Dei Verbum'." *Salamanticensis* 15 (1968) 291–315.

———. "La 'Dei Verbum' en el postconcilio español." *Lumen* 34 (1985) 434–45.

Baum, G. "Die Konstitution De Divina Revelatione." *Catholica* 20 (1966) 85–107.

———. "Vatican II's Constitution on Revelation: History and Interpretation." *Theological Studies* 28 (1967) 51–75.

Bavand, G. "Le mystère de la Révélation. Le Concile a-t-il favorisé le dialogue avec les protestants?" *Les Echos de Saint-Maurice* 67 (1971) 80–90.

Bea, A. "La parola di Dio nella vita della Chiesa" [On art. 21]. Annuario del Parroco 14 (1968) 131–42.

Betti, U. "De Sacra Traditione in Concilio Vaticano I." *Antonianum* 41 (1966) 3–15.

Blum, G.G. "Das II. Vatikanum—Selbstrechtfertigung oder ökumenischer Aufbruch?" *Quatember* 33 (1968/69) 36–37.

Bogacki, H. "Konstytucja II Soboru Watykanskiego o Bozym Objawieniu 'Dei Verbum' [The Constitution of the Second Vatican Council on Divine Revelation 'Dei Verbum']. *Collectanea Theologica* 36 (1966) 74–92.

Bopp, J. "Die Reform der römisch-katholischen Offenbarungslehre durch das II. Vatikanische Konzil." *Kirche in der Zeit* 22 (1967) 102–111.

Brajcic, R. "Objava i naravna spoznaja Boga" [Revelation and the natural knowledge of God]. [On art. 6]. *Bogoslovska Smotra* 37 (1967) 168–70.

Brayley, I. "The Written Word in the Church." *The Way, Supplement* 3 (1967) 41–49.

Brootcorne, J.C. "La parole de Dieu, source de notre foi." [On chap. I] *Confront* 1 (1968) 84–102.

Butler, C. "The Vatican Council on Divine Revelation." (An interview with C. Butler). *Clergy Review* 50 (1965) 659–70.

Caprile, G. "Tre emendamenti allo schema sulla Rivelazione." *La Civiltà Cattolica* 117 (1966/I) 214–31.

Carev V. "Ekonomija objave 'cinima i rijecima' [The economy of revelation by deeds and words]." [On art. 2]. *Bogoslovska Smotra* 37 (1967) 134–41.

Castro, L. de, "A VI Semana Portuguesa de Teologia [A teologia da Revelaçao, à luz de 'Dei Verbum']." *Brotéria* 86 (1968) 199–203.

Cerfaux, L. "Traditie en Schrift." *Collationes Brugenses et Gandavenses* 12 (1966) 338–52.

Chantraine, G. " 'Die Verbum.' Un enseignement et une tâche." *Nouvelle Revue Théologique* 107 (1985) 823–837; 108 (1986) 13–26.

Chenu, M.-D. "Verité évangélique et métaphysique wolffienne à Vatican II." *Revue de Sciences Philosophiques et Théologiques* 57 (1973) 632–40.

Chmiel, J. "Konsekwencje duszpasterskie Konstytucji dogmatycznej o Objawieniu Bozym [Pastoral Consequences of the Dogmatic Constitution on Divine Revelation]." *Duszpasterz Polski Zagranica* 17 (1966) 267–273.

Christ, F. "Ein grundlegendes Dokument des zweiten Vatikanischen Konzils. Die dogmatische Konstitution von der göttlichen Offenbarung." *Reformatio* 15 (1966) 11–18.

Cipriani, S. "Riflessioni sulla costituzione 'Dei Verbum'." *Presenza Pastorale* 43 (1973) 43–56.

Comblin, J. " 'Dei Verbum' después de diez años." *Teología y Vida* 16 (1975) 10–117.

De Armellada, B. "La Tradición en el Concilio Vaticano II." *Naturaleza y gracia* 13 (1966) 3–29.

Defois, G. "Révélation et societé: la Constitution 'Dei Verbum' et les fonctions sociales de l'Écriture." *Recherches de Science Religieuse* 63 (1975) 457–503.

de la Potterie, I. "La vérité de la Sainte Ecriture et l'histoire du salut d'après la Constitution dogmatique 'Dei Verbum'." *Nouvelle Revue Theologique* 98 (1966) 149–69.

De Surgy, P. "La Constitution 'Dei verbum' sur la Révélation." *Prêtres aujourd'hui* 280 (1966) 423–35.

Dexinger, F. "Die Darstellung des Themas 'Heilsgeschichte' in der Konstitution über die göttliche Offenbarung." *Bibel und Liturgie* 41 (1968) 208–32.

Dominic, F. "Dogmatic Constitution 'De Divina Revelatione'." *Eucharist and Priest* 72 (1966) 85–94.

Dulles, A. "The Constitution on Divine Revelation in Ecumenical Perspective." *American Ecclesiastical Review* 154 (1966) 217–31; reprinted in his *Revelation and the Quest for Unity,* 82–99.

Dupuy, B.-D. "Lignes de force de la Constitution 'Dei Verbum' de Vatican II." *Irénikon* 43 (1970) 7–37.

Ferrando, M.A. "La interpretación de la Biblia según el Concilio Vaticano II." *Teología y Vida* 16 (1975) 118–36.

Fucak, J. "Istina Svetoga Pisma [The Truth of Sacred Scripture]." *Bogoslovska Smotra* 37 (1967) 44–52.

Galbiati, E. "Aspetti ecumenici della 'Dei Verbum'." *Ut unum sint* 7 (1968) 46–54.

Galeota, G. "Aspetti ed istanze ecumeniche della costituzione 'Dei Verbum'." *Rassegna di Teologia* 8 (1967) 305–12.

Geißer, H. "Viva vox in ecclesia. Beobachtungen an der dogmatischen Konstitution 'Über die göttliche Offenbarung'." *Materialdienst des Konfessionskundlichen Instituts* 17 (1966) 41–50.

Ghidelli, C. "La 'Dei Verbum' dieci anni dopo." *Humanitas* 31 (1976) 737–53.

Giavini, G. "La Costituzione sulla Divina Rivelazione." *Ambrosius* 42 (1966) 109–16.

———. "La Costituzione dogmatica sulla divina Rivelazione." *Parole di Vita* 11 (1966) 189–96.

Gnilka, J. "Die biblische Exegese im Lichte des Dekretes über die göttliche Offenbarung (Dei Verbum)." *Münchner Theologische Zeitschrift* 36 (1985) 5–19.

Gnutek, W. "Cztery ewangelie w swietle Konstytucji Soborowej Dei Verbum [The four Gospels in the light of the conciliar Constitution 'Dei Verbum']." *Ruch Biblijny i Liturgiczny* 20 (1967) 13–24.

————. "Konstytucja Dei Verbum a cztery Ewangelie [The Constitution 'Dei Verbum' and the four Gospels]. *Ibid.*, 20 (1967) 129–135.

Golub, I. "Duh Tjesitelj uvodi u svu istinu [The Paraclete guides into all the truth]." [On arts. 8, 19, 20] *Bogoslovska Smotra* 37 (1967) 159–67.

Greehey, J. "Vatican II on the Bible." *Search* 2 (1979) 41–46.

Grelot, P. "La Constitution sur la Révélation." *Études* 324 (1966) 99–113, 233–46.

Grillmeier, A. "Die Wahrheit der Heiligen Schrift und ihre Erschliessung. Zum dritten Kapitel der Dogmatischen Konstitution 'Dei Verbum' des Vaticanum II." *Theologie und Philosophie* 41 (1966) 161–87.

Hermann, T. "Czytanie Pisma swietego w swietle Soboru Watykanskiego II [The Reading of Sacred Scripture in the light of Vatican Council II]." *Ruch Biblijny i Liturgiczny* 21 (1968) 40–47.

Höslinger, N. "Volk unter dem Wort. Zur dogmatischen Konstitution 'Über die göttliche Offenbarung'." *Bibel und Liturgie* 38 (1966) 26–29.

Holstein, H. "La Constitution sur la divine Révélation." *Bible et Vie chrétienne* 73 (1967) 43–59.

————. "Les 'deux sources' de la Révélation." *Recherches de Science Religieuse* 57 (1969) 375–434.

Homerski, J. "Pismo swiete—zbawczy dialog Boga z ludzmi [Sacred Scripture—God's salvific dialogue with men]." *Ateneum Kaplanskie* 77 (1971) 29–38.

Horst, U. "Wort Gottes und Konzil. Das II. Vatikanische Konzil über Offenbarung und Kirche." *Die Neue Ordnung* 21 (1967) 95–113.

Hotta, Y. "The Relation between Scripture and Tradition according to the Constitution on Divine Revelation of the Second Vatican Council." [Art. in Japanese. English summary: p. 211] *Katorikku Shingaku. Catholic Theology* [Tokyo] 6 (1967) 43–78, 211.

Hughes, P.E. "The Council and the Bible." *Christianity Today* 12 (1967) 65–68.

Ibáñez Arana, A. "La verdad de la Escritura." *Lumen* 15 (1966) 3–16.

———. "Escritura y tradición en el Vaticano II." *Ibid.*, 15 (1966) 244–55.

———. "Inspiración, inerrancia e interpretación de la Sagrada Escritura en el Concilio Vaticano II." *Scriptorium Victoriense* 33 (1986) 5–96, 225–329.

James, E.E. "The Unity of Scripture and Tradition. A Comparative Study of 'De Revelatione' of Vatican II and the Second Section of the Faith and Order Conference of Montreal 1963." *Indian Journal of Theology* 16 (1967) 221–32.

Jankowski, A. "Konstytucja dogmatyczna o Objawieniu Bozym [The Dogmatic Constitution on Divine Revelation]." *Znak* 18 (1967) 177–86.

Kasper, W. "Die Bedeutung der Heiligen Schrift für Kirche und christliches Leben nach der Konstitution 'Über die göttliche Offenbarung'." *Bibel und Kirche* 21 (1966) 54–67.

Kishi, A.H. "La Révèlation chrétienne et les autres religions à la lumière du Concile Vatican II." *Bulletin du Secretariatus pro non Christianis* 10 (1969) 31–38.

König, A. "Die Bybel in die Nuwere Rooms-Katolieke Teologie." *Nederduitse Gereformeerde Teologiese Tydskrif* [Capetown] 11 (1970) 247–59.

Klawek, A. "Uwagi do Konstytucji o Bozym Objawieniu [Remarks on the Constitution on Divine Revelation]." *Ruch Biblijny i Liturgiczny* 19 (1966) 26–32.

———. "Znaczenie Konstytucji [The significance of the Constitution] 'Dei Verbum'." *Znak* 18 (1967) 159–76.

Kloppenburg, A. "A Constituicao Dogmática sôbre a Revelacao Divina." *Revista Eclesiástica Brasileira* 25 (1965) 444–50.

Kolanovic, J. "Djelotvornost Bozje rijeci [The efficacy of the Word of God]." [On arts. 8, 3 and 21] *Bogoslovska Smotra* 37 (1967) 176–84.

Kopec, E. "Pojecie i przekazywanie objawienia w nauce Soboru Watykanskiego II. [The concept of Revelation and of its transmission in the teaching of Vatican II]." [French summary] *Roczniki Teologiczno-Kanoniczne* 14 [1967] 53–60.

Kopic, I. "Krist—punina objave [Christ, fulness of Revelation]." [On arts. 2 and 4] *Bogoslovska Smotra* 37 (1967) 115–20.

Kresina, A. "Povjesnost Evangelja [The Historicity of the Gospel]." *Ibid.*, 37 (1967) 176–84.

Kruse, H. "On Divine Revelation." *The Japan Missionary Bulletin* 20 (1966) 215–23.

———. "Die Zuverlässigkeit der Heiligen Schrift." *Zeitschrift für Katholische Theologie* 89 (1967) 22–39.

Kudasiewicz, J. "Powstanie i historycznosc Ewangelii w duskusji Soborowej [The origin and historicity of the Gospels in the light of the Conciliar discussion]." *Ruch Biblijny i Liturgiczny* 21 (1968) 1–24.

Lach, S. "Pismo Swiete w nauce Soboru Watykanskiego II [Sacred Scripture in the teaching of Vatican II]." [English summary] *Zeszyty Naukowe Katolickiego Uniwersytetu Lubelskiego* 10 (1967) 17–31.

Lafont, G. "La Constitution 'Dei Verbum' et ses précedents conciliaires." *Nouvelle Revue Théologique* 110 (1988) 58–93.

Latourelle, R. "La Révélation et sa transmission selon la Constitution 'Dei Verbum'." *Gregorianum* 47 (1966) 5–40.

————. "La Constitution sur la Révélation: points d'émergence." *Relations* 304 (April 1966) 99–101.

————. "Le Christ Signe de la Révélation selon la Constitution 'Dei Verbum'." *Gregorianum* 47 (1966) 685–709.

————. "Vatican II et les signes de la Révélation." *Ibid.*, 49 (1968) 225–52.

————. "Le Christ, signe de la Révélation, selon la Constitution 'Dei Verbum'." *Sélection-Receuil-Théologie du Vietnam* 1 (1969) 7–18.

————. "La Rivelazione come storia." *La Civiltà Cattolica* 120 (1969/III) 482–84.

Legrand, L. "Vatican II on Bible Translation." *Indian Ecclesiastical Studies* 5 (1966) 237–47.

————. "Vatican II et la Traduction des Écritures." *Revue Biblique* 64 (1967) 413–22.

Lohfink, N. "Erste Randglossen zur dogmatischen Konstitution 'Dei Verbum' (Über die göttliche Offenbarung), verkündet am 18. November 1965." *Orientierung* 29 (1966) 254–56.

————. "Bibel in der Gemeinde in katholischer Sicht." *Stimme* (1966) 719–33.

Loretz, O. "Die Wahrheitsfrage in der Exegese. Interpretationen der Konzilskonstitution 'Dei Verbum'." *Theologische Revue* 63 (1967) 1–8.

Lourenço, A. "Two Sources?" *Eucharist and Priest* 72 (1966) 340–48.

Maly, E.H. "The Council and Divine Revelation." *Hartford Quarterly* 6 (1966) 6–19.

————, W.J. Burghardt, F.L. Moriarty, J. Grassi, J.D. Quinn and J.F. Whealon. "The Constitution on Divine Revelation." *Bible Today* 35 (1968) 2418–60.

Martini, C.M. "Alcuni aspetti della Costituzione dogmatica 'Dei Verbum'." *La Civiltà Cattolica* 117 (1966/II) 216–26.

McNamara, K. "Divine Revelation." *The Irish Theological Quarterly* 34 (1967) 3–19.

Meis, A. "El Concepto de 'Revelación' en la Constitución Dei Verbum." *Teología y Vida* 31 (1990) 5–15.

Molino, A. del. "Iluminación interior y Magisterio a la luz de la 'Dei Verbum'." *Claretianum* 7 (1967) 133–73.

Mühlen, H. "Die Lehre des Vaticanum II über die 'hierarchia veritatum' und ihre Bedeutung für den ökumenischen Dialog." *Theologie und Glaube* 56 (1966) 303–35.

Murray, R. "The Inspiration and Interpretation of Scripture. Some Recent Work in the Light of the Constitution 'Dei Verbum'." *Heythrop Journal* 7 (1966) 428–34.

Neidl, F. "Tat- und Wortoffenbarung." *Österreichisches Klerusblatt* 100 (1967) 55–57.

Ochoa, J. "Biblia y Concilio." *Vida Espiritual* [Bogotá] 15 (1967) 10–25.

O'Collins, G. "At the Origins of 'Dei Verbum'." *Heythrop Journal* 26 (1985) 5–13.

———. "Divine Revelation." *Month* 221 (1966) 332–36.

O'Flynn, J.A. "The Constitution on Divine Revelation." *The Irish Theological Quarterly* 33 (1966) 254–64.

Olsen, A.L. "The Constitution on Divine Revelation." *Dialog* 5 (1966) 182–87.

Paino, M. "Un convegno a Napoli sulla costituzione conciliare 'Dei Verbum'." *Asprenas* 14 (1967) 172–76.

Pathrapankal, J.M. "The Problem of 'History' in the Gospels in the Light of the Vatican's Constitution on 'Divine Revelation'." *Indian Journal of Theology* 16 (1967) 86–96.

Peter, M. "Nauka Soboru Watikanskiego II o Pismie Swietym [The Teaching of Vatican Council II on Sacred Scripture]." *Ruch Biblijny i Liturgiczny* 20 (1967) 312–31.

Prager, M. "Was lehrt die Kirche über die neue Exegese?" *Bibel und Liturgie* 41 (1968) 282–90.

Precedo Lafuente, J. "Comentario a la constitución dogmática 'Dei Verbum' sobre la divina revelación." *Compostellanum* 11 (1966) 437–502.

Prete, B. "Le posizioni teologiche della 'Dei Verbum' sulla Sacra Scrittura." *Sacra Doctrina* 13 (1968) 583–99.

Putz, J. "Vatican II on Revelation." *Clergy Monthly* 30 (1966) 209–11.

Ramos, F.F. "La constitución 'Dei Verbum'." *Studium Legionense* 8 (1967) 125–255.

Rezus, P. "Constitutia dogmatica 'Dei Verbum' a Concilului al II-lea de la Vatican si învatatura ortodoxa despre Revelatia divina [The Second Vatican Council Dogmatic Constitution 'Dei Verbum' and the orthodox view on divine Revelation]." *Ortodoxia* [Bucarest] 21 (1969) 264–81.

Rolla, A. "La storia biblica come rivelazione divina: il dibattito attuale." *Euntes docete* 25 (1972) 285–93.

Romaniuk K. "Problemy egzegezy NT w Konstytucji dogmatycznej o Boskim Objawieniu [Problems of NT exegesis in the dogmatic Constitution on Divine Revelation]." [French Summary] *Roczniki Teologiczno-Kanoniczne* 14 (1967) 5–18.

Rossi, M. "Scrittura e Tradizione nel cristianesimo contemporaneo." *Annuario della Facoltà delle Lettere di Perugia* 122 (1974) 257–85.

Rupcic, L. "Fenomen Bozje rijeci [The Phenomenon of the Word of God]. Mogucnost razgovora izmedu Boga i clovjeka. [The possibility of communication between God and man]." *Bogoslovska Smotra* 36 (1966) 287–96.

————. "Nacela 'Dei verbum' o prijevodima Svetoga Pisma [Principles of 'Dei Verbum' about the translations of Sacred Scripture]." *Ibid.*, 37 (1967) 185–89.

Salaverri, J. "Planteamiento, discusión y exito de la Constitución Dogmática 'Dei Verbum' sobre la Divina Revelación." *Estudios Eclesiásticos* 41 (1966) 515–523.

Salvador, J. "Alguns Acenos à Constituicao Dogmática 'Dei Verbum'." *Revista de Cultura Bíblica* 4 (1967) 22–33.

Sant, C. "Biblical Interpretation in 'Dei Verbum'." *Melita Theologica* 19 (1967) 1–12.

Sasse, H. "After the Council." [On arts. 9–14] *Reformed Theological Review* 25 (1966) 1–14.

Sawada, K. "The Concept of Divine Revelation—Considerations on the Constitution on Divine Revelation and Its Historical Background." [Art. in Japanese, English summary] *Katorikku Shingaku* 6 (1967) 243–53, 443–44.

Scheifler, J.R. "La 'Palabra de Dios' y la vida espiritual." *Manresa* 38 (1966) 203–22.

Schildenberger, J. "Die dogmatische Konstitution des Vaticanum II 'Über die göttliche Offenbarung'." *Erbe und Auftrag* 43 (1967) 263–78, 351–68.

Schnitzler, E. "Ministerium Verbi." *Theologie und Glaube* 57 (1967) 440–62.

Semmelroth, O. "Zur Bedeutung der Konzilskonstitution über die göttliche Offenbarung." *Die Sendung* 19 (1966) 98–109.

Silanes, N. "Trinidad y revelación en la 'Die Verbum'." *Estudios Trinitarios* 17 (1983) 144–214.

Skrinjar, A. "Proslov u Konstituciju o Bozanskoi Objavi [Prologue to the Constitution on Divine Revelation]." *Bogoslovska Smotra* 37 (1967) 111–14.

Slugic, V. "Provijest spasenja u konstituciji [Salvation History in the Constitution] 'Dei Verbum'." *Ibid.*, 37 (1967) 120–25.

Smith, J.J. "An Introduction to the Constitution on Divine Revelation." *Philippine Studies* 14 (1966) 410–17.

Socha, P. "Geneza soborowej koncepcji Tradycji. La genèse de la conception conciliare de la Tradition." *Roczniki Teologiczno-Kanoniczne* 17 (1970) 31–52.

Sousa, J. A. de. "A doutrina de G. Tyrrell sôbre a revelacao e os textos preprados para o Concílio Vaticano II." *Didaskalia* 1 (1971) 107–36.

Spadafora, F. "L'inerranza della Sacra Scrittura." *Renovatio* 1 (1966) 45–62.

⸻. "Origine apostolica e storicità degli Evangeli nella 'Dei Verbum'." *Ibid.*, 2 (1967) 563–87.

Stern, J. "Le developpement du dogme selon Newman et la Constitution dogmatique sur la Révélation divine du Vatican II." *Euntes docete* 33 (1980) 47–84.

Stepien, J. "Pismo Swiete w kaznodziejstwie w swietle Konstytucji o Objawieniu Bozym [Sacred Scripture in Preaching in the light of the Constitution on Divine Revelation]." [French summary] *Collectanea Theologica* 37 (1967) 29–44.

Stöger, A. "Die dogmatische Konstitution 'Dei Verbum' auf dem Hintergrund des Werkes R. Bultmanns." *Der Seelsorger* 36 (1966) 377–391.

Stramare, T. "La trasmissione della rivelazione." *Rivista Biblica Italiana* 15 (1967) 225–247.

Strele, A. "Vera kot clovekov odgovor Bogu razodevavcu. [Faith as the response to God who reveals himself]." [On art. 5] *Bogoslovska Smotra* 37 (1967) 126–33.

————. "Pojem vere po nauku konstitucije o bozjem razodetju. [Faith according to the teaching of the Constitution on Divine Revelation]." *Bogoslovni Vestnik* 27 (1967) 161–69.

Szymanek, E. "Novum Konstytucji 'Dei Verbum' o przekladach biblijnych [The novelty of the Constitution 'Dei Verbum' about biblical translations]." *Homo Dei* (1969) 213–19.

Tavard, G.H. "Commentary on De Revelatione." *Journal of Ecumenical Studies* 3 (1966) 1–35.

Thome, A. "Die Bibelkatechese im Lichte der Konszilskonstitution über die göttliche Offenbarung." *Trierer Theologische Zeitschrift* 77 (1968) 69–85.

Thurian, M. "Un acte oecuménique du Concile: le vote de la Constitution dogmatique sur la Revélation." *Verbum Caro* 19, no. 76 (1965) 6–10.

Tomaszewski, E. "Historyczna prawda Ewangelii wedlug konstytucji II Soboru Watykanskiego [The historical truth of the Gospel according to the Constitution of Vatican Council II] 'Dei Verbum'." [French summary] *Roczniki Teologiczno-Kanoniczne* 16 (1969) 21–39.

Tomic, C. "Bozansko nadahnuce i tumacenje Svetog Pisma prema Konstituciji o objavi [Divine inspiration and the interpretation of Sacred Scripture according to the Constitution of Revelation]." [On Chap. III] *Bogoslovska Smotra* 37 (1967) 149–58.

Trapiello, J.G. "La Biblia en el Concilio Vaticano II." *Cultura Bíblica* 23 (1966) 338–351.

Urdanoz, T. "De momento Traditionis tractandae in Ecclesiologia et de sensu Traditionis 'vivae'." *Angelicum* 43 (1966) 393–404.

Valkovic, M. "Uciteljstvo 'sluzi Bozjoj rijeci' [The Magisterium 'serves the Word of God']." [On art. 10] *Bogoslovska Smotra* 37 (1967) 171–75.

Van Balen, C. "A Revelacao Divina." *Revista da Conferencia dos Religiosos do Brasil* 12 (1966) 193–203.

Van Leeuwen, P., "The Genesis of the Constitution on Divine Revelation." *Concilium* 3, no. 1 (1967) 4–10.

Vargas Machuca, A. "Escritura y Tradición en la Constitución 'Dei Verbum' cap. II: perspectivas para el diálogo ecuménico." *Estudios Eclesiásticos* 47 (1972) 189–204.

Villasante, L. "La Constitución dogmática 'Dei Verbum' sobre la divina revelación." *Verdad y vida* 25 (1967) 211–23.

Volta, G. "La Rivelazione di Dio e la Sacra Tradizione secondo la Costituzione dogmatica 'Dei Verbum'." *La Scuola Cattolica* 97 (1969) 30–52, 83–115.

Vorgrimler, H. "Die Konzilskonstitution über die göttliche Offenbarung." *Bibel und Liturgie* 39 (1966) 105–10.

Voss, G. "Die dogmatische Konstitution 'Über die göttliche Offenbarung'." *Una Sancta* 21 (1966) 30–45.

Wasner, F. "Die beiden Tische. Variationen über ein konziliares Thema." *Theologisch-praktische Quartalschrift* 118 (1970) 19–28.

Widmer, G.-Ph. "Quelques réflexions d'un point de vue réformé sur la Constitution conciliare 'Dei Verbum'." *Irénikon* 42 (1969) 149–76.

Winiarski, K. "Stosunek Tradycji do Pisma Swiete wedlug Konstytucji o Objawieniu Bozym [The Relationship between Tradition and Scripture according to the Constitution on Divine Revelation]." *Ruch Biblijny i Liturgiczny* 21 (1968) 197–208.

Worden, T. "Revelation and Vatican II." *Scripture* 19 (1967) 54–62.

Zarella, P. "Chiesa e Sacra Scrittura nella Costituzione 'Dei Verbum'." *Parole di Vita* 12 (1967) 205–26.

———. "I rapporti tra Chiesa e Sacra Scrittura nella costituzione 'Dei Verbum'." *Ibid.*, 14 (1969) 205–19.

Zerwick, M. "De Sacra Scriptura in Constitutione dogmatica 'Dei Verbum'." *Verbum Domini* 44 (1966) 17–42.

————. " 'Per homines more hominum' in Evangeliis." *Ibid.*, 46 (1968) 65–79.

————. "Das Wort Gottes und die Schrift. Anmerkungen zur dogmatischen Konstitution 'Dei Verbum'." *Die Sendung* 25, no. 3 (1972) 16–25.

2.4 SECTIONS OF ARTICLES:

Alfaro, J. "Encarnación y Revelación." *Gregorianum* 49 (1968) 431–59.

Burghardt, W.J. [On chap. II] In "Constitution on Divine Revelation," by E.H. Maly et al., 2426–32.

Dejaifve, G. "Diversité dogmatique et unité de la Révélation." *Nouvelle Revue Théologique* 89 (1967) 16–25.

Grassi, J. [On chap. IV] In "Constitution on Divine Revelation," by E.H. Maly et al., 2441–46.

Hamel, E. "L'Écriture, âme de la théologie." *Gregorianum* 52 (1971) 511–35 (esp. 522–30).

Kothgasser, A.M. "Dogmenentwicklung und die Funktion des Geistparakleten nach den Aussagen des Zweiten Vatikanischen Konzils. *Salesianum* 31 (1969) 379–460 (esp. 401–57).

Kryvelev, I.A. "La crise de la théologie contemporaine." *Istina* 15 (1970) 96–112 (esp. 107–12).

Kubik, A. "Teoria o rodzajach literackich, jej dzieje i zwyciestwo w biblistyce katolickiej [The theory of literary form and its victory in Catholic exegesis]." *Rocznik Teol. Slaska Opolskiego* 1 (1968) 81–108.

Kubis, A. "Urzad Nauczycielski papieza w swietle I i II Soboru Watykanskiego. Le magistère pontifical selon les Ier et IInd Conciles de Vatican." *Analecta Cracoviana* 3 (1971) 273–93.

Maly, E.H. [On chap. I] In "Constitution on Divine Revelation," by E.H. Maly et al., 2418–25.

Miano, V. "Dio parla ancora? Il problema della fede oggi." *Salesianum* 32 (1970) 855–80.

Moriarty, F.L. [On chap. III] In "Constitution on Divine Revelation," by E.H. Maly et al., 2433–40.

Müller-Fahrenholz, G. "Das Verhältnis von Heiliger Schrift und Kirche." *Evangelische Theologie* 31 (1971) 244–264.

Nissiotis, N.A. "Report on the Second Vatican Council (With Special Reference to the Decrees on 'Divine Revelation,' 'Church in the Modern World,' and to the ecumenicity of the Council as a whole)." *Ecumenical Review* 18 (1966) 190–206. (esp. 190–96).

Ocvirk, D. "La révélation et le savoir. A partir et en marge de la Constitution 'Dei Verbum'." *Lumen Vitae* 36 (1981) 149–85 (esp. 151–66).

O'Riordan, S. "The Experience of God in Modern Theology and Psychology." [cf. art. 8] *Studia Moralia Academiae Alfonsianae* 5 (1967) 127–53.

Pottier, B. "Les yeux de la foi après Vatican II." *Nouvelle Revue Théologique* 106 (1984) 177–203 (esp. 192–97).

Quinn, J.D. [On chap. V] In "Constitution on Divine Revelation," by E.H. Maly et al., 2447–53.

Torrell, J.-P. "Chronique de théologie fondamentale [I. La Constitution 'Dei Verbum']." *Revue Thomiste* 66 (1966) 63–107 (esp. 63–85).

———. "Chronique de théologie fondamentale." *Ibid.*, 67 (1967) 439–65 (esp. 442–56).

———. "Chronique de théologie fondamentale." *Ibid.*, 69 (1969) 61–92.

Whealon, J.F. [On chap. VI] In "Constitution on Divine Revelation," by E.H. Maly et al., 2450–60.

INDEX OF NAMES